STAGE-COACH
— DAYS —
IN THE BLUEGRASS

*Being an Account of Stage-Coach Travel
and Tavern Days in Lexington
and Central Kentucky
1800-1900*

J. WINSTON COLEMAN, JR.

FOREWORD BY THOMAS D. CLARK

THE UNIVERSITY PRESS OF KENTUCKY

Publication of this volume was made possible in part by grants from The Thomas D. Clark Foundation, the Lexington-Fayette County Historic Commission, and the Lexington Historical Publishing Corporation.

Scholarly publisher for the Commonwealth, serving Bellarmine College, Berea College, Centre College of Kentucky, Eastern Kentucky University, The Filson Club, Georgetown College, Kentucky Historical Society, Kentucky State University, Morehead State University, Murray State University, Northern Kentucky University, Transylvania University, University of Kentucky, University of Louisville, and Western Kentucky University.

Editorial and Sales Offices: The University Press of Kentucky
663 South Limestone Street, Lexington, Kentucky 40508-4008

Library of Congress Catalog-in-Publication Data

Coleman, J. Winston (John Winston), 1898-
    Stage-coach days in the bluegrass : being an account of stage-coach travel and tavern days in Lexington and central Kentucky, 1800-1900 / J. Winston Coleman, Jr. ; foreword by Thomas D. Clark.
        p.   cm.
    Originally published: Louisville, Ky. : Standard Press, 1935.
    Includes bibliographical references and index.
    ISBN 0-8131-1914-6 (cloth : alk. paper)
    1. Kentucky—Social life and customs. 2. Coaching—Kentucky—History—19th century. 3. Taverns (Inns)—Kentucky—History—19th century. 4. Lexington (Ky.)—Social life and customs. 5. Coaching—Kentucky—Lexington—History—19th century. 6. Taverns (Inns)—Kentucky—Lexington—History—19th century. I. Title.
F455.C64   1995
976.9'403—dc20
                                                                95-21201

CONTENTS

ILLUSTRATIONS FOLLOW PAGES 94 AND 190

To
The Memory of My Father
JOHN W. COLEMAN
1852-1929

FOREWORD

When Kentucky entered the Union of States on June 1, 1792, the face of its land was laced with ancient game and Indian trails. Many of these at later dates converted into intersettlement roads as emigrants pushed westward. In 1792 few roads could accommodate more than packhorse trains, and certainly none were adaptable to stagecoach travel for any distance. Not until 1787 and James Wilkinson's famous journey home from New Orleans by way of Philadelphia and Pittsburgh and by flatboat to Maysville was a wheeled vehicle brought to Kentucky. From Maysville, Wilkinson traveled over the Limestone Road to Lexington.

During the second year of his administration as governor, Isaac Shelby prevailed upon the Kentucky General Assembly to enact legislation authorizing the widening and improving of a link of the old Wilderness Trail. This became the first publicly maintained road in Kentucky. Governor Shelby had raised private funds to pay for the project, which became known as Shelby's Wagon Road. A pressure for opening main roads in Kentucky was to facilitate the delivery of the United States Mail, first on horseback, then by stagecoach.

At the opening of the nineteenth century, widened and slightly improved highways had been opened from Lexington south to Cumberland Gap and north to Maysville and the Ohio River. The opening of these roads encouraged the organization of stagecoach companies, which endeavored to establish a semblance at least of scheduled passenger and mail service.

Stagecoach travel in Kentucky had more social and cultural significance than as a simple means of going from one place to another. The coaches were largely the conveyors of news from the outside world to the western settlements. This phase of Kentucky history was largely overlooked until J. Winston Coleman did the necessary research and writing of his book *Stage-Coach Days in the Bluegrass.* Coleman, an amateur historian with a burning zeal to know more of Kentucky's past, was in 1935 just beginning a distinguished career of writing and collecting Kentuckiana. He searched far and wide for the basic source materials pertaining to local stagecoach travel.

In his diligent search for documentary materials, Coleman was able to produce not only an incisive depiction of stagecoach travel during the formative years of Kentucky history but also an account of the roadside accommodations for travelers. The Kentucky county court order books contain scores of applications for licenses to operate taverns. These houses were combinations of lodging and dining rooms, bars, and appended livery stables. They were so much a part of the social and economic fabric of their communities that both the Kentucky General Assembly and the county courts exercised control over them by establishing annually a scale of prices that tavernkeepers could charge for everything from a bottle of wine to horse feed.

Stagecoach travel over the early nineteenth-century Kentucky roads was at best rugged and physically trying. Spending a night in a roadside tavern was hardly a relaxing experience. During winter seasons the roads were rutted quagmires, and in summer rough and dusty. It was not unusual for passengers to be forced to disembark and walk around mud holes. Traveling at rates of speed that ranged from three to seven miles an hour, stagecoaches from Lexington took three days to reach Cumberland Gap and most of two to reach Maysville.

Numerous foreign observers came west to view the expanding American democracy. Those who traveled through Kentucky prior to the railway age in 1850 described dining and lodging in a roadside stagecoach tavern as an ordeal approaching primitivism itself. Meals were served in the most informal manner. Backwoods dining habits lacked refinements; food, though plentiful, was often indifferently prepared, and diners gulped down their meals as if famine itself were impending. Lodging was equally crude; many times travelers were forced to sleep two and three abed with total strangers or to bed down on the barroom floor. Perhaps the only picturesque features of the early Kentucky taverns were their quaint names and colorful signs, and the fact that prices were officially regulated. All the taverns kept on hand a surprising selection of alcoholic beverages, some of them downright exotic.

In no aspect of frontier American life was the practice of democracy more visible than among stagecoach travelers. Lawyers, statesmen, preachers, laborers, and soldiers of high rank were all crowded into cramped stagecoaches shoulder to shoulder. None among them experienced the ordeals of travel more intimately than Henry Clay, who traveled back and forth from his Lexington estate, Ashland, to Washington aboard stagecoaches. On one occasion he was trapped in an overturned coach.

There were the elite among the stage lines and their drivers. Those carrying the United States Mail lorded it over their less fortunate competitors. The drivers, or jehus, of mail coaches believed they had license to take the road at will and sometimes treated passengers with contempt. The mail coaches were perhaps better maintained than other coaches because of postal inspection, and they held more faithfully to published schedules.

Moving around in Kentucky—and the nation, for that matter—and to places away from navigable streams prior to the building of railroads required a certain amount of daring and a nonchalance for the passage of time and for personal safety. The Kentucky General Assembly was typically reluctant to enact internal improvement laws. Most of the legislators were too tax shy or unimaginative to sanction the building of better roads. They were tolerant of the inefficient plan of warning "tithes," which required men between the ages of sixteen and sixty to contribute two or three days of labor to work the roads. It was not until the early decades of the nineteenth century, especially 1830-1850, that the macadam process of building and surfacing roads was introduced in Kentucky.

Along with the introduction of the modern process of building roads, toll companies were chartered by the state to operate segments of the public roads and collect tolls to finance them. Throughout almost all the latter half of the nineteenth century, turnpike companies virtually controlled most of Kentucky's public roads. In time, toll company officials became arbitrary, toll collectors impatient, and stagecoach drivers arrogant. There resulted in the 1880s and early 1890s a so-called toll gate war in which vigilantes destroyed toll gates, burned toll houses, and threatened toll collectors with violence.

By the end of the nineteenth century, the age of the stagecoach had drawn to a close. The railroads robbed the companies of their passengers, and the hard surfacing of roads greatly facilitated private traveling. The United States Postal Service deserted the "fast express stage lines" by awarding mail transport contracts to the railways. By the opening of this century, American travelers had become too impatient and time conscious to be jostled into physical discomfort inside a tossing stagecoach. Time became both a precious and a conscious consideration on the railway, which had set schedules of arrivals and departures. As the rickety old stagecoaches clattered down the road to oblivion, there departed with them a colorful American folk character: the jehu who handled the driving lines of a six-horse team with one hand and cracked his whip with the other. No longer sounded the loud trumpet warning that the stagecoach was arriving at the tavern door. Down came the toll gates and the tollkeepers' houses with the introduction of new stages of road building and management.

This book, the product of a young and diligent self-disciplined historian, captures the spirit and mores of a rich historical moment in both state and nation. In many respects J. Winston Coleman was much more capable of ferreting out basic primary sources than many so-called professional historians. In researching this book, the author was able to locate a satisfactory amount of primary and contemporary information and to organize and present it in a clearly written narrative steeped in human interest.

There is no lack of books about early American travel in

the stagecoach era. Too, almost every foreign visitor who crossed the Atlantic to view the spread of American civilization rushed home to write and publish a travelogue. Many of their journals include fascinating descriptions of life over the primitive roads. The formal books describing this mode of moving about the country in the formative years treat the subject of stagecoach travel in generalities. *Stage-Coach Days in the Bluegrass* not only measures up to standards set by other studies; in many cases it exceeds them.

This solid local history documents the way of life and travel in another age; it is also rich in social and cultural commentary. Paradoxically, this was a period when Kentuckians were in a great hurry for their society and economy to mature, but they had the patience to travel in stagecoaches. On the obverse of the historical coin, the stagecoaches brought news of the outside world to the provincial towns and communities of Kentucky. There lingers on the scene a treasured relic of the period covered in this book. The old coach that traveled the Burnside-Cumberland Valley circuit now resides in style in the foyer of the Wells-Fargo Bank in San Francisco. The spirit of the age, however, lingers on in J. Winston Coleman's rich trumpet call to a stirring moment in Kentucky history.

—THOMAS D. CLARK

PREFACE

L EXINGTON was early the commercial mart and cultural center of the western country, the "Athens of the West," situated in the heart of the beautiful Bluegrass region of Kentucky. Splendid taverns and inns afforded the traveler the most desirable stopping places, and Lexington soon became the concentration point for numerous stage-coach routes and lines.

The first regular stage-coach line was established in central Kentucky shortly after the beginning of the nineteenth century. This mode of travel served the people of the Bluegrass as an adequate means of conveyance, reaching its greatest height from 1835 to 1852. After that, railroads gradually crept in, destroying the usefulness of the stage-coach and the romance of travel, until the year 1889 saw the last stage line operating out of Lexington.

Much of the success of the old stage-coaches, their remarkable speeds and long schedules, was due to the fine system of "artificial" roads, or macadamized turnpikes, which came into existence in the Bluegrass in the thirties and forties. These were privately owned and operated, and were financed through the medium of the toll-gates.

Taverns and inns being closely associated with stage-coach travel are discussed, but, excepting the more prominent, no attempt is made to cover them in their entirety.

Much valuable information on the early stages and taverns was gained from the files of the old Kentucky

newspapers at the Lexington Public Library, from the
county and circuit court records of Fayette and surrounding counties, and by personal interviews with many of
the oldest and best informed citizens of this and other
counties. A great many sources have been examined, including those in the attached bibliography. To those
who have aided him, with personal recollections, valuable
family papers, pictures, or letters, the author makes grateful acknowledgments, his thanks being especially due the
late Fred K. Irvine, of Chicago, for a series of valuable
recollections, incidents, and anecdotes of the old stage-
coaches, and of his father—Thomas H. Irvine, for over
forty years the principal stage proprietor of the Bluegrass.
To the authors of *Six Horses,* Captain William Banning
and George H. Banning, the author is grateful for co-
operation and assistance, and for the use of photographs.
To Charles R. Staples, William H. Townsend, Dr.
Thomas D. Clark, John Wilson Townsend, James M.
Roche, and Dr. John S. Chambers, the author desires to
acknowledge his indebtedness for valuable assistance and
encouragement, and for enjoyable companionship on numerous excursions in search of data.

Also to Mrs. Thomas D. Clark and to his wife,
Burnetta, the author is greatly indebted for reading and
correcting the manuscript, and offering many valuable
suggestions which have materially improved each chapter.
In order to put the reader more in sympathy with the
period under consideration, generous use has been made
of the phraseology of the times.

If, even in the least measure, this book serves to stimu-
late interest in the bygone days of the stage-coach and
taverns in the Bluegrass region of central Kentucky, and
tends to keep their memories alive, it will have ful-
filled its entire mission.

J. WINSTON COLEMAN, JR.

March 23, 1935,
405 *Dudley Road,*
Lexington, Kentucky.

CHAPTER I
PIONEER ROADS AND TRAVEL

W HAT lay beyond the blue haze of the majestic mountains which stretched from Pennsylvania through Maryland, Virginia, and North Carolina was uppermost in the minds of the young and vigorous manhood of the Tidewater countries. After their raids the Indians always retreated across these mountains, as did the deer and buffalo when they were pursued. The extravagant reports of surveyors and hunters returning through the Gap only served to whet this desire for adventure in the West.

Lord Dunmore's Point Pleasant campaign of October, 1774, brought together many active militiamen from Virginia and North Carolina, along with a few who had crossed the mountains into what is now the Bluegrass state. Around the camp fires each night, *Kentucky* was a subject as interesting as the campaign itself.[1] After discharge from this duty, the soldiers carried homeward the idea of *Kentucky* and the discussion served to increase the desire for knowledge by personal experience. The struggle for Independence prevented any large emigration, but the Yorktown campaign closed the seven dreary years of the Revolutionary War and released many from service, who, ruined by the economic upheaval of the war,[2]

[1] *Autobiography of Daniel Trabue*, pp. 15–21.
[2] Harrell—*Loyalism in Virginia*, pp. 25–30.

now sought to restore their fortunes by a hunting and ex-
ploring trip.

Many of these who had received land grants for services during the French and Indian War either located
these claims on desirable acreage in the Bluegrass or sold
them to speculators who hurried westward to place their
claims.

The close of the war found Kentucky sparsely settled
by some who sought economic or religious independence;
others who fled from the depredations of camp followers
of both armies, and some who had maintained the posts
and settlements throughout the war. By 1783, the population of all the settlements of Kentucky was considered
to be about twelve thousand.[3] The suspension of Indian
hostilities and the return of peace invited emigration, and
the stockades of Kentucky received great numbers of settlers from the Atlantic states. In the spring of 1784, it
was estimated the population had increased to more than
twenty thousand.[4]

During 1784, the inhabitants were so increased by arrivals from Virginia and North Carolina as to number
thirty thousand, and the "district of Kentucke" began to
assume the character of a prosperous community. Schools
were opened, churches established, and agriculture flourished in all the fields that had been cleared of the giant
oaks, hickories, and elms. Canebrakes were plowed under to be planted in corn so necessary to the pioneers.
Settlements sprang up where the buffalo trails crossed and

[3]Monette—*History of the Mississippi Valley*, Vol. II, p. 143.
[4]Albach—*Annals of the West*, p. 419.

where a good spring was near by, and many of these trails became the public highways of our day.

During the prehistoric period of Kentucky's history, wild animals, particularly the buffalo, were the road-makers. When the Indians entered this region, they found innumerable buffalo trails or "traces," already plainly marked and beaten down by the trampling of countless herds. The buffaloes were migratory, visiting the interior of Kentucky year after year from the prairies of Illinois and Tennessee. They came more to drink the abundant mineral waters and to lick the saline earth, than to pasture on the luxuriant cane and other tempting herbage. Since these animals seldom remained stationary in Kentucky, it is easy to see why their trails became the main roads, as distinguished from the "varmint paths" or runways in small local areas, cut out and worn bare by the native fur-bearing animals which dwelt permanently in Kentucky.

The buffalo's great weight demanded that the thoroughfares should be stable, and, because of his ability to cover great distances,[5] that they should be practicable. The only course open for passage for the buffalo was the summits of the hills. From the hilltops the water shed most quickly, making the dryest land, and from here the snows of winter were quickest blown, lessening the dangers of drifted banks and erosion. Buffalo roads not only traversed the state, but were transcontinental in extent. Nor did they move in haphazard fashion. With marvelous instinct they generally picked out the most direct and

---

[5] Two hundred miles a day. Hulbert—*The Old National Road*, p. 16.

favorable routes. No wonder, therefore, that the Indians looked upon the buffalo as a benefactor.

In an account of the adventures of Colonel Daniel Boone, published by John Filson, in 1784, Boone states that he left "his family and peaceable habitation on the Yadkin River in North Carolina, the 1st of May, 1769, to wander through the wilderness of America, in quest of the country of Kentucke." After crossing the "mountain wilderness" he and his five companions camped on Red River, June 7, when Boone relates: "We found everywhere abundance of wild beasts of all sorts, through this vast forest. The buffaloes were more frequent than I have seen cattle in the settlements, browsing on the leaves of the cane, or cropping the herbage on those extensive plains, fearless, because ignorant of the violence of man. Sometimes we saw hundreds in a drove," and in 1780 "the inhabitants of Kentucky lived chiefly on the flesh of buffaloes."[6]

Another writer of this period, in describing the buffalo trails, said: "After remaining a few days at the lick [lower Blue Licks] and killing an immense number of deer and buffalo, they crossed the Licking [River] and passed through the present counties of Scott, Fayette, Woodford, Clark, Montgomery, and Bath, where falling in with another great buffalo trace, it conducted them to the upper Blue Lick, where they again beheld elk and buffalo in immense numbers."[7]

Filson wrote of the buffalo that roamed Kentucky: "The amazing herds of buffaloes which resort thither

---

[6]Filson—*History of Kentucke*, p. 73.
[7]McClung—*Sketches of Western Adventure*, p. 86.

[to the licks], by their size and number, fill the traveler with amazement and terror, especially when he beholds the prodigious roads they have made from all quarters, as if leading to some populous city."[8] There are other references to the abundance of the buffalo in Kentucky at the time this region was first visited by the white settlers. Just when the buffalo became extinct in this region is not definitely known, but Toulmin writing in 1792 said: "The buffaloes are mostly driven out of Kentucky at this date,"[9] and all agree that these animals survived at most points for only a few years after the first permanent settlements were made.

These broad trails or "traces" of the buffalo converged at the Ouasioto or Cumberland Gap, and through this gap they passed and repassed for generations, just as did the Indians and white men after them. The war roads of the Iroquois, Miami, and Shawnee nations to the North and West, and of the Cherokee, Catawba, and Creeks to the South and Southwest, also merged into a single trace through this famous gap, and it became known as the "warriors' path."[10]

Other "traces" of more or less importance stretched over the boundless tracts of Kentucky, and possibly the greatest of them all crossed the Ohio River at the present site of Maysville. It led straight up the hill to the high ridge and on to the lower Blue Licks. Here a branch led up Licking River to the upper Blue Licks, and thence on through the country to the Cross Plains, the present site

[8]Filson—*History of Kentucke*, p. 32.
[9]Toulmin—*Description of Kentucky*, p. 85.
[10]Filson, Map of Kentucky, 1784.

of Athens, Fayette County. From the lower Blue Licks the trail ran southwest, crossing Hingston at the Ruddell's Mill site, and from there it branched out into the rich grazing lands.

Another big branch crossed the Ohio River and came by Stamping Ground to North Elkhorn, passing on to Cross Plains, and thence across the Kentucky River near Boonesboro to the lower Cumberland region. From Stamping Ground the trail to Bryan Station passed over the dividing ridge to the waters of Boone's Creek, near Cross Plains, where it united with the trail from upper Blue Licks. Another branch from Stamping Ground passed through Great Crossings and on to the site of Lexington, and then led down what is now South Broadway and on to the Kentucky River, crossing the latter at the mouth of Dick's River.

Without the aid of the trail-blazing buffalo and the path-finding red man, the task of the white explorers and settlers, Dr. Thomas Walker, Daniel Boone, Christopher Gist, John Finley, and others, would have been much harder, and the advance of civilization into the valley of the Ohio and the great middle West would have been longer delayed. These trails were first of all just wide enough for a foot or bridle path, along which woodsmen might tramp single file. Frequently cattle or horses driven over these trails would stray into the cane or brush and get lost, thus subjecting their owners to danger and a great loss of time. The practice of "belling" cattle and horses was resorted to as a safeguard against losses. The pioneers soon learned that these bells betrayed the presence of the whites to the roving bands of hostile Indians, and more than once resulted in disastrous ambuscades.

It was dangerous for an individual to travel these "traces" or Indian trails through the wilderness from cabin to station. Those who traveled with any degree of safety banded together and traveled in "companies," for there was risk enough for the most daring in any case, but a "well armed company of so many guns" was a dangerous game upon which to prey. It was customary to advertise in local newspapers the formation and departure of an "armed company" either from Virginia or to Kentucky. One such advertisement of an intended departure appeared in the *Kentucky Gazette,* November 1, 1788:

> "A large company will meet at the Crab Orchard the 19th of November in order to start the next day through the wilderness. As it is very dangerous on account of the Indians, it is hoped each person will go well armed."

It appears that unarmed persons sometimes joined these companies and relied on others to protect them in time of danger. One notice in the *Gazette* urged everyone to go armed and "not depend on others to defend them."[11] Because of numerous Indian raids, a great deal of anxiety was felt by the early settlers of the Bluegrass, and one of them prophesied that this land "would never be settled for the Indians" and "a lot of people were

---

[11]*Kentucky Gazette,* November 29, 1788.

glad to get their money back by selling the land at low prices."[12] Some of these earlier settlers disposed of their holdings for what they could get and returned to their native states along the Atlantic seaboard.

It is "the proud boast of Kentuckians that in the center of their beautiful Bluegrass country was erected the first monument to the first dead of the Revolution." A party of hunters, while seated on logs and buffalo hides around their fire, discussed a name for a proposed town. John Maxwell suggested *Lexington,* for they had just heard of the battle of Lexington, which had been fought about fifty days before at Lexington, Massachusetts. Thus, in commemoration of the first battle of the American Revolution, this Kentucky site was called Lexington.[13] Nothing further, however, was done toward the settlement of Lexington, for Indian raids threatened and the scouting party abandoned its cabin and returned to Harrodsburg. In June, 1776, the name Fincastle County, Virginia, was changed to the "district of Kentucke," for the present state of Kentucky was then a part of Virginia.

Again the settlement of Lexington was undertaken by Colonel Robert Patterson and twenty-five men who arrived "on or about the middle of April, 1779," and erected a fort on the north side of the Kentucky River. This was "the first white man's residence on the beautiful region which now surrounds the city of Lexington."[14]

[12]Wymore to Shane—Draper Manuscripts, No. 11CC128–132, Wisconsin Historical Society, Madison.

[13]In the issue of the *Reporter,* July 29, 1809, appears an article: "Origin of the Name of the Town of *Lexington,*" and fixes the date of the naming of the town, June, 1775.

[14]Monette—*History of the Mississippi Valley,* Vol. II, p. 75.

Ten years later, a resident writing from Lexington,[15] September 25, 1789, described its growth:

> "It is astonishing how fast this town improves
> . . . it is by far the largest in the district and it is
> expected the emigration this fall will be greater than
> ever . . . report says there are seventy families now
> on their way to Kentucky . . ."

Many of these intrepid pioneers and settlers who had come to Lexington and other stations throughout the Bluegrass during this period brought their families with them. They made the entire journey on foot or horseback, just as the Boones, Harrods, and Logans of earlier days were obliged to do, and everything they brought with them had to be carried on the backs of patient pack-horses, marching single file over Indian or buffalo traces. Threat of Indian ambuscade was ever present. Roads were miry, creeks were flooded over their steep banks, and crossings were numerous. Often parties had to "tote" their packs across on logs and swim the horses.

There were no road houses or camps where travelers could stop at night.[16] They slept in the open, huddled near camp fires, with one or more of their number posted as look-outs for Indians. Often there was great suffering from storm, cold, and hunger. A vivid picture of the hardships of these sturdy pioneers is contained in Moses Austin's narrative of the year 1796:[17]

---

[15]Letter of Mrs. James Wilkinson—*Pennsylvania Magazine of History and Biography*, Vol. 50, p. 164.

[16]In 1790, the population per square mile of area averaged 1.8 in Kentucky and .8 in Tennessee, Meyer, p. 5.

[17]Barker—*Life of Stephen F. Austin*, p. 8.

> "Women and children in the month of Decem-
> ber traveling a wilderness through ice and snow,
> passing large rivers and creeks, without shoe or
> stocking, barely as many raggs as to cover their
> nakedness, without money or provisions except what
> the wilderness affords . . . To say they are poor is
> but faintly expressing their situation . . . can any
> thing be more absurd than the conduct of man,
> traveling hundreds of miles, they know not for
> what, nor whither, except it's—Kentucky! . . ."

So eager were the pioneers and settlers to reach Kentucky that, by a conservative estimate, seventy-five thousand persons had passed through Cumberland Gap prior
to the opening in 1796 of the "Wilderness Road" to
wagon traffic. Few movements of population in America
can compare in magnitude with this influx of immigrants
between 1780 and 1800.

Equipped with axe and Dechard rifle,[18] they forged
ahead with grim determination, fighting every inch of
the way against odds that were seemingly overwhelming.
These immigrants were settlers bent upon building a
permanent home in the wilderness. They brought their
household goods, their domestic animals, their books, and
even their printing presses. They received little or no
aid from the mother state, and were compelled to rely for
their protection upon their own efforts. Thus they developed an independence of thought and action which
resulted finally in statehood.

---

[18]Most of the early settlers in Kentucky were armed with this flint-lock
rifle, made by the celebrated riflemaker, Jacob Dechard, or Decherd, of
Lancaster, Pennsylvania.

No longer dependent upon regular army officers and troops sent over the mountains who were unaccustomed to Indian warfare, the Kentuckians fought their enemies in "Indian fashion" and drove the savages from the state.[19] They manifested a courage born of the very hardships encountered and founded a new American civilization whose culture was equal to that of the eastern colonies. All of this came West over the buffalo traces and Indian paths extending from the states of Virginia, Pennsylvania, Maryland, and North Carolina to the Bluegrass region of central Kentucky.

[19]"If any part of the inhabited earth could be said to have been peopled in tears and blood, that was, emphatically, Kentucky! If Tennessee is excepted, no other part of the United States was peopled under such accumulated difficulties as Kentucky," Darby, p. 203.

CHAPTER II

THE FIRST STAGE LINE

TRAVEL into central Kentucky during its formative period, the latter part of the eighteenth century, was not only by land but by boat down the Ohio River. During the Revolution and for sometime afterwards such travel was dangerous, because of Indian attacks and floods and swift currents in river navigation. Moreover, good boats were scarce and expensive, consequently a land route, although much longer, was preferred by many of the early pioneers and settlers.

For a decade after the Revolutionary War, practically all roads leading to Lexington and central Kentucky were merely buffalo traces[1] or Indian trails, over which the immigrants passed single file with their worldly possessions on the backs of pack-horses. Toward the end of 1793, improvements were being made by private enterprises on the main trails and traces leading into the Bluegrass, converting them into "waggon-roads" over which a wheeled vehicle might be drawn. By 1787 the Limestone Road[2] to Lexington had become a thoroughfare over which a line of wagons was plying, and, since a man named

---

[1] For a detailed list of these early roads and traces, see Samuel M. Wilson—*The First Land Court of Kentucky*, pp. 81–87.

[2] "Limestone," reported Josiah Espy, "is a little town, but the greatest landing place on the River" and it was here that nearly all the river travel halted and started overland for the settlements of central Kentucky.

The bridle-path and pack-train stage of our civilization began to fade with the opening of these "waggon-roads" into central Kentucky. By 1800 Lexington,[6] as the center of the Bluegrass region, was beginning to assume the appearance of a thriving metropolis of some 1795 inhabitants, consisting "in the main of refined and educated persons." Transylvania University attracted students from all over the South, many of whom later brought honor to their alma mater and left their imprint upon the life of their communities. Tobacco and whiskey assumed first rank as exports from the Bluegrass, and the Kentucky light leaf tobacco rapidly drove the British plug out of the market. Twenty-four retail stores in Lexington attracted shoppers from all over Kentucky. The imported nankeens, calimancoes, dimities, tamboured and jaconet muslins, Bertha laces, and Paisley shawls began to deck the shoulders of the pioneers' daughters, and the French heeled slippers covered dainty toes as they tripped lightly through the dance measures at Waldemard Mentelle's dancing school to the tunes of old Buford's bow.

Robert Frazer, Edward West, and other silversmiths of Lexington were busy turning out fine silver, while Nathan Burrows advertised a large stock of fine china and queensware, with a varied assortment of wine and toddy glasses. The "Great Revival," which had started in the Green River country, rapidly swept towards the

---

[6]"No where in America has the almost instantaneous change, from an uncultivated waste to the elegances of civilization, been so striking as to obtain for that town the title of Athens of the Western States." Darby, p. 206.

Bluegrass and, for many months, was the sole topic of conversation.[7]

Ginseng, hemp, tobacco, flour, pork, and country products found a ready market in the port of New Orleans. Ropewalks, bagging and duck factories brought wealth to local capitalists. Marsh and Studman manufactured all kinds of spindles and carding machines for use in the plants of William Tod and others, while Samuel Wilkerson advertised himself as a manufacturer of textile machinery. The Manchester settlement, adjoining Lexington, turned out large quantities of linens and woven materials, soon to be loaded in wagon trains for Baltimore or Philadelphia, or down the river for the merchants at Natchez and New Orleans. Joseph Bruen opened his foundry and machine shop on Spring Street and hauled the iron ore to Lexington from the eastern counties. In the fall of 1800, the Kentucky Iron Works began the erection of a furnace and splitting mill. It is of no wonder then that the little town of Lexington,[8] the cultural metropolis and the commercial mart of the western country, should rightly claim the title of "Athens of the West."

Communication with the outside world and with relatives and friends was impossible unless the early Lexingtonians availed themselves of the services of traders and such travelers as journeyed eastward, to deliver their messages and carry their letters, as the government was

[7]Cleveland—*The Great Revival in the West*, pp. 90–108.
[8]"This town which promises to be the great inland city of the Western World is situated in the center of an extensive plain of the richest land in Kentucky." *Niles Weekly Register*, Vol. VII, p. 339, January 28, 1815.

slow in extending the postal services to the West. After John Bradford set up the *Kentucky Gazette,* in 1787, he employed "post-riders" to deliver the paper to subscribers in the outlying districts and to bring in news from correspondents at different points. These "post-riders" made regular trips to Limestone and other points for mail, particularly eastern newspapers, and Bradford further accommodated his readers by opening a letter box in his printing office where all papers and letters brought to town were held "until called for."

There was nothing that caused more excitement in the little town of Lexington than the arrival of the "post-rider" on his foam-flecked pony. He always carried a horn, which was vigorously blown to announce his coming. When he dashed up to Bradford's printing office, there was always a crowd to meet him. As soon as he deposited his mail bag, he became the center of an inquisitive throng, to whom he related the news he had gathered along his route. Each individual in the crowd went away and repeated the news until everyone in the community had been informed of what had happened in the other settlements.

Newspapers from New York and Philadelphia were eagerly awaited, and, on days they were expected, crowds gathered about the office to hear the news which was read aloud by some strong-lunged individual, occupying a position of prominence on a chair or box. These facts illustrate the crude and uncertain methods by which Lexington and central Kentucky had to communicate with the outside world. However, the first post-office was established in September, 1794, when Lexington was only a city of one thousand inhabitants, with Innes Baxter Brent, postmaster.

Until the opening of the nineteenth century, the accepted means of travel for the citizens of the Bluegrass was horse-back, while a few dared the perils and pains of wagon travel, which was as rough as it was slow. It was not many years, however, before the citizens of Lexington and the surrounding territory could travel with more ease and comfort in wheeled vehicles, with two and four horse teams.

On Wednesday, August 9, 1803, John Kennedy, a resident of Lexington, announced that he had started the first regular stage-coach line in Kentucky,[9] and that it would run from Lexington by Winchester and Mt. Sterling to the Olympian Springs in Montgomery County, a distance of about forty-seven miles. Bradford's *Kentucky Gazette* carried the notice of this first stage line:[10]

"Lexington and Olympian Spring STAGE: J. Kennedy, respectfully informs the public, that he has commenced running his Stage-Coach, on the line between Lexington and the Olympian Springs, at Mud Lick, every Thursday morning, at Four o'clock precisely, to arrive at the Springs the same day. Passengers may engage places with R. Bradley, at the Stage-Office, Travellers Hall, in Lexington,

FARES	S	d
To the Springs	21	–
Mount Sterling	15	–
Winchester	9	–

[9]Collins, Vol. I, p. 514, "First Stage Route in Kentucky."
[10]*Kentucky Gazette*, August 9, 1803.

With Mr. Galloway, Winchester

To the Springs	15	–
Mount Sterling	7	6
Lexington	9	–

With Mr. Simpson, Mount Sterling

To the Springs	9	–
Winchester	7	6
Lexington	15	–

With Mr. Botts, at the Springs

To Mount Sterling	9	–
Winchester	15	–
Lexington	21	–

Each passenger will be allowed 10 lbs. baggage, for all extra baggage from Lexington to the Springs, will be charged three cents per pound—from Winchester to do. two cents per pound—and from Mount Sterling to do. one cent per pound, or one cent per pound between any two of the adjoining places— He will also undertake to convey packets of papers, etc., at a reasonable rate."

From this initial move toward faster and more convenient transportation, Kennedy expected much, "as he had already expended upwards of 2000 dollars in starting it." This expense was made in the purchase of stage-wagons, horses, and equipment, and in the employing of his stage agents, Messrs. Galloway, Simpson, and Botts, along with his drivers and stock tenders. Having met with some degree of patronage with his initial stage line,

Kennedy, two months later, entered into partnership with William Dailey of Lexington and started another line in a different direction:

"LEXINGTON AND FRANKFORT STAGE

"The public are respectfully informed, that my Stage will start from Mr. Bradley's Inn, Lexington, every Monday and Friday morning, at day-break; and from Frankfort every Tuesday and Saturday at noon —Passengers may engage places at 9s each allowing 10 lb. baggage, and 1½ cents per lb. for extra baggage.

"JOHN KENNEDY."

Having started this line from Lexington to Frankfort, the capital, Messrs. Kennedy and Dailey rented for a term of three years the lot and dwelling of Horatio J. Offutt in Leesburg, Woodford County. Offutt "obligated himself to put the said dwelling house and kitchen in good repair and to erect a log stable 24 feet by 20 feet and finish it with stalls for eight horses." This early stage stable and tavern was rented for eleven pounds per year, beginning April 1, 1804, and the stage proprietors reserved the right to cancel the lease if "the seat of government should be moved from Frankfort before the expiration of the said time of three years."[11]

This stage tavern and half-way house in the now extinct town of Leesburg, Woodford County, was the first to be established for the accommodation of stage travelers

<hr>

[11]William Dailey *vs*. John Kennedy, file 234, Fayette Circuit Court, January 10, 1808.

and was half way between Lexington and Frankfort, on the Leestown Road.

With the introduction of the stage line between Lexington and Frankfort, and the one to the Olympian Springs by way of Winchester and Mt. Sterling, the mail was soon transferred to the stage-coach and the post-rider became an institution of the past.[12] Little is known of the stage-coaches that left Lexington on the first runs in 1803, but they were nothing more than home-made affairs. A stage-wagon was of light construction, with backless benches and makeshift top, with curtains to be let down in the rainy season. The arrangement of the benches was such that a passenger entered the wagon at the front and climbed over all seats to reach those in the rear.

These stage-wagons accommodated from six to eight persons, with the baggage limited to ten pounds. Baggage was carried inside the vehicle under each passenger's seat. There was little comfort for the passengers, who shared the interior with bulky merchandise and bumped and jolted against each other, as the wagon creaked on its way at the rate of three or four miles an hour. The distances covered by these early stage-wagons were considered remarkable. John Kennedy advertised with considerable pride that his stage "would arrive at the Springs the same day" after leaving Lexington before daylight. Such snail-paced movements and such discomforts in travel would be regarded as unendurable now; yet passengers were patient and some of them remained even cheerful.

[12]*Kentucky Gazette,* May 3, 1806, announced: "The conveyance of the mails in the stages does not take place until June, 1806."

These rates of movement were typical of the speeds maintained throughout the Bluegrass for some years, until the "artificial" or hard-surfaced roads came into use in the middle thirties.

CHAPTER III

IMPROVEMENTS OF STAGE TRAVEL

W ITH the coming of winter, 1803, Kennedy discontinued his stage line to the Olympian Springs because of the roads "becoming a vast sea of mud," but he continued the run to Frankfort for the entire session of the Legislature. It is not known what financial return this initial line netted its owner, but the chances are he lost money, for, the next year, a proprietor who had heretofore driven the stage to Frankfort was operating the line to the Springs:

> "I will start with the Stage from Mr. Bradley's door every Monday and Thursday morning at daylight, and run to the OLYMPIAN SPRINGS during the present season without fail—Passengers may engage places on each preceding evening, at the latest. "GEORGE SOWERBRAY."

Early in the nineteenth century it became popular with the elite of Lexington to leave the "sickly climate" of the city and visit the well known watering place, Olympian Springs,[1] which the owner, George Coleman,

---

[1]This was one of the earliest "watering places" in Kentucky and was noted for its "most pure and salubrious air" where the traveler "found himself in a high mountainous country, embellished with scenery of a bold romantic character." Henry Clay was one of the early owners of the resort and gave it the name of Olympian Springs.

announced is "now elegantly furnished for the season and ready for the reception of *genteel visitors.*" The fame of this resort in Montgomery County was largely responsible for the continuance of the stage line, and, after several years, the proprietor of the stage was the well known Cuthbert Banks, who advertised:

"THE STAGE

"For the Olympian Springs

Will leave Major Wagnon's in Lexington, every Monday morning, and return on Saturday. The Stage is now furnished with excellent horses and a good careful driver.   "CUTHBERT BANKS."

For those who did not intend to make extended trips, this notice was made:[2]

"A STAGE-COACH, COACHEE & CHARIOT

"Will be constantly kept for hire, at the Travellers Hall. Parties may engage the above carriage with good horses and careful driver upon the shortest notice to   "ROBERT BRADLEY."

With the opening of the stage line, it was necessary to have places where travelers could congregate, deposit their baggage, buy tickets, and make connections with the stages. These were the stage offices and each had

[2]*Kentucky Gazette,* October 24, 1805.

a stage agent in charge. On this stage agent rested the responsibility of properly routing the travelers, checking their baggage, selling tickets, keeping stage office, and, most important of all, making out and checking the way-bills.

The Travellers Hall, owned and operated by Robert Bradley,[3] was selected as the first stage office for Lexington. Increased patronage forced Bradley to purchase an additional lot of ground, upon which he built a dining and assembly room 50 feet by 32 feet. He stated that "neither his time or his purse shall be spared in attempting to render the Travellers Hall a house of entertainment for *Genteel Guests only,* equal to any in America." This first Kentucky stage office and tavern was located on the "publick square," directly opposite the northeast corner of the courthouse.

Kennedy and Dailey's stages still left Travellers Hall every Monday and Friday at sunrise, and left Bush's Tavern in Frankfort every Tuesday and Saturday at noon—the fare being one shilling six pence cheaper than the previous year. Schedules were arranged so passengers could "breakfast and dine" at the proprietors' half-way house at Leesburg on certain days.[4]

These early stage-wagons or coaches were essentially fair-weather vehicles, and, at the end of summer, notices

[3]Tavern license of Robert Bradley, July 9, 1804, in author's collection. Bradley was under a bond of one hundred pounds to provide "good cleanly lodging and diet for travelers, stableage, and provender for horses," and, "he shall not suffer any unlawful gaming in his house or suffer any one to tipple or drink more than is necessary, or at any time suffer any disorderly or scandalous behaviour to be practiced in his house. . ."

[4]*Kentucky Gazette & General Advertiser,* April 10, 1804.

appeared as follows: "The Proprietors of the stage-coach beg leave to inform their friends and the public in general that their coach left off running on Saturday, the 15th of October instant."[5]

One English traveler visiting Lexington in 1806 reported in his published account of his travels,[6] that, in that year, there had been established "a mail-coach from Pittsburgh to Lexington in Kentucky, through Philadelphia, Wheeling, and Chillicothe, a distance of upwards of seven hundred miles, to be performed by contract in fifteen days." He said of the inns along this route: "they were generally log huts of one apartment, and the entertainment consists of bacon, whiskey, and Indian bread." Of this early "mail-coach" service little is known, as the newspapers failed to mention anything of so great importance. This same traveler reported "from Lexington to Limestone, and to Cincinnati, on the Ohio, a distance of each of seventy miles, the roads with a few exceptions are no more than buffalo traces . . ."

Of the travel at this period, a passenger in the first stage-coach or, possibly, stage-wagon, to make a trip from Lexington to Paris in 1808 relates that: "George Walls, of Lexington, drove up on the first coach which ever dawned upon the startled gaze of the inhabitants of Paris. For our driver with much loud winding of the horn and many sharp cracks of his long whip dashed up at a speed calculated to toss the swaying coach from its creaking running gear. It rocked so alarmingly on

---

[5]In 1804, there were six four-wheeled carriages and two two-wheeled ones owned by the citizens of Fayette County, making a total of "28 wheels of carriage." Each vehicle was listed and taxed at the rate of six shillings per wheel.

[6]Ashe, p. 171.

its springs that we feared for our lives and clutched desperately at our best bombazine bonnets to keep them from being demolished." Upon reaching Paris, the stage drew up in front of Buckhanon's Tavern, where the steps of the coach were let down for the passengers to dismount, to receive a cordial welcome from the host, Henry Buckhanon. His handsome broadcloth suit, consisting of long coat and knee breeches, his white ruffled shirt and stock, were quite elegant and, as this early passenger remarked, "made a sharp contrast to the round waistcoats with sleeves, bright woolen girdles, coarse linsey shirts, and leather breeches worn by some of the hunters we passed on the way from Lexington."[7]

During the next decade and a half, after the introduction of the stages, there seems to have been no regular line of stages operating. Several of the taverns and inns, notably the Columbian in Lexington, had for the accommodation of travelers and guests "a stage-coach sufficient for the conveyance of six or seven passengers, which will run from this place to the Mudlick[8] and Greenville Springs, or to any of the neighboring towns, at any time when a sufficient number of passengers will justify the trip."[9]

One Kentuckian, an early stage traveler, said "he did not mind walking when he had paid his fare to ride in the stage, but he did not like to walk and 'pack' a rail

---

[7] *Register*, Kentucky State Historical Society, January, 1922.

[8] Olympian Springs was earlier known by that name. In 1791, a patent was issued by the Governor of Virginia to Jacob Myers for a tract of land "including a large mud-lick, with log cabin and improvements in the mountains." The Greenville Springs, later known as Graham, were at Harrodsburg.

[9] *Kentucky Gazette*, June 13, 1814.

to help pry the stage-coach out of the mudholes which
frequently punctuated the customary line of travel." Undoubtedly, early stage traveling had many drawbacks, and
not the least among these was the extreme ease with
which the coach upset, an instance of which is shown by
an entry in a letter from Dr. Charles Wilkins Short, professor at Transylvania University, to his uncle, in April,
1815: "The greater part of the distance I walked, pre-
ferring that fatigue to the danger of the upsetting of the
stage, which at this point frequently happens."[10]

Another early traveler in this section, after experiencing several "oversettings" of the stage, said of the
roads: "in passing over the corduroy roads, the stage-
coach or wagon bounced from one log to another,
enough it seemed to have dislocated all the bones in the
human body." Yet the happenings on a stage journey
were accepted and endured with complaisance and forti-
tude. This early clumsy transportation was considered
the height of travel luxury, and it was seldom that complaints were made by the public of the uncomfortable
and weary condition that inevitably attended stage-
coach travel. One early traveler[11] tells of the difficulties
met in keeping the stage from upsetting in the deep ruts
with which the roads abounded. The driver frequently
called upon the passengers for assistance: "Now, Gentlemen, to the right," upon which all passengers leaned
their bodies half way out of the coach to balance that
side; "Now, Gentlemen, to the left," and so on.

---

[10]Referring to a part of the road between Frankfort and Middletown.
Letter in the Filson Club library, Louisville.
[11]Weld—*Travels through the States of N. America*, Vol. 1, p. 36.

"After riding a few miles, I left the coach," related Flint, an early English traveler, when going by stage-coach in 1818 from Maysville to Lexington, in describing the perils of travel. Continuing he reported: "There is no great degree of comfort in traveling by this vehicle; stowed full of people, baggage, and letter bags; the jolting over stones and through miry holes is excessively disagreeable, and the traveler's head is sometimes knocked against the roof with much violence. A large piece of leather is let down over each side, to keep out the mud thrown up by the wheels. The front was the only opening; but, as the driver and two other persons were occupying it, those behind them were almost in total darkness, and a peep at the country was not to be obtained."

After lying over for some hours and trying his luck in another stage-wagon or coach, he was forced to travel some distance after sunset when "the coach stopped at Millersburg, from eight o'clock till three in the morning. It overturned[12] on my journey hither, and though I received no injury I resolved upon going no further with that vehicle in the dark, and over such bad roads."

Continuing on the way to Lexington, Flint spent the next night in Paris and said of the taverns: "Several of

[12]An English clergyman, Rev. Wm. Milton, in 1810, published a small book entitled: *The Danger of Travelling in Stage-Coaches*, in which he devised a scheme for a "patent stage-coach to prevent the fatal and disastrous consequences of breaking down and oversetting." Milton's plan was to place a strong box with small wheels below the body of the coach "ready in case of a wheel coming off or breaking, or an axle breaking, to catch the falling carriage, and instantly to continue its previous velocity, thereby preventing that stop to rapid motion, which so frequently proved fatal to the driver and passengers." Several coaches were built upon Milton's plans, but like "so many other patent coaches were speedily forgotten." Straus, p. 218.

the taverns were large, and, like many of the others in
the western country, have bells on the house tops which
are rung at meals." On reaching Lexington, this traveler
sought quarters in the best known tavern of the town—
Postlethwait's—and there he "found the people very
polite and obliging in their manner. Some of them are
interesting in their conversation, and some talk of horses
and horse-racing, and the latter kind of discourse is mixed
with much swearing."

Evidently the city[13] made a good impression on our
traveler, who said: "Lexington is still [1818] considered
the capital of fashion in Kentucky. There are many
genteel families, a few of which keep coaches. The town
on a whole exhibits a well-dressed population, and is
regularly built of frame houses. It has an University,
brick Mason's hall, several places of worship (three
Presbyterians, one Episcopal, one Baptist, one Methodist,
one Roman Catholic). Three printing presses where
three weekly newspapers are published; a branch of the
United States bank, and two other banking houses; seven
mercantile houses, and some good taverns. The population is supposed to be about seven thousand; but the
increase has been slow for several years past . . ."[14]

At this period Colonel James Johnson, of Great Crossings, Scott County, was the prime mover of the stage-
coach industry, operating in the Bluegrass. In 1817 he
announced:

---

[13]"Lexington is the seat for a great commerce and has many flourishing
manufactures. The population is already between six and seven thousand
souls." *Niles Weekly Register,* Vol. III, p. 339, January 28, 1815.
[14]Flint, pp. 137–138.

"Having determined to establish a line of stages from Louisville to Wheeling, at which point the stages run to the Eastern termini, it becomes necessary to inform the public that the line will commence from *Louisville to Lexington* on Monday week, this day and in less than a week from that time they will continue to Louisville, and by the first of July to complete operation to Wheeling. Its progress till then will be noticed as arrangements are made. The stages will carry passengers at an average of 60 miles a day, to run three times a week; as often as the Philadelphia and Washington stages run to Wheeling. In case any accident should happen with the stages, arrangements will be made to carry the passengers on horse-back till the next stage can take them. Of course, passengers may rely on it, that when they take a seat they shall be on a certainty as to their progress . . . the overseers of the roads are particularly requested to turn their attention to making the roads as good as circumstances will permit. Apply to me for terms—

"JAMES JOHNSON."

Colonel Johnson[15] was associated with numerous enterprises of early travel and transportation, and was proprietor of a freight line which maintained the steamboat Providence, carrying freight from Leestown on the Kentucky River at Frankfort to Natchez and New Orleans. This was the accepted means of disposing of the

[15]Brother of Colonel Richard M. Johnson, Vice-President of the United States, and reputed slayer of the Indian chief Tecumseh.

produce of central Kentucky; and Johnson would have made a great deal of money had not "misplaced confidence led him astray in pecuniary affairs and involved him in losses which ruined his fortune."[16] It has been stated that he lost over forty thousand dollars alone in the stage-coach enterprise. He died at his home in Scott County, August 13, 1826, leaving a family of ten children,[17] one of whom, Edward P. Johnson, later acquired considerable prominence in the stage-coach industry of central Kentucky.

Close onto the inauguration of through stage service from Lexington to Louisville, was the establishment of the first stage line from Lexington to Cincinnati, May 6, 1818, with Abner Gaines as proprietor, who informed the public:

"LEXINGTON & CINCINNATI MAIL STAGE

"Commenced running for the first time, Wednesday May 6th inst. It will leave Cincinnati every Wednesday, at 8 o'clock A. M. and arrive at Lexington on Thursday at 6 o'clock P. M.

"Leave Lexington at 2 o'clock P. M. and arrive at Cincinnati on Monday at 8 o'clock A. M.

"Fare for passengers 10 cents per mile, with an allowance of 14 lbs. baggage; 100 lbs. baggage considered equal to one passenger. Books for the entrance of passengers will be kept at the Cincinnati Hotel, at Keen's Inn, Lexington, and at Capt.

---

[16]Obituary of Colonel James Johnson, *Kentucky Gazette,* August 18, 1826.

[17]Gaines—*History of Scott County,* Vol. 1, p. 146.

Brenin's, Georgetown.   The proprietor who lives on the road will make every exertion to promote the comfort of passengers.

"ABNER GAINES—Proprietor."[18]

Not only did the proprietor, Abner Gaines, live on the road, but he kept a tavern in Williamstown, Grant County, for the accommodation of the passengers on the first permanent stage line from Lexington to Cincinnati.[19]

Travel by this new line to Cincinnati was both expensive and tedious. It was dusty in summer and muddy in winter. Frequently fallen trees made detours necessary, yet it was the shortest route to Cincinnati. This road climbed the hills north of Eagle Creek and then ran along the top of the ridge until within sight of Covington. From the advertisement of Abner Gaines, it will be seen that the fares of eight or nine dollars per passenger were charged, and two days consumed in making the trip, with one hundred pounds of baggage considered and charged as an extra passenger.

By means of more commodious stages and convenient taverns along the roads, overland transportation improved greatly during the period prior to 1818. This was a period of expansion, with emigrants coming from the states along the Atlantic seaboard, and a great portion of new country being opened up with almost unparalleled rapidity. It is not surprising that in these new

---

[18]*Western Monitor*, Lexington, May 16, 1818.
[19]Gaines *vs.* Robert Clark, Pendleton Circuit Court, file 11, October 12, 1818.

regions the roads did fail to keep pace with the expansion of the population.[20]

Many of the sturdy pioneers of central Kentucky who were accustomed to make long trips by horse-back and exposure to all kinds of weather, looked upon the introduction of stage-coaches and the establishment of stage lines as a detriment to the community, tending to render the traveling public "effeminate and idle." Furthermore, stage-coaches were bad for business "as people used less clothes than when they had to travel on horse-back or on foot"; and "they were bad for the health of the passengers, owing to the long stages and late arrivals." The strongest outburst of opposition to the new method of travel was "that the coaches were destroying the breed of good horses" and that "saddlers and spurriers would be ruined by the hundreds."

Objections of this character have been made against every innovation and advancement in travel and transportation to the present day. They showed the spirit of the times when the stage-coach was fast supplementing the horse as a means of public conveyance.[21] Notwithstanding the perils and inconveniences of stage travel and the opposition and ridicule hurled against the "crazy four-wheeled carriages," the popularity of the stage-coaches continued to grow. After the establishment of the first stage line from Lexington to Louisville in 1817, the stage-coach system was firmly planted in the Blue-

[20]"The roads in Kentucky are in the situation which might be expected in a country so lately settled; generally not good." Morse, p. 496.
[21]"Lexington was noted as early as 1817 for her number of carriages, which was twice that of any town of its size in the United States." Ranck, p. 289.

grass, and travel was maintained on a much more reliable basis. Heretofore, it was only periodic travel, stages being run "whenever there was a sufficient number of passengers to justify them" or on very irregular schedules, with frequent mishaps and bad connections.

Now the system had undergone great improvement. Regular schedules were being maintained, stage offices operated in the cities, on the termini, and way stations, all in charge of stage agents, or ticket agents, whose principal duties consisted of making out and checking the passenger way-bills. This consisted of a paper, prepared by the agent at the starting point of the coach, in the nature of a bill of lading or manifest, termed the "way-bill." This bill was given the stage driver, and by him delivered to the agent at the other end of the line immediately upon the arrival of the coach. It contained the name and destination of each passenger, the number of seats engaged, distance traveled, and the several sums as fares. If a passenger got on at a way station, or along the road, he paid his fare to the driver, which was duly noted on the way-bill, together with the passenger's destination. On some of the stage lines the way-bill carried a list of the passengers' trunks or boxes, exclusive of the hand baggage, which was in most cases limited to fifteen pounds per person.

In addition to the stage agents, there were the "division agents" or general agents of the stage lines, who possessed functions somewhat, but not altogether, like those of railroad conductors or superintendents of safety. Some of these agents passed constantly over the road, paying bills, hiring and dismissing the drivers and stock tenders, supplying horses and provender, and giving general instructions as to the running of the line and conduct of the officers. Others were stationary, attending to local business. Their jobs must have been difficult at times, judging from the letter of one, to the proprietor of the line, who stated: "I am constantly going from one road to another to keep the stock in order, for there is no dependence in stage agents or drivers."[22] These division agents, usually risen from the ranks of drivers, were prominent characters of the road, and popularly esteemed as men of high position.

The connection of Lexington with Louisville by stage was considered by Kentuckians as quite a feat for long distance travel, but, as early as 1786, there was a line of stage-coaches operating from the state of New Hampshire to Savannah, Georgia, which, the newspapers of that period stated, "go and return regularly and carry the several mails by order and permission of Congress."[23] And, in 1824, a trip could be made by stage from "Lexington to Washington City in six days" providing the roads were at all suitable for travel.[24]

Consistent with the improvement of travel and the regular schedules were the stage-coaches themselves, which by this time had evolved from the home-made ones to those of qualified coach and body builders. Several "coach repositories," or manufacturing establishments, were located in Lexington, and to these the stage pro-

---

[22]Letter from J. Yontz to Col. Dunning R. McNair, in author's collection.
[23]*Worcester* (*Mass.*) *Gazette*, January 5, 1786.
[24]Collins—*History of Kentucky*, Vol. 1, p. 31.

prietors turned for their finished products. For the next decade the local coach builders held full sway. The early coach had an egg-shaped body, suspended on wrought iron springs. No great improvement was noted in coach design until 1827, when the famous Concord coaches began to make their appearance in the eastern states. By the year 1833, Concord coaches were running over the Bluegrass routes, and these revolutionized travel, being pronounced by many "the only perfect vehicle for traveling that has ever been made."

This famous vehicle was manufactured by the Abbott-Downing Company, Concord, New Hampshire, a firm founded in 1813, which from the early thirties to the late eighties supplied coaches[25] for all the important lines in central Kentucky. The coach usually employed on the Bluegrass routes had provision for nine inside passengers, three to a seat, and one or more on the outside. The body of the coach was built of stout white oak, braced with iron bands, and a stout top capable of carrying a number of pieces of baggage. It was suspended upon two leather "thorough-braces" extending lengthwise of the coach and attached at each end to a standard protruding up from the axle.

These "thorough-braces" were made of leather straps placed on top of each other to a thickness of about three inches. The leather swing was used in place of the steel springs to absorb the jars, and it permitted the coach to rock slightly forward and backward. Not only did

[25]About 1834 or 1835, the Troy coach, made by Eaton & Gilbert, of Troy, New York, was introduced in Kentucky. These two coaches, Concord and Troy, were the most popular ones on the routes of the Bluegrass.

the "thorough-braces" serve the purpose of springs, but they acted as shock absorbers for the horses, in that violent jerks upon the traces, due to any rut or obstruction in the road, were automatically lessened and generally eliminated. It was the force of inertia—the forward lunge and the upward lurch of the rocking body—that freed the wheels promptly upon impediment, and thus averted each shock before it came upon the animals.[26]

Behind the body of the coach was the triangular compartment or "boot" for mail, express, or baggage, and, at the front, under the driver's seat, was another "boot," but more commonly referred to as the "box," which carried various small articles and valuable packages. These "elegant Concord coaches"[27] were the marvel of many, and their introduction marked the beginning of the palmy days of stage travel in Kentucky.

[26]Banning and Banning—*Six Horses,* p. 25.
[27]"Such qualities of durability in a coach weighing about 2500 pounds, may not appear at once to be the soundest boast, but when it is added that no other vehicle of equal capacity, and a few enough of any capacity, ran as easily over the average road, there is little more to be added." *Ibid.,* p. 26.

CHAPTER IV

EARLY TAVERNS

STAGE-COACH travel in the Bluegrass would not have been so picturesque and colorful, perhaps, had it not been for the part the taverns and inns played in the accommodation of travelers and townsfolk. Taverns in the Bluegrass, unlike those of New England, were the outgrowth of the times and modes of travel. At first there were so few towns and villages that hospitality was shown the traveler at every cabin, station, farm, or plantation; every man's house was an inn; every settler was a landlord. In general, no charge was made for the entertainment of the chance visitor, whose stay was deemed a pleasure in the secluded life of the Kentucky backwoods.

The first inns or taverns were built mostly of log, though a few were of stone. They were ordinary wilderness cabins, rendered professionally hospitable by stress of circumstance. They were more often of but one or two rooms where, before the open fireplace, guests were glad to sleep together upon the puncheon floor, wrapped in their traveling blankets or bear skins. The fare was such as hunters had—game from the surrounding forests and neighboring streams, and the product of their nearby clearing, potatoes and the common cereals.

With the improvement of the roads and the advent of the stage-wagons and coaches, these log buildings were soon replaced with comfortable inns and taverns, which were established in the settlements, at the country cross-roads, and at frequent intervals in between these points. They were favorably situated along the principal stage routes, convenient for the accommodation of the travelers as well as for the relief of the horses. Taverns were some-times called "ordinaries," universally pronounced "or-naries," and "it is highly likely the pronunciation hit the nail upon the head more appropriately than the spelling."

Sometimes the terms inn and tavern were employed to distinguish between a mere drinking place and one where meals were also served.[1] Coffee-house was another term used in the towns for a house of accommodation of travel-ers. It was not until after 1825 that the words hotel and house were in general use, and some localities scorned the term "inn" as "too English."

Lexington in the early days had many taverns, "veri-table old English Inns, with quaint signs, smiling boni-faces and everything to match." Probably the first in Lexington and central Kentucky was kept by James Bray, in 1785, who had a little sign swinging in front of his log house bearing the arms of Virginia and announcing to travelers that he could furnish "entertainment for man and beast." This was shortly followed by other taverns in Lexington, of more or less importance. Some of these were the "Sign of Cross-Keys," "The Eagle Tavern," "The Fried Meat Tavern," the "Sheaf of Wheat," and the "Indian Queen."

---

[1]Tippling houses were common in this section, and were places where whiskey and other drinks were sold, without providing accommodations for travelers.

Throughout the country, the tavern prices for food, lodging, and drink, wavered up and down according to the needs of the landlord. In 1803, the magistrates of Fayette County, in consideration of the welfare of the travelers and with a desire to regulate the sale of liquor, deemed it important enough to meet and fix the tavern rates.[2] The accounts were figured in English money as late as the year 1815, when one American dollar or Spanish piastre was worth six English shillings.

There were numerous smaller taverns in the private residences of Lexington, much as the present-day tourist home, and one such tavern is noted wherein:[3]

"Leave is granted him [Jeremiah Murphy] to keep a tavern at his dwelling house in Lexington, for one year from this date, agreeable to law."

Anyone wishing to open and operate a tavern or inn made formal application to the board of magistrates with suitable surety for his good behavior and the peace and

[3]Breakfast........[hot]........1/3 ....cold.......1/
Dinner............[hot]........1/6 ....cold.......1/
Supper............[hot]........1/3 ....cold.......1/
Whiskey per half pint 4d
Brandy per half pint 6d
French brandy per half pint 1/
Rum per half pint 1/
Madeira wine per bottle 9/
All other wines per bottle 6/
Lodging per night 6d
Oats per gallon 4d
Corn per gallon 4d
Hay and stableage, 24 hours 9d
Pasturage, 24 hours 9d
Cyder per quart 6d
Strong beer per quart 6d
Fayette County Court, Order Book I, p. 30, May Term, 1803.
[2]*Ibid.*, p. 131, April, 1804.

order of the establishment. Upon the fulfillment of the conditions, license was granted for one year, as follows:[4]

> "On motion of Joshua Wilson, license is granted him to keep a tavern at the house lately occupied by John Postlethwait, one year from the date hereof, who came into court and entered into bond with George M. Bibb his security as the law directs."

Another entry upon the order books of Fayette County for August, 1809, shows:

> "Tavern license granted John Postlethwait agreeable to law, upon his entering into bond with Joseph Hawkins as surety."

It was the duty of each county clerk, once a year, to prepare a list of all the tavern-keepers in his county and present it to the clerk of the circuit court, who in turn submitted it to the grand jury, that they might look over the list and hear any complaints registered against the tavern-keepers for that year. Any violation of the law subjected the tavern-keepers to a suspension of their license,[5] which clearly stated that "they shall constantly provide wholesome, cleanly lodging and diet for travelers and stableage for horses." Any tavern-keeper found

---

[4]Fayette County Court, Order Book 1, p. 153, May, 1804.

[5]Gideon Woods, tavern-keeper at the settlement of Athens, Fayette County, had his license suspended for "suffering persons to tipple and drink more than is necessary in his house and on his premises and by suffering scandalous and disorderly conduct and behaviour in his house and about his premises to the great disturbance of the peace and happiness of divers good citizens of the Commonwealth." Fayette County Court, file, 1812–14.

guilty of overcharging his guests was fined thirty shillings for each offense. To further protect travelers, the tavern-keepers were required by law to obtain from the county clerk a copy of the tavern rates as fixed by the magistrates, and post the same in the public room and bar of his tavern, and keep the same up, under a penalty of twenty-five pounds.[6]

Judging from the large number of inns and taverns scattered throughout the Bluegrass, it is evident they played a very important part in the political and social life of the people. Many were the reasons that could be given to explain and justify attendance at the old-time tavern; one was that often the only newspaper that came to the village was kept therein. This small sheet often saw hard usage; for when it went its rounds some could hardly read it; some but pretended to read it. The extent and purpose to which this frail news-letter might be applied can be guessed from the following notice, posted over the bar of one tap-room:

"Gentlemen learning to spell are requested to use last week's newsletter."

It was most natural that people should frequent taverns in order to learn what was going on in the eastern states and to acquire the latest local gossip. It was to these places of refuge that the traveler came and imparted information which he had gathered on his journey across the country. It is not surprising that the tavern of the town became the civic center from which radiated

⁶Littell, Vol. 1, p. 195.

much of the social and intellectual life of the community. In fact, the importance of the tavern to its neighborhood was far greater than to travelers.

In the earlier days of our settlements, all diversions centered at the nearest tavern. Very often the only suitable assembly room in the town would be the large public room of the inn. This hall was the favorite place for performances of all sorts; small shows, petty fakers, and for the exhibition of small and amusing inventions of skill. Tavern-keepers, as a rule, encouraged these showmen, giving them part of the stables or an outbuilding, because the crowd they drew would patronize their bar. Fortune tellers, exhibits of dwarfs and freaks, musical clocks, wax-works—truly the number and variety of these petty fakers were legion.

Citizens of Lexington and travelers stopping over had the opportunity to see the "Siamesse Twin Brothers" at Postlethwait's Inn, and so popular were they, in response to public request, they announced "they will remain for another fortnight." Farther down the street at Candy's Tavern could be seen the "Gigantic Giraffe or Camelopard" which its owner proudly remarked "was never brought before to this continent and but rarely seen in any part of the civilized world," or, at Satterwhite's Tavern could be seen "an African Lyon," the largest ever seen in America.[7]

Another popular diversion of the early Lexingtonians was attending the exhibition of wax-works, usually held in the ball room of Robert Bradley's Travellers Hall,

---

[7]*Kentucky Gazette*, June 1, 1805.

where the exhibitor, Mr. Davenport, was registered. These
life-like figures depicted scenes of love, humor, pathos,
and tragedy, as well as great historical events. For winter
amusement, the citizens were treated to numerous feats
of ventriloquism, natural magic, and exhibitions of "optic
views" by Mr. Rannie, at the long room of the Eagle
Tavern, and the following season at Satterwhite's Tavern.[8]

For the first decade and a half of the nineteenth century, the citizens of the Bluegrass as well as travelers passing through Lexington were thrilled with the exhibitions
of balloon ascents and fire-works, usually held on the
green in front of the tavern, or lot adjacent. Mr. Gaston,
an early exponent of the art, announced with handbills in
the tavern tap-rooms that he would have "a great display
of fire-works and the ascent of a balloon sixty-five feet in
diameter." A week later, the *Gazette* in speaking of the
terror this strange "vertical air coach" caused to the country folk in an adjoining county, where it alighted, said:
"The strange appearance of so singular a stranger drop-
ping from the clouds excited considerable alarm and
terror among the good people of the neighborhood where
it alighted."

Not only were the taverns used for the shows and
exhibitions of skill, but they were often the scene of
brilliant balls and dances, entertainment of distinguished
guests and famous visitors, as well as "concerts of music."
Most exciting of all were the drawings of lotteries at
the tavern, which was thronged with the excited ticket

[8] *Kentucky Gazette,* June 11, 1805.

holders. This was the favorite means used by schools, churches, and benevolent institutions for raising sums of money quickly.[9] Various military companies used the taverns of Lexington for their meeting place. A great day of sport at the early taverns was preparation for a turkey shoot or a shooting match; usually taking place on Thanksgiving day or other holidays. Handbills posted in the taverns of Postlethwait, Satterwhite, Keiser, and Downing announced that there would be a very unusual match on the green at Manchester, adjoining Lexington. The prize was a lot and two-story brick house, with a stone-smith house, all valued at $3000, or 30 shots at one hundred dollars each at sixty yards off. The captains of the various military companies were requested to subscribe one shot and to send their best marksmen.

There were other sports offered at the taverns and private homes, as shown by an advertisement in the *Western Citizen*[10] of December, 1814:

"RARE SPORT

"To the Lovers of Sport, their attention is called that on the 29th of December there will be a

"BEAR BAITING

"At my house on the Cynthiana Road, one mile from Paris at 10 o'clock A. M. when a three year old HE BEAR will be turned loose and five dogs will be entered every half hour to fight him; according

---

[9]"On September 16, 1809, all ticket holders for the Episcopal Church lottery are requested to be present at Satterwhite's Tavern, to proceed with the drawing of tickets." *Kentucky Gazette*, September 5, 1809.
[10]*Western Citizen*, Paris, December 10, 1814.

to the regulations to be made known at the time of entering.

"ALSO, the half of a SHE BEAR will be barbecued and as good a dinner furnished as the country can provide. No quarrelsome person will be permitted to remain a guest as peace and harmony will be promoted and expected.

"O. A. FORSYTHE."

One of the most important and, needless to say, frequented rooms of the tavern was the tap-room. Here travelers congregated to refresh themselves, renew acquaintances, and in winter to enjoy the large open fire upon which was kept a huge back-log. This room was generally the largest of the tavern, with rough floor and ample seats and chairs. Usually there was a tall, rather rough writing desk at which a traveler might write a letter, or sign a contract, or where the landlord made out his bills and kept books. There was nothing of particular beauty about the bar itself, which in most cases was constructed by the neighborhood carpenter of rough lumber, but it served its purpose in ample fashion. Across this bar were dispensed drinks of whiskey, French brandy, peach brandy, rum, Madeira wine, and "cyder," at prices ranging from four and one-half cents to two shillings three pence.[11]

Metheglin was a favorite drink in Kentucky for many years, as well as in Virginia and other southern states, whole plantations of honey locust being set out to supply metheglin. The long beans of the locust were ground

---

[11]Fayette County Court, Order Book 2, p. 278.

and mixed with honey, herbs, and water, and fermented. Beer being hard to obtain in the taverns of the Bluegrass, the patrons soon drifted to cider drinking, the fixed price being six pence "for strong cyder per quart."[12]   So great was the demand for cider in the South that apple orchards were deemed the most desirable leasing property. Claret wine being expensive was not popular with tap-room patrons.

In order to remind dilatory customers that cash was to be desired, broad hints were sometimes hung in plain view over the bar of the tap-rooms, one of which read:

> "My liquor's good, my measure's just;
> But, honest Sirs, I will not trust."

To such of those early travelers as sought more privacy and were desirous of being removed from the tap-rooms, the proprietor of the Love Tavern in Frankfort appealed:

> "Private parties may have rooms undisturbed by the bustle of a Tavern, and Gentlemen disposed to have private boarding can be accommodated to their wishes."

Young men in Lexington and vicinity, desiring instruction in the art of self defense, attended classes at Travellers Hall, where Aaron Cipriani, the well known and skillful professor, gave lessons in the use of the "broadsword, backsword, spadroon, and dagger."[13]   Great movements were organized in the assembly rooms of the taverns.

[12]Fayette County Court, Order Book 2, pp. 278–280.
[13]*Kentucky Gazette*, August 12, 1812.

Frankfort was chosen the capital of Kentucky in Brent's Tavern, Lexington; and the sitting of courts were often held in the public rooms of taverns, not only in small towns, where assembly rooms were few, but in larger cities. Notices were posted about the tavern walls offering rewards for runaway slaves, and traders and slave-drivers frequented these places for gossip and information that would lead to their capture. The tavern was the place for assemblages of all kinds: recruiting rendezvous; meeting of town trustees; taking depositions; examining applicants for law licenses; caucuses and town elections.

We imagine the host of the early inns and taverns had very little difficulty in preparing the daily menu, with his choice of venison, bear, wild turkeys, and other small game, fresh from the hunters' prowess; a slightly heavy fare, but those "were strenuous times when a heavy fare was most necessary." This with the well-stocked supply of "johnny-cake," wild berries, vegetables, and fruits gave the traveler a hearty meal suitable for the hard trips.

Manners were rough enough at many of the country taverns, as well as some of the villages and cities, until well into the nineteenth century. There could be no putting on of airs, no exclusiveness. Many of the rooms were double bedded, and three or four who were strangers to each other often slept in each other's company. When a traveler came into an inn and found all the beds taken, his peace of mind was quite undisturbed. The landlord considered it his duty to give shelter to all who opened his door, and usually did so. After the normal capacity of the tavern was filled, late arrivals were told of the

situation and knew what to do.   At bedtime they simply
spread their blankets on the floor of the large public room,
lay down with their feet toward the fire, and rolled themselves up in blankets or buffalo robes for a good night's
rest.   Often the assembly room was so crowded with the
forms of weary men that a late arrival had to explore by
candle light and careful steps in order to find a place for
himself.   In the early morning, the guests arose fully
clothed, ready for another day's trip upon the road.

Travelers and tavern patrons in the early period of our
country were often confronted with the difficult problem
of making change in the payment for their meals, lodging, and keep of their horse.   With the scarcity of small
coins and the use of the Spanish piastre, Mexican and
American dollar, the problem of small change gave rise
to our present terms, "two-bits" and "six-bits," whereby
the dollars were cut in eight pieces or "bits" for circulation.

Thomas Ashe, who visited Lexington in the fall of
1806, remained overnight at one of the taverns, and, on
leaving the next morning, asked the proprietor what he
owed, at the same time throwing down a silver dollar on
the rough counter of the barroom.   The tavern-keeper
called in his Negro man servant and told him to *"chop* it,
I want it changed" and to take out of the dollar one-
quarter and one-eighth; in other words, one shilling and
three pence for his lodging and meals and nine pence for
his horse.   The servant executed his master's orders with
great dexterity and returned the dollar to the guest with
nearly one-fourth cut out, making "an angle running to
the middle, which gave it the appearance of three-fourths

of a circle."[14]   Learning that this was the legal mode of procuring change, the English traveler had the Negro transform a couple of dollars with his chisel, into quarters, eighths, and sixteenths, and as he later stated: "I received a handful of small change which I found of great advantage on the road."

It was of common occurrence for Lexington merchants to send pack horses loaded with "cut silver" to the eastern markets once or twice a year to square their accounts with Philadelphia and other merchants from whom goods had been purchased and extensive credits given.[15] As everybody was entitled to make that division of the coins, there were some "who did it for the sake of gain; at the same time in the retail trade the seller will generally abate in his articles for a whole dollar, than have their full worth in six or eight pieces."[16]

"It is the custom in all American taverns from the highest to the lowest," wrote an English traveler in 1807, "to have a sort of public table at which the inmates of the house and travelers dine together at a certain hour." One of the most interesting phases of the life in Lexington in this period was that of the taverns and inns, and the only full account that we have is by the English traveler, Henry Bradshaw Fearon, in his *Sketches of America*. In describing the customs around the local tavern where he was stopping, he wrote: "These hotels are conducted different-

---

[14]Ashe—*Travels in America*, p. 190.

[15]Michaux—*Early Western Travels*, Vol. III, p. 204; Ranck, p. 232.

[16]This crude method of making change often left the wedge-shaped pieces with rough edges; some filed these off for easier handling—hence there was always a loss in weight of the metal. In 1813, the Legislature passed an act subjecting all "cut money" to a 3 per cent discount when offered in payment for state debts.

ly from those with which you are acquainted. A person desiring to put up at one of them applies to the bar-keeper, and he must not feel disappointed should he be refused accommodations for want of room. The place for washing is in the open yard, in which there is a large cistern, several towels, and a Negro in attendance.

"The sleeping room commonly contains from four to eight bedsteads, having mattresses, but frequently no feather beds; sheets of calico, two blankets, a quilt. The bedsteads have no curtains, and the rooms are greatly unprovided with any conveniences. The public rooms are— a newsroom, a boot-room, in which the bar is situated, and a dining room. The fires are generally surrounded by parties of about six, who gain and keep possession. The usual custom is to walk up and down the newsroom in a manner somewhat similar to walking the deck at sea. Smoking segars is practiced by all without an exception, and at every hour of the day.

"But to return to the tavern; at half-past seven, the first bell rings for the purpose of collecting all the boarders, and at eight the second bell rings; breakfast is then set, the dining room is unlocked, a general rush commences, and some activity as well as dexterity is essentially necessary to obtain a seat at the table. A boy as clerk attends to take down the names, in order that when bills are settled no improper deductions should be made. The breakfast consists of a profuse supply of fish, flesh, and fowl, which is consumed with a rapidity truly extraordinary; often before I had finished my first cup of tea the room which when I had commenced was crowded to suffocation —had become nearly empty.

"At half-past one the bell rings, announcing the approach of dinner; the avenues to the dining room become thronged. At two o'clock the second bell rings, the doors are thrown open, and a repetition of the breakfast scene succeeds. At six, tea, or what is here called supper, is announced, and partaken of in the same manner. This is the last meal, and usually affords the same fare as breakfast. A billiard table adjoins the tavern, and is generally well occupied. At ten o'clock, nearly all have gone to bed, or what they call '*turned in.*' At table there is neither conversation or drinking; the latter is effected by individuals taking their solitary 'eye-openers,' 'toddy,' or 'phlegm dispensers' at the bar, the keeper of which is in full employ from sun-time to bedtime . . . every house of this description that I have seen is thronged to excess, and there is not a man who appears to have a single earthly object in view except spitting and smoking segars . . ."[17]

In another description of tavern life in the Bluegrass region, Fearon gives us the prices of board[18] at Lawes' Hall, and the rules posted:

    I.   All Gentlemen to give in their names to the bar-keeper.

[17]Fearon—*Sketches of America*, pp. 247–249.

[18]Board for horse, per year	$120.00
Board for horse, per week	3.00
Board for horse, per night	.50
Board for horse, per single feed	.18½
Dinner for man	.37
Supper for man	.25
Breakfast for man	.12½
Board for man, per year	120.00
Board for man, per week	3.00
Board for man, per day	1.00

II. No Gentleman shall enter the dining room
     until the second bell rings.
III. No gambling allowed in the bedrooms.
IV. The door will be closed at ten o'clock, except
     on nights of public entertainment.
V. No Gentleman shall take the saddle, bridle, or
     harness of another Gentleman without his
     consent.

Travelers coming to Lexington by horse-back and by
stage were those who, in some measure, were looking
about for homes, farms, or family connections. The best
people necessarily "stopped" at some tavern while they
looked around for suitable locations for the new home or
business, or tarried awhile to enjoy the pleasures offered
by this thriving frontier town before pushing "on to the
West." Famous visitors came from time to time. The
tavern, large or small, made bids for patronage in the accepted way of that day. It was considered a great feature
to be able to entertain a celebrity, and that too served as
publicity, not only for the time being, but for future generations as the fame of the hostelry would be carried far
and near.[19]

Lexington by 1810 had grown to be the cultural, intellectual, and commercial center of the western country, and
had firmly laid claim to the title of "Athens of the West,"
which may be better judged by the description left by an
English traveler[20] who stopped here at this period:

"Lexington is the seat of justice of Fayette County and
is situated in the heart of a most beautiful country, on a

---

[19]Such was the case when LaFayette visited Lexington in 1825, also
James Monroe and Andrew Jackson.   [20]Melish—Vol. II, pp. 186–189.

branch of Elkhorn River. It is one of the earliest settlements in the western country, and is coeval with the battle of Lexington, the news having reached the early settlers, they conferred on it the present name. It has since flourished in a wonderful degree and now contains 4326 inhabitants. By the census of 1800, it contained 2400, so that it has nearly doubled its population in ten years; and as it is progressing in manufactures and wealth and the adjoining country is rapidly settling up, there is every probability that it will increase in the same ratio for a considerable time to come.

"Lexington has a very neat court-house, market house, jail, four churches, and a bank. There is a very excellent seminary of learning, under the management of special trustees, which is supported by 70,000 acres of land. There are a number of valuable manufactures; and a steam mill was recently put in motion, which is of great advantage to the town and neighborhood. There are four principal taverns, all under good management, and there are about thirty retail stores, and two book stores. The principal manufactures of Lexington are hemp, to which the labor of the black people is well suited, and of which the country yields amazing crops, at the low price of four dollars per cwt.; being at the rate of eighteen pound Sterling per ton. There are eighteen extensive ropewalks, five bagging manufactures, and one of duck. The other principal manufactures are eight cotton factories, three woolen factories, and one oil-cloth factory.

"The state of society is much improved in Lexington. Education is well attended to, and there are plenty of good schools. Perhaps the church is not on a footing with the sentiments of the people, which are very liberal on the subject of religion. They are polite and affable in their manners, and are hospitable in a high degree. They are high spirited, independent, and republican in their sentiments; and, as might be expected from a people sprung from Virginia, they are warm admirers of Mr. Jefferson, whose inaugural speech I saw elegantly printed on white silk, and hung up in the hall of Postlethwait's Tavern. The streets of Lexington are nearly all paved, and the country round about is remarkably fertile and well cultivated . . . and very little land is now to be had under twelve dollars per acre . . ."

Had overland transportation prevailed, Lexington might have maintained her commercial supremacy over the neighboring towns of Louisville and Cincinnati, but, after the successful trip of the steamer *New Orleans,* in 1811, the first steamboat to ply western waters, the commercial doom of Lexington was sealed. Even though Lexington at this period was beginning to lose some of its commercial supremacy, it was still a place of culture and refinement, as is stated by Samuel R. Brown who visited the Old Postlethwait's Tavern, then Wilson's, in 1817: "Wilson's tavern is excelled by none in America for extensiveness, style, and good living." Even the Lexington of today would not need to feel ashamed at the account of the material prosperity of that village in 1817, which, according to Brown's account, compared favorably with any of the cities of the Atlantic seaboard.

With the opening of the stage lines out of Lexington and radiating through the Bluegrass, it can be seen that the need of taverns and inns was great. They soon sprang up at frequent intervals along the main roads and at all cross-roads.[21] Comforts incidental to stage travel were not commonly met with in the journeys over the long dusty roads; and the place where a bath could be obtained attracted more than ordinary notice. Travelers through Lexington had their attention called to Boshart's:[22]

"BATH HOUSE

The subscriber has his *BATH HOUSE* in good order and is now ready for bathing. All the troughs are new; the pump is in a good spring; the water is plenty; the house is inclosed with a high fence of plank. Every attention should be paid to accommodate those that please to call. Bathing 1s 6d"

Passengers arriving in stage-coaches in Lexington late at night, or departing before daylight, would frequently hear that important personage—the town night-watchman—making his hourly rounds and crying out his watches "in a shrill, unearthly voice, the time of night and the weather." This protection to the citizens of Lexington was established in the spring of 1811, being the first city in Kentucky to have a town crier or night-watchman.

It was the unique custom in those days to advertise in rhyme. Luke Usher, proprietor of the well-known tavern, urged travelers to Lexington to refresh themselves with him:[23]

---

[21]For a list of these early taverns and inns, see Appendix.

[22]J. Boshart—*Kentucky Gazette*, May 30, 1814.

[23]Usher's Tavern was the "Sign of the Ship." *Kentucky Gazette*, May 1, 1818.

"When the weary and hunger to *Lexington* trip.
Let them stop and regale at the sign of the Ship,
Where I promise to treat them as well as I'm able,
With a larder well stored, and good liquors and
    stable."

In this glimpse of tavern and inn life in the Bluegrass
of a century and a quarter ago, we see many of the customs and traits that were typical of all frontier towns.
Many of these traits that the foreign visitors found here
were still holding in the remote sections of Kentucky well
into the twentieth century.

CHAPTER V

PALMY DAYS OF STAGE TRAVEL

IT IS doubtful if any description written today could adequately portray the importance, in its relation to the affairs of the people, which stage-coach traffic assumed during the period between 1830 and 1845 in the Bluegrass. During the years in question it was the only means by which a large part of the population could accomplish overland journeys. Even when railroad and rivers were available for some portions of the trip, travelers had to resort to the stages for the major parts of the distances traveled.

Early in this period, Lexington and central Kentucky were visited by the disease commonly known as Asiatic cholera, which resulted in the great cholera plague of 1833. Lexington had scarcely gotten into the harness of civic progress[1] when the plague broke out. Modern methods of sanitation were not then known, and in June, 1833, the cholera crept like a thief in the night into the gaieties of the little metropolis. Within the short space of one month, fifteen hundred people were stricken and not less than five hundred died.[2] This epidemic of cholera was brought to Lexington in the stage-coaches, after having come down the Ohio River to Maysville, and thence to

---

[1]The city was incorporated in 1832, with Charlton Hunt as its first mayor.
[2]Davidson—*History of the Presbyterian Church in Kentucky*, p. 334.

the various towns and villages[3] along the stage route to central Kentucky.

The *Observer and Reporter* gave a fairly complete list of those who died, and from it we learn that two hundred and fifty-two whites, one hundred and eighty-four slaves, and forty-six free blacks were among the victims.[4] While the death rate was chiefly among the poorer classes, it did not spare those in the higher walks of life. A letter written June 16, 1833, from a resident of Lexington to a friend in another city,[5] gives some idea of the devastation of cholera in Lexington, and the attempts of the citizens to leave the scene of horror: "That awful scourge of God broke out in Lexington and its ravages have been dreadful and desolating beyond example—not even excepting New Orleans. It is the opinion of the best informed that not far short of four hundred have fallen victims in fourteen days—and this too, with a greatly reduced population. More than one-half, probably two-thirds, fled soon after its commencement.

"The progress of the disease has been frightfully rapid. Many have gone to their beds well, and have been in their graves before the next noon. The panic has been dreadful, and the more so, as it was wholly unexpected. The city authorities disappeared, no hospitals for the poor provided, no boards of health formed, no medical reports made or required, and now, no mode of ascertaining our

[3]"In like manner it [the cholera] burst out at the lower Blue Licks, a watering place thronged with visitors." *Niles Weekly Register*, Vol. XLIV, p. 305, June, 1833.

[4]*Lexington Observer & Reporter*, August 22, 1833.

[5]*National Gazette & Literary Register*, Philadelphia, June 27, 1833.

exact loss. Stores have been shut, hotels and taverns[6] shut, public houses, printing offices all shut; and in short, nothing open but graveyards and their premonitories, apothecary shops. Our physicians are either dead or broken down. Graves could not be dug or coffins made as fast as they are wanted. A number of coffins or boxes were sometimes put into one hole. Ten or a dozen boxes have been left in the graveyard, unburied, until their turn came the next day. When we retired at night, we could not expect, and hardly dared hope, to meet again well. All those that could fly—fled . . ."

Great crowds gathered around the old stage office in Brennan's Tavern, hoping to secure seats in the stage-coaches leaving the city, and so great was the rush, that extra coaches were put on all the lines and still the stage proprietors were not able to accommodate all the fleeing citizens. Those who could not secure passage in the stage-coaches left the panic-stricken city by various means; some walked, some by horse-back, and a great many left in wagons, gigs, and private carriages. "Our city is literally depopulated," remarked one of the citizens who remained behind.[7]

Olympian Springs, eight miles southeast of Owingsville, in Bath County, was a favorite objective for many of the fleeing citizens, as the proprietor of that well known watering place advertised in the Lexington papers: "There has been no cholera at this place."

---

[6]Minutes of the trustees of Lexington, May 6, 1833, showed licenses had been issued for "3 porter-houses, 5 coffee-houses, 10 victuallers, 6 taverns."

[7]*Lexington Observer & Reporter*, June 5, 1833.

As a carrier of news in those dreadful times, the stage-coach figured prominently in keeping stricken communities posted on the growth and progress of the pestilence in other places: "We learn that the Paris stage this morning brings account of eight deaths in that place yesterday evening and last night."[8]   Another news item stated: "Passengers on the stage from Louisville to Shelbyville reported a violent outbreak at Simpsonville and in the country along the route."

This large exodus from Lexington during the cholera epidemic was a boon to the stage-coach business, clearly demonstrating the important part this method of conveyance played in the lives of the Bluegrass citizens. At this period, 1834, there were more than a dozen principal stage routes through the Bluegrass.[9] In addition to these principal routes, as shown by S. Augustus Mitchell on his

---

[8]*Lexington Observer & Reporter,* June 22, 1833.

[9]From Louisville, by Frankfort, Lexington, Paris, and Washington, to Maysville, 140 miles, daily.

From Louisville, by Elizabethtown and Munfordsville, to Bowling Green, 111 miles, 6 times a week.

From Louisville, by Shepherdsville and Bardstown, to Lebanon, 69 miles, 3 times a week.

From Lexington, by Georgetown to Frankfort, 30 miles, daily.

From Lexington, by Winchester, Mt. Sterling, and Owingsville, to Cattlesburg, Va., 124 miles, 3 times a week.

From Lexington, by Nicholasville to Harrodsburg, 32 miles, 3 times a week.

From Lexington, by Cynthiana, Falmouth, and Newport, to Cincinnati, 86 miles, twice a week.

From Lexington, by Lancaster, Mt. Vernon, Barbourville, and Cumberland Gap, to Bean Station, Tenn., 174 miles, twice a week.

From Lexington, by Athens to Richmond, 25 miles, 3 times a week.

From Frankfort by Harrodsburg, Lebanon, Glasgow, and Gallatin, to Nashville, Tenn., 206 miles, 7 times a week.

From Georgetown, by Williamstown, Florence, and Covington, to Cincinnati, 62 miles, 3 times a week.

From Harrodsburg, by Lancaster to Richmond, 44 miles, twice a week.

From Danville, by Stanford to Somerset, 45 miles, 3 times a week.

stage map of Kentucky for the year 1834, there were numerous smaller routes, over which stages ran as connecting links. These were for the most part purely local. One example of this was the stage line from Cave City to Mammoth Cave, in Edmonson County.

After 1830, stage-coach travel in the Bluegrass was on the upward trend. The increase of business resulted in several companies starting lines and running over the same routes. This developed great rivalry between the different stage lines. The passenger and mail coaches were operated very much like the railroads and bus systems of today. A perfect network of routes covered the Bluegrass. The rival lines fought each other with bitterness, in lowering rates and in outdoing each other in points of speed and accommodations.

New inventions and appliances were eagerly sought in the hope of securing a larger share of the public patronage. This rivalry extended into every phase of the business, with fast horses, comfortable coaches, well known and companionable drivers, and favorable connections. The rivalry of coach owners and drivers extended to passengers, who became violent partisans of the road on which they traveled, and a threatening exhibition of bowie knives and pistols was often made.

At this time, the "Old Line" stage had been in operation for some years, with its stage office at the Postlethwait or Brennan's Hotel, and was under the ownership of Edward P. Johnson, Philip Swigert, John H. Hanna, and Jacob Swigert, who "were trading and staging under the partnership name and style of Edward P. Johnson &

Co."[10]   Their lines covered the Bluegrass region of Kentucky and extended as far south as Bean Station in Tennessee.[11]   During the palmy days of the stage travel Edward P. Johnson,[12] son of the former stage-coach proprietor, Colonel James Johnson, was the most important figure.   He had numerous connections and companies, operating over many Bluegrass routes.   Each of these companies co-operated with each other so as to form connecting links for through travel between distant points.   One
of the companies was Johnson, Weisiger & Co., which
operated out of Frankfort to Louisville, and one from
Maysville to Lexington was in partnership with John H.
Hanna.[13]

Johnson's stage office was convenient for travelers, as
it was located in one corner of the barroom in Brennan's

[10]A. M. Poage *vs.* Edw. P. Johnson & Co., file 1013, Fayette Circuit
Court, July 6, 1832.

[11]GENERAL STAGE OFFICE, Brennan's Hotel, Lexington, Ky. Arrivals and Departures of the Mail and Accommodation Stages. Louisville
Mail Stage, via Versailles, leaves Lexington every day at 9 o'clock P. M.
and arrives at Louisville at 10 o'clock the following morning.

Maysville Stage leaves every night at 12 o'clock and arrives at 10
o'clock A. M. the following day at Maysville.

Also *another* leaves at 10 o'clock A. M. and arrives same day at
9 o'clock P. M.

Nashville and Bean Station [Tenn.] Mail Stage, by Harrodsburg,
leaves every other day at 4 o'clock A. M.

Richmond and London Mail Stage, *intersecting the Bean Station
Stage at London,* leaves every other day at 4 o'clock A. M.

Winchester and Owingsville Mail Stage leaves on Mondays, Wednesdays, and Fridays at 5 o'clock A. M.

Georgetown and Cincinnati Mail Stage leaves every night at 9 o'clock.

Extra Stages for any point can be furnished whenever called for and
tickets can be taken at Brennan's Hotel either for Frankfort or the
whole way to Louisville. J. H. Penney, Gen'l Agent.

[12]He lived at "Johnson's Grove" on North Limestone, Lexington. On
September 27, 1855, he sold the property for $15,900 to David A. Sayre,
who established Sayre College on the site. Fayette County Court, Deed
Book 31, p. 406.

[13]Alex. Preston *vs.* Johnson & Hanna, Fayette Circuit Court, file 1213,
January 17, 1834.

Hotel, Lexington. He evolved what we now term the "limited" and "accommodation" service of the railroad. In fact, the term "limited" originated with mail-carrying coaches limiting passengers to a specific number. The fast mail line took but four passengers in each coach on a certain day of the week, the slower line charging lower fare and taking all applicants, even putting on extra coaches if necessary.

Fare on the "limited" or mail stages from Paris to Maysville was three dollars per passenger, while on the "accommodation" slower stage the fare for the same distance was two dollars. It was twenty-five cents cheaper to take the slower stage from Lexington to Paris, making the price of passage seventy-five cents. Leaving from the stage office in Lexington at Brennan's Hotel, this line stopped ten miles out of Lexington on the Maysville Road at William Moreland's Tavern and post-office, then at Charles Talbutt's Hotel in Paris, James Bassell's in Millersburg, Mrs. Pryor's at lower Blue Licks, and concluded the run at Mrs. Goddard's Inn at Maysville.[14]

It usually happened that a stage-coach company owned, or had an interest in, several of the taverns and inns along its route, and all their coaches stopped at those particular places. The success or failure of a stage line often hinged upon the favorable connections of well known inns and stopping places along its route.[15] Experienced travelers were wise in "booking" passage with

[14]*Western Citizen*, Paris, March 22, 1839.

[15]"Dickey is very hostile to us and at Paris has both taverns and I could not get in any," wrote Weaver to his partner, Col. McNair, of the line of McNair & Weaver, Lexington, January 2, 1838. Letter in author's collection.

stage lines that stopped for relays and meals at the well known and popular taverns of the time.

Another prominent figure of this time, in the stage-coach traffic, was Colonel Dunning R. McNair, who maintained a large line of stages from Wheeling, West Virginia, to Pittsburgh and Washington. He came to Lexington in the fall of 1837, in company with John W. Weaver, "bringing all their stages, horses, and drivers out from Pennsylvania."[16] They started an "accommodation line" of stages under the name of "Good Intent Line" or General Opposition, and managed to secure the mail contract from Lexington to Maysville:

GOOD INTENT OR GENERAL OPPOSITION LINE UNITED STATES MAIL

Leaves Lexington daily at 3 o'clock A. M. for Maysville, running through in 8½ hours.

Leaves Lexington daily at 5 o'clock A. M. for Louisville.

This company is supplied with substantial Troy and Lancaster Coaches, excellent teams, and careful sober drivers; all racing is expressly forbidden and baggage or parcels at the risk of owners thereof.

McNAIR & WEAVER, Proprietors[17]

The stage office of the Good Intent Line was in charge of Harbert McConathy,[18] and was located at 13 South

[16]Recollections of Henderson G. Banta, Kentucky State Historical Society, Frankfort.

[17]*Lexington Intelligencer*, January 8, 1838.

[18]John W. Weaver in a letter dated February 4, 1838, to his partner, Col. McNair, said: "I have opened an office opposite the railroad office in Lexington, for Louisville, and have employed Mr. McConathy as agent, as he is the most popular young man and best acquainted with our business." Letter in author's collection.

Mill Street, at the corner of Water Street. Great stress
was laid upon the qualifications of the drivers, as this had
a lot to do with public patronage, and rival lines advertised that "their drivers were experienced, sober, and careful." Then another line at this period was the "Opposition Reliance" line of stages, between Lexington and
Louisville, under the proprietorship of Griffin and Mc-
Archran. They selected M. D. West as their stage agent
in Lexington and with their office in Todd's Hotel announced:

OPPOSITION RELIANCE LINE OF STAGES
between
LEXINGTON AND LOUISVILLE

Leaves Lexington every morning at 4 o'clock A.
M. Arrives at Louisville same evening at 6 o'clock
P. M.

Returning

Leaves Louisville at 4 o'clock A. M., and arrives
at Lexington by 6 o'clock P. M. They have also a
line of Stages running every other day from Lexington to Harrodsburg, by way of Frankfort.

GRIFFIN & McARCHRAN, Proprietors

The stage proprietors, at variance on most matters, all
agreed that the nomenclature of coaches and stage lines
and the painting of names on them very materially in-
fluenced their reputation and the class of their customers.
This fact being indisputable, coach proprietors vied with
each other to invent names which would appeal to the

public and indicate to a great degree the nature of the coach and the people it especially catered to. As old ladies and gentlemen formed no inconsiderable portion of travelers, they were provided with steady easy going names as "Peoples Line," "Good Intent Line," "The Reliance"; names as familar to the traveling public as New York Central, Southern, and other railroads of today. The best coaches, like their counterparts on the railways of today, were named for statesmen, warriors, states, presidents, generals,[19] nations, and cities; besides such fanciful names as "Ivanhoe," "Mayflower," "Pathfinder," "Clarenden," and "Sultana" were called into requisition.

Of the main stage routes out of Lexington, the ones to Louisville and to Maysville were the most overworked,[20] and on the latter, another stage company, the "Peoples Line," made its appearance in 1839. Keiser's Hotel was the stage office for this new line:

PEOPLES LINE—LEXINGTON TO MAYSVILLE

Will leave Lexington and Maysville at 6 o'clock A. M., running through in DAY-LIGHT. Having comfortable Coaches, their stock fleet and true, experienced and accommodating drivers, the Proprietors solicit a share of the public patronage.

J. SURDAM, Agent at Lexington

---

[19]General Taylor was a well known and favorite coach of C. A. Hawkins, on the Lexington-Georgetown stage route. *Georgetown Herald,* May 2, 1849.

[20]The speeds and fares charged for stage travel of this period may be summed up in the notice of the opposition line, Griffin & McArchran, who agreed to transport passengers from "Frankfort to Louisville in 9 hours, fare $4.00." *Lexington Intelligencer,* October 24, 1838.

With three companies operating over the Bluegrass routes, great rivalry sprang up among the drivers, whose great delight would be to whip up the horses and pass the other stage just as it entered the town or village. Hard down Main Street flying before its cloud of dust would come the stage, the high and red-splotched body swaying above racing wheels, the horn blasts, and the four spirited foaming horses, the commotion of the halt, sliding in with a whirlwind of excitement and driver's shouts. The stage was brought to a stop before a waiting, loafing crowd about the tavern or inn, and "the stage was in" for all the townsfolk.

News can never have the same vital importance as in the days when it was taken through the town from the tavern or inn yards by word of mouth. The in-coming coaches were the chief intelligencers of the day, and within a few minutes after their arrival there was an eager buzz of gossip drifting away to the homes and byways. At moments of national importance, the coaches were waylaid by a continuous ambush of inquiry along the roads; a farmer would shout his question from the plough handles, well pleased with a word of answer, and the population of hamlets too inconspicuous for official notice would besiege the driver of the stage for some distance into the country, eager for news of war, invasion, or peace.

Everybody would rush out to see the stage go by and to hear the news, and to catch a glimpse, if possible, of that great man—the stage driver. What a hero he was! "But to see him in his glory is to see him when he starts out in the morning with a fresh team," proudly remarked one of the summer boarders, who often witnessed the departure of the stage in front of Brennan's Inn and stage office in Lexington. Continuing in his admiration for the "knight of the ribbons," who was the acme of many a young man's ambition, he gives us this picture:

> "He comes up in front of the stage office flying; the horses are nervous and uneasy while the passengers are getting aboard, but he is master of the situation; he is happy for he knows that he is the observed of all by the small boys and loungers gathered to see him off. Baggage all strapped; passengers all in; everything ready, he is prepared to act—he is not yet ready—first he slaps his hat over one side of his head, gives the ends of the lines a professional swing over the top of the coach, places his foot firmly on the footboard, pulls up his lines, whip in hand, rolls his quid of tobacco around to the right spot, and then issues the command to the horses. Each horse is expected to press into his collar at that instant and do his best to forge ahead. This speed is kept up until he is out of sight of the loungers and small boys, when he slackens the pace and settles down to a square trot, and the regular day's journey has begun."

Fanciful appellations were often-times bestowed upon the stage drivers, as "knight of the ribbons," "whipster," "knight of the reins," or "whip," but the sobriquet most used, and perhaps better suited was "jehu."[21] The term coachman or coachmaster was never used in the American stage-coach world. It was used in a few cases by passengers, usually Englishmen who were accustomed to hearing that name in their own country, and it was about as equally disagreeable to a stage driver to be called a coachman as to be offered a tip. He might accept a cigar, a drink, a box of cigars, or even a ten-dollar bill, but the typical tip offered the ordinary coachman was far beneath his dignity. His professional vocabulary did not include the word coachman—the operation was one of staging.

Of the stage drivers, some owned their own coaches, some owned part, but the majority were merely employed as drivers. On the road the much envied and esteemed person, the stage driver, was a very busy man. He was lookout, pilot, captain, conductor, brakeman, flagman, and engineer. From his position and duties he came into constant contact with men of political, social, and commercial fame of the country. The esteem in which the "knight of the ribbons" was held may be obtained from the picture drawn by one who was reared on the Old National Pike, or Cumberland Road, who said: "My earliest recollections are intimately associated with coaches, teams, and drivers, and like most boys raised in an old stage tavern, I longed to be a man when I could aspire to the greatness and dignity of a professional stage driver. In my boyish eyes no position in life

[21]A humorous allusion to a fast driver. Jehu, son of Jehoshaphat and King of Israel, as captain of the host, conspired against Jehoram, making a furious attack with chariots, during which Jehoram was killed. ". . . and the driving *is* like the driving of Jehu, for he driveth furiously." II Kings, IX:20.

had so many attractions as that of driving a stage-coach. A Judge, a Congressman, even Henry Clay, or President Jackson did not measure up to the character of John Mills or Charley Howell in my juvenile fancy."[22]

These stage drivers were a dignified and interesting class of men, and on their stages they carried from country to town, from house to house, news of the health of loved ones, gossip up and down the roads, and matters of national importance. They were character readers of men and horses alike, and were autocrats of their own special domain and respected everywhere. The drivers on local lines developed most friendly intimacy with dwellers along the route; they bore messages, brought news, carried letters and packages, transacted exchanges and did all kinds of shopping at the city end of the route.[23] To keep all the letters and messages clear, the driver often wore a big hat, or a small satchel over his shoulder, in which he enclosed these papers.

Mark Twain, in *Roughing It,* gives a remarkable picture of the old stage driver and his position. "In the eyes of the station-keeper and the hostler, the stage driver was a hero—a great and shining dignitary, the world's favorite son, the envy of the people, the observed of the nations. When they spoke to him, they received his insolent silence meekly, as being the natural and proper conduct of a great man . . . The hostlers and the station-keepers treated the really powerful conductor

---

[22]Searight—*The Old Pike,* p. 182.
[23]N. Parker Willis, who visited Mammoth Cave in 1854, wrote: "A Judge drove the stage in which I crossed the country from Harrodsburg, and the women came out from the farm houses and gave him sixpenny errands to do in the village, with unhesitating familiarity."

or division agent of the stage line merely with the best of what was their idea of civility, but the *driver* was the only being they bowed down to and worshipped. How admirably they would gaze up at him in his high seat, as he gloved himself with lingering deliberation, while some happy hostler held the bunch of reins aloft, and waited patiently for him to take it. And how they would bombard him with glorifying ejaculations as he cracked his long whip and went careering off. . ."

Whips were seldom used to strike the stage horses, the belief of old stagers was that driving them willingly and cheerfully accomplished better results than driving them by force. Those drivers, or "whips" as they were known to each other, could make those crackers unwind at any point they chose with several different degrees of explosive crash, and this had a far greater effect on the horses than beating them. Much stress was laid on the chanteys of the old drivers, because with their chanteys they controlled the cadence of the stride of the team. Stage horses were peculiar in this respect; the confident voice of their master on the box gave them assurance that everything was all right and kept them pulling in unison.

The stage driver's most cherished possessions were his whip[24]—the badge of his profession—and the stage

---

[24]The old stage drivers were expert with their whips, and often indulged in the game of "penny-on-the-bottle" during their spare time around the old stage barn and yard on Limestone, just back of Brennan's or the Phoenix Hotel. There was a big yard adjacent to the stable, where the coaches were washed off after the runs. One of the old copper one-cent pieces, or "penny," was placed flat on the neck of a quart whiskey bottle, and the bottle set on the bare ground. Three, four, five, or any number of drivers could play the game. The players, in turn, would put one foot close to the bottle, take four strides away

horn or bugle. The former he even hesitated lending a trusted brother driver who had been unfortunate in losing his own, and the latter he cherished with almost equal devotion. When approaching a hamlet, village, or town, a vigorous blast was blown to apprise the towns-folk of his coming, or within a half mile of the tavern the bugle was sounded for the table to be in readiness to eat and for fresh horses to be brought forth and changed. Every driver blew two blasts on his horn to start, three to clear the road, and one long blast when a station or tavern was reached.

These were the regulations, but accomplished drivers did a lot more with their horns. Instead of blowing two blasts to start, they would blow a pipe of about eight notes that would put all the horses dancing to go, and then, on taking up the lines, a cluck of the tongue was enough to send them off with a swinging trot. Others, instead of blowing the regulation three blasts when a load of hay was in the road, would play the notes on their horn that could be sung:[25]

"Clear the road for we are coming,
Do not delay the U. S. Mail."

Without their chanteys and horn music, the old stage drivers would have been no better than a farmer boy on

from it, turn suddenly and take a crack at the "penny" to lift it off the bottle without upsetting it. The whip crackers would pop like a pistol about a quarter of an inch above the coin, and it would glide off nearly every time, and the bottle only quivered slightly. Four or five rounds would be played before some driver overset the bottle, and then the drinks would be on him at Dennis Mulligan's across the street.

[25]This was to the tune of "Let the Lower Lights Be Burning."

the job. Toll-gate keepers strained their ears for the blast of the stage horn, in order to have the "gate" lifted and ready to note the number of passengers as the stage passed. "Five for you today, Charlie," was frequently heard as the driver cracked his whip and passed on to the next toll-house.

So regular were the arrivals of the stage that the inhabitants along the route knew almost the hour and minute when the welcome sound of the post horn would reach them and the lead horses appear around the curve. The stage marked the time of day for the laborers in the field, who leaned on hoe or scythe until it was lost to view. The plough stopped in the furrow and the smith rested his sledge on the anvil, as the old stage rolled along. This was the welcome sight to both young and old, and the one big event of the day.

Due to the comparatively level and rolling country of the Bluegrass and the even loads of the stages, along with the good turnpikes, four-horse teams[26] were used mostly. In case of bad roads during the winter months, some lines used six horses, while on some of the short routes two horses were deemed sufficient. Teams of the stage-coaches were designated, in order, from front to rear, as for a four-horse complement the front ones were the "leaders," and those next to the stage were the "wheelers" or wheel horses. *Off* meant *right; near, left.* One spoke of the *off leader,* for example, meaning the

---

[26]The sterling characteristics of the stage horses in the Bluegrass were known at an early date, when the *Kentucky Gazette,* for January 16, 1826, carried the following notice: "Horses Wanted!—The Philadelphia, Dover, and Norfolk Steamboat and Transportation Company desires to purchase one hundred young and first rate horses suitable for the stages of said Company. Apply at Dover, Del."

right-hand leader as seen from the driver's seat; or *near wheeler* meaning the left-hand animal as seen from the driver's box.[27]

Many stage routes of the Bluegrass had a peculiar nomenclature familiar to the tens of thousands who traveled over them in their palmy days. The names applied to peculiar localities along the routes of importance and blended harmoniously with the unique history of each. As example we read of Foxtown, Burnt Tavern, Slickaway, Catnip Hill, Little Hickman, Flat Rock, Stony Point, and Elm Corner. Rich memories always clustered around these names, old stage drivers delighting to relate the scenes with which they were associated, and the stories lost nothing in the telling. Blue Licks was "The Springs"; Paris was "Bourbontown"; but Lexington was always "Lexington."

Along these routes of central Kentucky, taverns and inns were the most important landmarks of the journey, and it was the universal custom for travelers and business men to compute the distance from them, instead of from one town to another. A traveler in the stage-coach days was not tantalized by the fleeting half glimpse of the places as in railroad or automobile travel today. He had ample time to view any unusual, beautiful, or historic spot, as he passed. He had leisure to make inquiry, he had many hours to hear his fellow traveler's tale, or that of the driver. The frequent traveler grew versed in the lore of the road, and its history. He knew the gossip of each house he passed, and he knew the traditions and tales of each community.

---

[27]Banning and Banning—*Six Horses,* p. 401.

The traveler by stage-coach learned the constant lessons from nature. The city-bred man learned of the rounds of work on the farm, the season of crops, the various kinds of trees, grains, grasses, and wild flowers, heard the songs of birds, and witnessed the flights of the wild creatures. Truly, nothing could have been more inspiring and entertaining than a journey through the Bluegrass in the early days of stage-coach travel. Congenial companionship made all the difference in the pleasure of the ride, and passengers usually assorted themselves accordingly; sporting folk whose chief interest lay in horses, gravitated naturally to the front of the coach, where they could talk "horse" and enjoy staging to an extent not imaginable to the passengers behind who did not know an off-wheeler from a near-leader. These long journeys, when the passengers were thrown in such close relationship to each other, were often replete with memorable incidents and developed pleasing and lasting friendships.

This pictures the romantic side of stage-coach travel in central Kentucky. The prosaic side attracts attention when we look at the schedules of some of the lines, which invariably announce departures at three, four, or five A. M.—all before daylight.[28] It mattered little how long was your journey, or where you were going, your coach always started before daylight. You had to arise in the dark, dress in a room most feebly illuminated, eat a

[28]"It is generally the custom in traveling in stages all over the United States to stop early in the evening, generally not later than the hour of seven, so that passengers may go soon to bed, and be ready to start very early in the morning." Stuart, Vol. II, p. 229.

hurriedly prepared breakfast, and start out in the blackness of the night or depressing chill of early morning.

Any number up to nine or ten would be loaded in the stages on an early morning start, and you "traveled in total darkness without your having the least idea of who your companion might be." Another old traveler said of the early morning starts: "The way was very dark, so that, though I rode with the driver, it was some time before I discovered we had four horses." It was not unusual on those early starts to ride ten or fifteen miles before breakfasting.[29]

There were wealthy persons who had their own private carriages and were not dependent upon the stagecoach. These private carriages, or traveling coaches, were a distinctly aristocratic vehicle and deemed a great luxury. General Leslie Combs, of Lexington, stated that one of the few things that Henry Clay and President Jackson ever agreed upon was the improvement of the Zanesville-Florence mail stage route, as that road "extended to both of their homes." General Jackson seldom traveled from the "Hermitage" to Washington in the stage-coaches, but went in his own private coach,[30] driven by his servant, "faithful Albert." It took the General one month to make the trip from his home near Nashville, by way of Lex-

---

[29]"Next morning, May 16, 1830, the stage started early, conveying us to Rice's Tavern, about half-way to Lexington [from Frankfort], twenty miles to breakfast." Stuart, Vol. II, p. 271.

[30]General Jackson's private carriage caused great wonderment to some of the backwoods settlers, one of whom remarked: "I saw General Jackson once riding in the elegantest carriage that ever mortal man *sot* his eyes on—with glass winders to it like a house, and *sort* o' silk *curtings.* The harness was mounted with silver; it was *drawd* by four blooded nags, and *drove* by a mighty likely *nigger* boy." Hall—*Legends of the West*, p. 185.

ington and Maysville, to the nation's capital. Henry Clay
also traveled from "Ashland" across the country in his
private coach,[31] as did other people of wealth and rank
of that period.

The "post-horses" for the use of the private carriages
were obtained from the stage barns en route, swapping
them at the same places the stages did. The keeping of
"post-horses" for hire was one of the money-making accounts of the stage-coach business, and there was always
extra stock in the barns for this purpose. Ten cents per
mile for a two-horse team was the usual price, and twenty-
five cents for a four-horse complement.

Certain stage lines patronized certain taverns and inns
in the towns and along the route. Of these taverns, all
had a sign swinging out in front, fashioned for the most
part of wood, and announcing to the traveler that entertainment could be furnished for both man and beast.
Before named streets and numbered houses came into general use, and when few persons could read, painted and
carved sign-boards were more useful than they are today,
and not only innkeepers, but men of all trades[32] sought
signs that would attract the eyes of the customers and
visitors and fix in their memory the exact spot of the ad-

[31]This coach was presented to Henry Clay by admiring citizens of New-
ark, New Jersey, in 1833, and was used by him in making many trips
from Lexington to Washington. It is now in the possession of Jacob
Edinger & Sons, 1012 Story Avenue, Louisville. Jackson's private coach
is still to be seen at the "Hermitage" near Nashville, Tenn.

[32]Dr. Chipley had his drug store at No. 7 Cheapside, Lexington, at
the "sign of the Red Mortar"; Hugh Crawford's boot and shoe manufac-
tory at the "sign of the Golden Boot and Shoe"; M. Fishel's tin and
copper shop at the "sign of the Still," and S. Oldham's "toilette saloon"
at the "sign of Dr. Franklin," where he had for sale "an assortment
of wigs and top pieces of all colors. Also false whiskers of various
shades."

vertiser. It was an old English custom reproduced in this country, and landlords vied with each other to see who could design the most attractive one.

There was a wide range of subjects on these signboards. Some of the signs displayed before Lexington taverns were: "Sheaf of Wheat," "Cross Keys," "Indian Queen," "Don't Give up the Ship," "Green Tree," and "Free and Easy." These signs were not always elaborate—often simply a broad board with the owner's name—"Bright's Inn," "Bradley's" or "Inn by M. Thornton."[33] As time passed, these signs were less used, and in many cases left swinging on account of their humor and sometimes because they were a guarantee of an old established business.

Other tavern signs that graced the places of refreshment and cheer around the Bluegrass region were: "Sign of Rising Sun" (Frankfort); "Sign of the Golden Eagle" (Bardstown); "Sign of the Buffalo" (Lexington); "Sign of the Indian Queen" (Winchester); "Sign of Square and Compass" (Maysville); "Sign of Golden Bee Hive" (near Shelbyville), and "Sign of George Washington" (Harrodsburg). These and many other noted places of entertainment and refreshment were familiar stands to stage-coach travelers of a century ago.

---

[33]Bright's Inn, near Stanford, Lincoln County; Thornton's Inn at Midway, Woodford County, and Bradley's Inn, the first stage-coach office in Lexington.

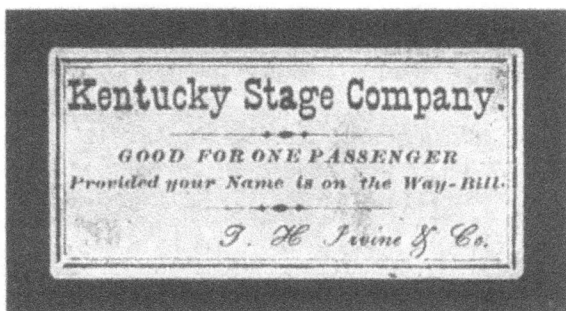

A stage-coach ticket of 1865-70

Henry Clay's traveling coach, photographed by D.B. Elrod.
Courtesy of the Henry Clay Collection, University of Kentucky
Libraries.

WILSON'S TAVERN,

(LATELY POSTLETHWAIT'S.)

I HAVE rented the House and Tavern, lately occupied by me, in this town, to *Joshua Wilson*, formerly of Bairdstown. I beg leave to return my sincere thanks to my numerous customers, for their preference in my favor whilst in that house, and am happy, and confident in assuring those who continue their favors to Mr. Wilson, that they will find every accommodation that the house and situation is capable of affording—which, I hope I do not presume in saying, will be equal to any in the Western Country.

J. POSTLETHWAIT.

Lexington, (K.) June 4, 1804.

An early tavern notice

Postlethwait's Tavern, Lexington, 1830

Blue Licks Springs Hotel, Nicholas County, 1845

STAGE RULES!

I.   The names of passengers must be entered on all way bills, and stage fare paid before they enter.

II.   Passengers will be permitted to carry fifteen pounds weight in the stage, trunks at owner's risk.

III.   No trunks or baggage of any kind can be put in the stage at one office, to be paid for at another; but must be paid for where they are entered.

IV.   Stage agents will carefully examine way bills on arrival of stages, to see that all entries check with passengers and trunks.

V.   No stage driver will be allowed to receive stage fare, or sign his name to a way bill; but it shall be his duty to take in passengers on the way, and have them entered on the way bill at the stage office or stand.

VI.   The mail bags must at all times be carried inside the stage, to avoid injury from rain, or otherwise.

VII.   No person whatever is to go on the stage free, without written authority from the proprietors or agent.

VIII.   It shall be the duty of the stage driver to pay strict attention to the accomodation of passengers, and treat them with the utmost politeness.

IX.   Only in case of sickness shall a stage driver employ another to perform his duty, under forfeiture of one month's salary.

X.   All accounts against the stage company for work, must be attested by the driver who had it done, or by some disinterested person.

XI.   All stage drivers on approaching a town, village or hamlet, shall sound his trumpet, so as to give timely alarm; also in overtaking or meeting waggons or carts; and if any waggon or cart driver on having timely notice, refuses to give the road, so that the mail is detained, the drivers are to report such waggoner or cart driver to the proprietors of the line.

XII.   Stage agents are requested to post these rules in some part of the stage office or building most convenient for passengers and drivers to see.

GRIFFIN & McACHRAN,
PROPRIETORS.

Stage rules for the Lexington-Louisville Line, 1838-1840.
Courtesy of the J. Winston Coleman Photographic
Collection, Transylvania University Library.

GENERAL STAGE OFFICE

BRENNAN'S HOTEL,
LEXINGTON KENTUCKY.

Arrivals and Departures of the Mail and Accommodation Stages, and the Cars from Lexington to Frankfort.

LOUISVILLE MAIL STAGE, via VERSAILLES, leaves Lexington every day at 9 o'clock, P. M. and arrives at Louisville at 10 o'clock the following morning.

RAIL ROAD CAR FOR FRANKFORT, connecting with Accommodation Stages to Louisville, leaves every day at 6 o'clock, A. M. and 2 o'clock, P. M. through to Frankfort in 3 hours, and to Louisville in 11 hours.

MAYSVILLE STAGE leaves every night at 12 o'clock, and arrives at 10 o'clock, A. M. the following day at Maysville. ALSO, another leaves at 10 o'clock, A. M. and arrives same day at 9 o'clock, P. M.

NASHVILLE AND BEAN STATION MAIL STAGE, BY HARRODSBURG, leaves every other day at 4 o'clock, A. M.

RICHMOND AND LONDON MAIL STAGE, intersecting the Bean Station Stage at London, leaves every other day at 4 o'clock, A. M.

WINCHESTER AND OWINGSVILLE MAIL STAGE leaves on Mondays, Wednesdays and Fridays, at 5 o'clock, A. M.

GEORGETOWN AND CINCINNATI MAIL STAGE leaves every night at 9 o'clock.

GEORGETOWN ACCOMMODATION leaves every evening at 4 o'clock.

EXTRA STAGES, for any point, can be furnished whenever called for.

SEATS FOR THE CAR can be taken at the General Stage Office, Brennan's Hotel, either for Frankfort, or the whole way to Louisville.

J. H. PENNEY,
GENERAL AGENT,
Brennan's Hotel, Lexington, Ky.

Oct 27, 1839 51-tf

A time table of 1839

OPPOSITION RELIANCE
LINE OF STAGES.
BETWEEN
Lexington and Louisville.

Leaves LEXINGTON every morning at 4 o'clock.
Arrives at LOUISVILLE same evening at 6 o'clock.
RETURNING,
Leaves LOUISVILLE at 4 o'clock, A. M, and
Arrives at LEXINGTON by 6 o'clock, P. M.

☞They have also a line of Stages running every other day from LEXINGTON to HARRODSBURG, by way of Frankfort.

☞Offices in Lexington, at *Todd's Hotel*, and on the *corner west of Brennan's Hotel.*

M. D. WEST, *Agent.*
GRIFFIN & McACHRAN,
Proprietors.

A sign of early competition between stage lines.
Courtesy of the J. Winston Coleman Collection,
University of Kentucky Libraries.

UNITED STATES MAIL.

GOOD INTENT LINE.

LEAVES LEXINGTON
DAILY,
AT 8 O'CLOCK, A. M.
FOR MAYSVILLE;
Running Through
IN 8 1-2 HOURS.

For Seats apply at their Office opposite the the Rail Road Warehouse, or at KEISER'S HOTEL.

THE OPPOSITION
GOOD INTENT LINE,
Leaves Lexington

BY RAIL ROAD to *Frankfort*, there connecting with the STAGES at 9 o'clock, A. M., and arriving at Louisville at 5 P. M.

This company is supplied with substantial Troy and Lancaster coaches, excellent teams, and careful sober drivers; all racing is expressly forbidden, and baggage or parcels at the risk of the owners thereof.

Passengers will confer a favor on the proprietors of this Line, by reporting to the agent at Louisville, Maysville or Lexington, the names of any drivers who may attempt to race.

McNAIR & WEAVER,
PROPRIETORS.

January 6, 1837.   40-tf

A stage-coach notice, Lexington, 1837. Courtesy of the J. Winston Coleman Collection, University of Kentucky Libraries.

Bluegrass stage routes in 1834

CHAPTER VI

OPPOSITION LINES AND DRIVERS

S HORTLY after competitive stage lines entered the field, the drivers of the various lines developed greater speed, which resulted in racing of the stages and endangering the lives and safety of the passengers. Newspaper editors constantly were trying to decrease the danger of stage driving through the streets of the cities by citing damages[1] in other places and the liability of the drivers:

"CAUTION TO STAGE DRIVERS!

"A Gentleman of Louisville while driving in a gig through the streets of that city was overset by the carelessness of a stage driver in his eagerness to pass another stage. The Gentleman had his collar bone broken and was awarded by the Jury the sum of nine hundred dollars damages."

Despite the efforts of the town fathers of Lexington to regulate the speed of the stage-coaches over the streets, numerous complaints continued to reach the officials. With this in mind, ordinances were passed for the protection of the pedestrians as well as travelers, which limited the speed of "the wind-splitting demons of the turnpike" over the streets of Lexington to "a moderate trot." In go-

---

[1]*Kentucky Gazette*, October 5, 1837.

ing around corners or on narrow streets "a slow trot" was to be observed and a violation of these statutes subjected the owners to a fine of five dollars. This checked the speeding of rival drivers for a while, but in the June 8, 1837, issue of the *Kentucky Gazette,* we read:

> "The stage drivers have been for some time violating the city ordinances by driving through the streets with a speed contrary thereto. Yesterday morning one of those jehus, in giving a display of his prowess in making a short turn on Main Street, upset the stage with several passengers, by which Mrs. David Laudaman was considerably injured, though it is hoped not fatally."

Bradford, in his paper for June 15, appealed to the citizens of Lexington: "Will the Corporation take no steps to arrest this dangerous practice?" It was extremely hard for the proprietors of the different stage lines to keep their drivers from engaging in races with the other drivers,[2] although they were in some cases urged on by the passengers. This was much against the rules of the company which invariably stated that "all racing is expressly forbidden."

Some of the mail stage drivers considered themselves kings of the road, and looked with a great deal of disdain

---

[2]"I wish you would send me about four or five good drivers, and make a positive bargain how much we are to pay a month, for they are all turned out for higher wages and I was compelled to give or have our line stopped, as drivers are very scarce here. Agree to give them sixteen dollars a month for one team, and twenty-two for two teams." John W. Weaver to Col. McNair, Frankfort, January 20, 1838. Letter in author's collection.

upon the slower moving vehicles. They would shout "clar the road" and other such warnings as they rode along, and when not heeded would occasionally crowd the vehicle into the ditch. One victim complained in the *Gazette* that "we have been at a loss to know *why* it is that waggons, carriages, gigs, shays, or sulkys, are bound to give the road, no matter at what hazard, to the stages, knowing as we do that there is no law compelling us to do so." He finished his article by saying "there is no law that requires anyone to give the *whole road* to a mail stage, more than to any other vehicle."[3]

Dr. James B. Riley and family, of Madison County, were returning from church in the late fall of 1842, when the stage of Hawkins and Company, traveling from Lexington to Richmond, came in sight of the Riley buggy about three-fourths of a mile on the Madison side of the Kentucky River. On seeing the slower moving vehicle in the road, the driver, John Roswell, gave the customary three blasts on the stage horn, but kept the middle of the road. He ran against "the buggy and knocked off the left hind wheel." The impact upset the Riley vehicle and dragged it ten feet. Dr. Riley and two of the children were seriously injured. Passengers on the stage assisted in extricating the wrecked vehicle, and one of them, Joseph E. Gilbert, stated: "We had considerable difficulty in getting the buggy loose and from under the stage." Dr. Riley blamed the driver for the accident whose language after the mishap was "very abusive, profane, and insulting," and who later stated that he "was behind time and

---

[3]*Lexington Observer & Reporter*, May 16, 1833.

would have to spur up to make it," as the "United States mail was due in Richmond at 7 o'clock that evening."[4]

After much litigation and carrying the case to the Court of Appeals, damages of two hundred and fifty dollars were awarded the injured.[5] In giving the decision, the court held that "the stage driver was grossly negligent and the accident was wholly unexcusable," and admonished the proprietors in the future to employ only "skillful and prudent" drivers on all their stage routes.

Regardless of the warnings and protests of the citizens through the press, racing of the stages continued, and the rivalry of the drivers and lines grew more intense. The usual way to settle rivalry was by trial of speed, and though stage-coach owners publicly deplored this dangerous practice, there is every reason to believe that many of them secretly enjoyed it. The jehus openly gloried in it, and so jealous were they for the reputation of their respective coaches that the very sight of an opposition coach caused their blood to boil, and race they would, despite public sentiment and the safety of their passengers. The drivers were deaf to all entreaties, conscious of nothing but the opposition coach thundering in the rear and a grim determination not to allow it to pass at any price, while the passengers clung despairingly to their seats, and threatened to report everything and everybody when they got safely to their destination.

A short time after the upsetting of the stage on Main Street of Lexington, the readers of the *Kentucky Gazette*

---

[4]Riley *vs.* C. A. Hawkins & Co., file 50, Madison Circuit Court, January 6, 1845.

[5]Hawkins *vs.* Riley, Kentucky Reports, B. Monroe, 17, p. 101.

were informed that the stages of the "Old Line" and the "Good Intent Opposition Line" had run together, one crowding the other over an embankment, resulting in the breaking of the driver's leg, and in serious damage to some of the passengers. This accident occurred on the Louisville to Frankfort route, near Shelbyville, each of the rival stage agents attempting to throw the blame on the other, and, in the words of Thomas N. Lindsey of the "Old Line": "The *Old Stage Line,* as it is called, belongs to Johnson, Weisiger & Co., and was ahead of the *Good Intent Opposition Line,* the former with eight passengers, and the latter with two or three. In passing an embankment this side of Shelbyville, the opposition driver ran his stage and horses against the other stage and horses and forced them over the embankment. The old line was not racing, on the contrary, drew up to the left, giving the other two-thirds of the road and plenty of room to pass . . . When the opposition came upon the road,[6] directions were given not to race at any time, to all the drivers, but to take a regular gait, so as to make their hours without regard to the fact whether they were before or behind the other line.

"Mr. Laughlin, the driver, said that he had been quarreled with that day by some of his passengers because he let the other line pass rather than race his horses. . . . He has had no accident—nor injured a single horse in the four teams driven by him daily for about eight weeks, until the accident above . . . As evidence of his

<hr/>

[6]Edward P. Johnson & Co., of the "Old Line," regarded the opposition lightly and thought it to be only temporary: "This line is to be permanent, and during the opposition will carry passengers cheaper than any other." *Kentucky State Flag,* Paris, May 2, 1837.

care for the passengers, when the stage had fallen over
the embankment, breaking his leg and twisting his foot
over until it rested on his knee, he got up hopping on one
foot and holding his horses until the passengers who
were not injured came to his assistance . . ."[7]

From the agent of the "Opposition Line," Harbeth
McConathy, came a statement in the *Kentucky Gazette*
disclaiming any blame for the accident,[8] and stating that
they had made seventy-four trips between Frankfort and
Louisville without an accident, while the "Old Line'" had
eight or ten during that period, causing considerable
injury to both drivers and passengers. Whether the
"Opposition Line" was guilty of the accident or not, it
caused quite a stir among the users of the stage-coach,
and one who viewed the wrecked coaches said: "A more
wicked and malicious act has not been committed in our
country within the last century."

The driver of Johnson and Company's "Old Line"
stage, Isaac Laughlin, had "one foot and ankle crushed
to pieces," and as a result of the accident "was made a
cripple for life." He sued McNair and Weaver, the
proprietors of the "Good Intent Opposition Line," for the
injury, alleging the wanton conduct of their driver as
the cause.[9] In the Shelby Circuit Court a verdict of
nineteen hundred dollars was given in favor of Laughlin; a new trial was granted upon the application of the
defendants and the case was removed to the Henry Cir-

---

[7]*Lexington Intelligencer*, September 26, 1837.

[8]Mr. McConathy reported: "the subject has been judicially investigated" and our driver "has been triumphantly acquitted of all the blame in the matter." Copied in the *Lexington Intelligencer*, November 17, 1837.

[9]*The Commonwealth*, Frankfort, October 20, 1840.

cuit Court, where a verdict of two thousand dollars was given the injured driver in the last week of October, 1840.[10]

As a result of this stage-coach opposition, one grave in a Lexington cemetery is marked with this melancholy epitaph:

IN MEMORY OF

MRS. EUNICE LOCKWOOD

FORMERLY

MRS. AYRES

WHO DIED ON THE 15 NOVEMBER 1837

AGED 59 YEARS

HER DEATH WAS OCCASIONED BY THE

UPSETTING OF THE STAGE BETWEEN

LOUISVILLE AND FRANKFORT.[11]

Public sentiment was strongly against this form of unnecessary speed, with increased risks to the traveling public, and strongly urged that legislation be brought into play as had been done to regulate steamboat racing. So dearly did the jehus love to race that, if they could not pit themselves against an opposition line, they were ready to make a trial of speed with anyone of

---

[10]Laughlin *vs.* McNair & Weaver, file 132, Henry Circuit Court, February 15, 1840.

[11]"Mrs. Eunice Lockwood (late Mrs. Ayres), consort of Mr. Caleb Lockwood, of Liberty, Clay County, Mo., died in this city on the 15th inst. Mrs. Lockwood's death was caused by an injury received from the upsetting of the stage between Louisville and Frankfort, near Shelbyville, on the 25th of September last . . ." *Kentucky Gazette,* Lexington, November 30, 1837.

a sporting tendency. Frequent wagers were laid on horses and ponies backed to race the coaches for certain distances.

To regain some of their lost patronage after the mishap near Shelbyville, the "Good Intent Opposition Line" posted handbills in the taverns, stage offices, and along the lines stating that they had again instructed their drivers "to drive at a moderate or regular gait" and "not to regard the wishes of the passengers at the risk of their lives." Similar notices were posted by the "Old Line" notifying passengers and travelers that "they will confer a favor on the proprietors of the line by reporting to the stage agent at Louisville, Maysville, or Lexington, the names of any drivers who may attempt to race."[12]

But racing continued with the inevitable results. "The Louisville and Lexington stage-coaches belonging to both lines, as they left Versailles Sunday morning, were upset, and several of the passengers severely injured. We understand that the accident was caused by racing and running the stages against each other."[13] "Let someone who is injured," remarked the *Louisville City Gazette*, "bring an action against the proprietors and we will hear nothing more of the troubles that have existed on the Louisville and Lexington roads for so long."[14] This did not seem to be the public feeling, since it was the drivers and not the proprietors responsible for the continued mishaps and "oversettings" of the stages, and urged "that it was high time that a stop should be put to the accidents, which so

[12]*Lexington Intelligencer*, January 8, 1838.
[13]*Ibid.*, July 10, 1838.
[14]*Louisville City Gazette*, October 3, 1838.

often are produced by either the recklessness or carelessness of the stage drivers."[15]

"Anything for the honor of the coach," was the jehu's
motto, so it is little wonder that accidents became dis-
tressingly frequent with the newspapers containing har-
rowing accounts. The following notice taken from the
Cincinnati Whig for August 22, 1838, is a typical example:

> "A distressing stage accident occurred on Sun-
> day morning last, August 20, 1838, at the 'Ten Mile
> House' north of Lexington on the Maysville turn-
> pike.[16] The stage contained nine passengers besides
> the driver and an extra driver on the outside. The
> house stands back from the road some seventy or
> eighty yards, and when the driver started he gave the
> horses the whip, and they pitched off at full speed.
> In turning the acute angle from the yard to the
> road, the stage upset with great violence, dashing
> the top *into a thousand pieces*. The forewheels be-
> came immediately disengaged from the other parts
> of the stage, and the horses ran off with them with
> great fury for several miles. Every person in or
> upon the stage was more or less injured. Judge
> Underwood, of Kentucky, and his daughter were
> both seriously wounded in the head, and a young
> man by the name of Love from Tennessee, on his
> way to West Point, had his collar bone badly broken,

---

[15]*Lexington Observer & Reporter*, October 13, 1838.
[16]William Moreland's Tavern and post-office, in Bourbon County
just over the Fayette-Bourbon line.

and a Gentleman from New York was seriously injured in the right side.

"The driver had his ankle dislocated and the extra driver was badly hurt internally, and the blood streaming profusely from his mouth. The rest were less, though considerably, injured. It is almost a miracle that not one of the passengers was killed, as the accident occurred through the recklessness and imprudence of the driver, for whose conduct there seems to be no extenuation or apology."[17]

The stage-coaches in use at this period, due to their short coupling and the rough roads, were continually being upset, even in the streets of Lexington, as the local newspaper reported: "We learn from the Gazette that the Georgetown and Lexington stage upset on Sunday morning last and injured Mr. Ficklin, who was a passenger. On Monday, the Lexington and Winchester stage upset injuring four passengers. On the same day, the stage for Versailles upset in Mulberry Street, none of the passengers however were injured."[18]

Mail service to the Bluegrass was greatly handicapped by the stage accidents, as these "disasters" frequently broke the stages and injured the horses. It was some time before the lines were in operation again, and the newspapers continually complained that "the mails have become so irregular as to exhaust all patience."[19]

Minor accidents were constantly taking place in the operation of the stages, but it was seldom that a mis-

---

[17]*Cincinnati Whig*, August 22, 1838.
[18]*Lexington Intelligencer*, May 4, 1838.
[19]*Ibid.*, February 20, 1838.

hap resulted in such unfortunate circumstances as those
which accompanied the upsetting of the "Old Line" stage
near Shelbyville. In winter, hot bricks were put in the
stages to warm the feet of the passengers, and for their
general comfort. On one occasion a local stage caught
fire from this heating arrangement and "burned with
such rapidity that the passengers, six in number, with
difficulty made their escape." Invitations to drink caused
the drivers in one or more cases to leave their coach in
the hands of a stable boy, resulting in mishaps. Mrs.
Charles Wickliffe, of Louisville, was seriously injured
in that city, "when the horses ran off without the driver
who left the stage to enjoy himself with a little grog."
Fondness for drink caused the Lexington-Louisville stage
to "overset" in Frankfort, early in the spring of 1838,
severely shaking up and bruising Mrs. Blakey, of that
city. She testified in court that the driver left his coach
to visit the tavern bar, and "the driver of the overset
stage was not the driver employed for that purpose,
but a stable boy whose business was to take care of the
horses."[20]

Usually when a stage "overset" its occupants received
a bad shaking up or some bruises and occasionally someone suffered a broken limb. Nor were the elect of the
land more immune from such happenings than the most
humble traveler. Chief Justice John Marshall, in his
eightieth year, died from injuries to his spine result-

[20]Blakey *vs.* McNair & Weaver, Shelby Circuit Court, file 333, August
12, 1838. Mrs. Blakey stated that her "skull was fractured, and her
constitution materially and radically impaired." She sought $5,000
damages, and, after hearing the testimony, the jury returned a verdict in
her favor for $500.

ing from "the post-coach fall and oversetting" on one
of his visits to Washington.[21] Even Henry Clay himself, to whose influence more than that of any other man
the creation of the National Road was due, was involved
in an upset on one occasion. He was on his way to Washington, when the driver upset the coach on a pile of limestone in the streets of Uniontown, Pennsylvania.[22] The
Idol of the West was unhurt, and when dragged out of
the vehicle, humorously remarked: "This is mixing the
Clay of Kentucky with the limestone of Pennsylvania."
Sam Sibley, the driver of the stage, was thrown from his
lofty perch by the impact and, alighting on his head,
suffered a broken nose.

On another trip, the Sage of Ashland was involved
in a stage accident:[23]

> "We regret to learn, as we do from the Wheel-
> ing (Va.) Times, of Thursday last, that Messrs.
> Clay and Crittenden, our distinguished Senators,
> were both severely injured in the overturning of
> the stage near Brownsville, Pennsylvania. Mr. Crit-
> tenden's collar bone was broken, and the injury
> to Mr. Clay was such as to have him remain at
> Brownsville for a day or so . . ."

These mishaps of Henry Clay seemed to have been
purely accidental, but the rivalry of drivers grew more
intense along the Bluegrass stage routes, and, on September 16, 1838, the stages of the "Old Line" and "Oppo-

---

[21]Beveridge—*Life of John Marshall*, Vol. IV, p. 587.
[22]Searight—*The Old Pike*, p. 16.
[23]*Lexington Intelligencer*, December 7, 1838.

sition Line" on the Lexington and Maysville Road, ran
against each other at Moreland's Tavern,[24] ten miles
north of Lexington, and upset the stage of the "Opposition Line." The local newspaper reported the accident: "We understand that the OLD LINE and OPPOSI-
TION LINE of stages coming in from Maysville on Saturday afternoon ran against each other at Moreland's,
ten miles from town, and upset the latter. Both coaches
were filled with passengers, the lives of all of whom
were jeopardized by the encounter. Mr. G. P. Richardson, of this city, a passenger in the OPPOSITION LINE,
had his arm broken, a lady was seriously injured, and
most of the other passengers in the coach upset were
more or less bruised. The OLD LINE had stopped at
Moreland's Tavern and changed horses. The tavern is
situated several rods from the road and is approached
by a semi-circular carriage path.

"The OLD LINE coach was just ready to start when
the OPPOSITION coach drove into the post-office to leave
the mail. The post-office is kept in a building a few
rods nearer the road than the tavern house, and in the
direction of Lexington, so that to reach it the OPPOSI-
TION coach had to pass the point where the OLD LINE
coach stood. At the moment when the OPPOSITION coach
at full speed was crossing the carriage path leading out
to the road the OLD LINE coach started and the horses

---

[24]This was operated and owned by William Moreland, and was also a
post-office. It was a two-story brick, ell on the north side, with a large
dance hall on the second floor, and the wing in the rear was used for a
dining room and bar. This old building was torn down in 1913. Robert
Meteer owns the site of the old tavern, which is located in Bourbon
County, about half a mile north of the Fayette County line and on the
west side of the road.

of both lines came furiously in contact. The consequence was that the horses of the Opposition were driven shortly around, and the coach overturned, as before stated."[25]

The "oversetting" of a stage-coach was not as disastrous as a modern train wreck; nevertheless it provided plenty of excitement.

A statement signed by several of the passengers in the overset stage declared that the wreck was caused "by the pre-determined hostility and wilful intent of the driver of the stage owned by Dickey & Co.," and added that the driver "drove off after the accident without giving assistance which humanity alone would have dictated under circumstances of a less aggravated nature."

On Saturday afternoon following the accident the various stage drivers after delivering their passengers at their respective stage offices and delivering the way-bills to the stage agents drove down to West's stage stable in the rear of Brennan's Hotel where they signed the register.[26] This stable[27] of Preston West was used by Messrs. Johnson, Dickey, Gaines, and other stage proprietors to keep the stage horses and coaches, and was

---

[25]*Lexington Intelligencer,* September 18, 1838.

[26]On leaving the stage barn every driver signed the register, showing the time of his departure and his destination, also the name of the stage and the inspector. At the conclusion of their runs, the drivers also signed the register, giving the number of passengers conveyed in their coach, time of arrival, notes on the weather and incidents of the trip, such as a horse "throwing a shoe" or a passenger becoming sick and requiring medical attention. All the old registers burned with the stage stable in 1886.

[27]This stable was in the rear of Brennan's Inn, now the Phoenix Hotel, and was located on the east side of Limestone, where Vine Street comes into Limestone. Fayette County Court, Deed Book 14, p. 289, December 20, 1837.

a general gathering and loafing place for the stage drivers of all the lines. On this Saturday afternoon, some of the drivers got into an argument over the wreck at Moreland's Tavern and almost came to blows. It was pretty well known that there existed open hostility between the rival drivers. Later in the evening there was a personal encounter at the circus between two of the drivers, Powell and Cameron, of the "Opposition Line" and the "Old Line," respectively.

Powell was too much for his rival and whipped him so severely that, at the time, it was supposed his life was endangered. Immediately after the affray at the circus, Justice Daniel Bradford issued a warrant for the apprehension of Powell. Between eleven and twelve o'clock that night the officer proceeded to the place where the drivers usually loafed, Keiser's Hotel, hoping to find Powell there. On entering the barroom, he inquired of a driver of the "Opposition Line" where Powell could be found. After some words had passed between the officer and the driver, several drivers of the "Old Line" made their appearance and immediately "a general melée commenced" between the drivers of the two lines.

In the course of the fight several pistols were discharged, one striking an "Old Line" driver named Crabster in the back of the head, causing instant death.[28] Crabster had discharged a pistol which had burst, and the handle of his piece was grasped in his hand after he fell. Two or three of the drivers of the "Opposition Line" were wounded with buckshot, but none of them seriously.

---

[28]*Lexington Intelligencer,* September 18, 1838.

This shows the intense hatred and hostility maintained by the stage drivers, or jehus, of the opposition lines.[29] Through the press, appeals of this nature were constantly finding their way into print: "It is high time that the strife among stage drivers on the two lines from Lexington to Maysville, which has already resulted in the death of one of their number and the crippling of another and the severe injuries of numerous stage passengers, should be put to an end; and if public opinion cannot act to do so, the laws should be enforced until the end is accomplished and the safety of travelers assured . . ."[30]

Whenever a new stage line was established the older organization whose field was thus invaded reduced the price of passage in the hope that the new company would thereby find its business unprofitable.[31] If the new company met the lower passenger fare, the established lines would promptly make another reduction. When both parties entered this rate-cutting controversy with a grim determination to win, the results were sometimes peculiar and also highly satisfactory to the traveling public. After much fighting among the proprietors, the result would be swifter schedules and better connections. A truce

[29]This hostility also extended to the proprietors of the lines: "We learn that Weisiger's stable at Frankfort was burned by *design*, and not by accident, this being the second attempt to accomplish the object." *Lexington Intelligencer*, October 17, 1838.

[30]*Ibid.*, September 18, 1838.

[31]"I think Dickey will drive one of the three lines off the road in a little. Dickey has injured us very much, and stated that you and me [McNair & Weaver] was broke and would not be able to run three months." Weaver to McNair, Lexington, January 10, 1838. Letter in author's collection.

would be reached finally, after giving the public much travel over the lines at no profit to the owners.[32]

The swifter mail coaches demanded exorbitant sums for passage; thereby making the rates too high for the majority of the passengers, but the rival lines brought the fares within the reach of nearly everyone. In other parts of the United States, the rate-cutting practice grew so intense that one line offered to carry the first applicant without charge and furnish a dinner free each day at the end of the run. The newer line, not to be outdone, agreed to do this and also add a bottle of wine for the passenger's meal. This continued for several weeks, much to the passenger's enjoyment; but a compromise was reached between the stage proprietors and they agreed upon a uniform scale of prices.

While stage-coach owners and operators were having their keenest competition and rate-cutting war, the country was swept by the panic of 1837, which made it doubly hard for the proprietors to keep in business. A letter written from the stage agent of McNair and Weaver at Maysville to Colonel Dunning McNair gives additional light on the financial difficulties of staging at this period:

> "I have just returned from Lexington where I found everything in confusion and claims out to the amount of $4000 and not all yet presented. They have attached the whole line from Lexington to Mays-

---

[32]"We are beginning to do a fair share of the business, but not clearing expenses." Stage agent at Lexington, January 15, 1838, writing Colonel McNair of the stage firm, McNair & Weaver. Letter in author's collection.

ville and locked up the teams and coaches at Maysville, besides having attached those six new coaches
on the road. They said they would do nothing unless I could give them some responsible man as security for the money, which I could not do . . ."[33]

Before the rate-cutting campaign was begun the fare
from Lexington to Maysville, a distance of sixty-four
miles, was $4.25. Between Frankfort and Louisville the
stage ticket commanded the fare of $4.00, while from
Lexington to Paris, a distance of eighteen miles, it was
$1.00. While these rates were high, it was only twenty
years before that the rate from Lexington to Cincinnati
had been ten cents per mile, or nearly nine dollars. Whatever the disastrous results of the period of racing and
rate-cutting competition,[34] there was the one good result of lower fares and better connections over the Bluegrass lines.

As a result of this competition, greater speeds were
maintained and this naturally told considerably on the
horses employed.[35] Although the distance between stage
stables or relay stations was materially reduced, it was not
often that the period of usefulness of the horses exceeded
three or four years. This did not necessarily mean that

[33]Letter from W. A. Moyston, Maysville, January 3, 1838. In author's
collection.

[34]John W. Weaver writing to his partner, Colonel McNair, February 8,
1838, said: "I caught M. W. Dickey and his agent playing a double-
handed game on us last week. He was carrying passengers in his morning line for two dollars and the line that runs with us, we charge four
dollars." Letter in author's collection.

[35]"Our stock on the Louisville-Lexington road is a good deal cut down
on account of opposition." McNair to Weaver, January 5, 1838.

they were worn out, but that they were no longer equal to the pace the coach had to maintain year in and year out. The horses on the slower stages lasted proportionately longer. One stage owner in Scott County had a mare that traveled seventy-five miles a week in a four-horse coach for ten years, and at the end of that time was still considered a good stage horse.

Edward P. Johnson and Company, still the most important factor in the stage-coach business in central Kentucky, advertised that the rates were reduced and that an agreement had been reached with the other lines, putting the fares down on a uniform basis. Such notices appeared:

"FARE REDUCED!

"Two Daily Lines of Post Coaches
from
Lexington to Maysville

"The Mail Pilot Coach leaves any time the passengers prefer; between supper and daylight next morning. The Express Coach leaves every other day at half past one o'clock, fare as low as any line. Speed not less than eight miles per hour. Racing positively forbidden, and not apprehended, as no other coach is expected to go out at the same time. For seats, apply at Brennan's Bar, or at the Railroad Office—

"J. H. PENNY, Agent
"M. W. DICKEY & Co., Proprietors."[36]

---

[36]*Lexington Intelligencer*, February 16, 1838.

In the same issue of the *Lexington Intelligencer,* the Good Intent Opposition Line posted a similar notice:

"FARE REDUCED!
from
Lexington to Maysville

"U. S. MAIL—GOOD INTENT LINE

"For seats apply at the General Stage Office opposite the Railroad warehouse, or John Keiser's Hotel, Lexington, and at our offices on the line.
"H. McCONATHY, Agent,
"Good Intent Line."

From the notice of Dickey and Company relative to the reduced fares, it is found that more attention was being paid the travelers' comforts and safety. In order to stop the racing, only one stage was allowed to leave at a time. Then again, they would not leave until the passengers had finished their supper, thus saving them the discomfort of rushing through their meals as had often been the case. A speed of eight miles an hour would be maintained. This change of fare and better service[37] to the traveling public made stage travel more popular, with a decided increase in the patronage of the lines at the time the future of the stages seemed unquestioned.

---

[37]*Western Citizen,* Paris, February 8, 1838, announced: "An accommodation stage will leave Paris expressly for the convenience of 'Old Bourbon' every morning for Lexington, leaving Paris at 8:30 A. M. and returning at 3 P. M., giving passengers four hours *to do business in Lexington.*"

CHAPTER VII

THE COMING OF THE RAILROAD

W ITH this seeming prosperity for the stage-coaches, there loomed upon the horizon the much heated question of a railroad, which spelled the ultimate doom of stage travel in central Kentucky. Situated in the center of the fertile agricultural belt of the Bluegrass region, Lexington was without an outlet to the southern markets, except by river boats. The citizens, as well as the merchants of Lexington, saw the possibilities for a railroad from Lexington, by way of Frankfort, to "some point" on the Ohio River, possibly Louisville. They were certain of securing the railroad, but were faced with the problem of preserving Lexington's position as the macadamized road hub of the state, and, at the same time, securing for her a similar honor in railroad building.[1]

This question brought on heated discussions, with some claiming "that railroads would create a monopoly of shipping which the country would be unable to control." When it was first suggested that steam should be utilized for draft purposes in place of horses, there was occasion for much merriment up and down the stage routes. The jehus, in particular, regarded it as a huge joke. "The iron horse drive us off the road!" they would

---

[1] *Cf.*—Thomas D. Clark, The Lexington & Ohio Railroad, A Pioneer Venture, *Register*, Kentucky State Historical Society, Vol. 31, pp. 8–16, January, 1933.

exclaim with hearty guffaws at the very presumption of the thing. "It can never come to pass," they exclaimed emphatically, "No place in the country has such traveling as we have." "What do we want with a railroad?"

Owners of stage lines, turnpikes, and bridges were bitter opponents of the railroad, foreseeing that their business might be, as indeed it was in many cases, ruined by the new enterprise. Many other groups were hostile.[2] Farmers feared the loss of their market for horses, hay, and grain, and foresaw a rise in insurance rates to cover the increased danger of fire. Tavern-keepers, whose source of income was the stage and horse-back traveler, set every possible obstacle in the way of the railroad construction. The wagon drivers themselves joined the stage lines in opposing the new means of transportation whenever possible.

While there was much opposition to the building of the railroad, there were many citizens of Lexington who favored it, one of whom, in pointing out the relative merits of steam to stage travel, said: "All the accidents which occur from drunken drivers, restive horses, brittle harness, and broken axletrees would be avoided; for we presume that locomotive engines would not be given to running off, to taking fright, or to oversetting."

Those in favor of the proposed railroad stressed the disaster that had recently befallen a party of four hacks which had left Lexington at nine o'clock in the morning for Frankfort. Three of the vehicles reached their

---

[2]Anti-railroad broadsides were distributed in Philadelphia and other cities in 1835 opposing the building of railroads and referring to them as "demons of destruction" from which "there would be no safety or peace for anybody." Copy in author's collection.

destination sometime during the night, after encounter-
ing numerous perils along the way, while the fourth
was left in the road with a yoke of oxen endeavoring
to pull it out of a mud hole where it had stuck fast. It
had previously overturned, nearly killing a woman, and,
in order to reach Frankfort, where she might receive
medical attention, it was necessary to hire a team and
wagon to complete the journey, and then it was three
o'clock in the morning before the party arrived.[3]

Economic demand, however, overcame all objections,
and on March 6, 1830, the Lexington and Ohio railroad
was organized. Plans were immediately laid to build the
road from Lexington by way of Frankfort, to the Ohio
River. This was the first railway venture in Kentucky, and
one of the first in the West. On April 16, 1831, the
promoters of this infant railroad met at Postlethwait's
Tavern in Lexington when stock to the amount of six
hundred thousand dollars was subscribed. Henry Clay,
at this time an ardent supporter of railroad schemes, was
in the chair.[4] The plan was for a railroad to Louisville
and a turnpike to Maysville further up the Ohio River.
These two roads were expected to increase the market
for products of Lexington manufacturers and farmers of
central Kentucky.[5]

Late in the fall of this year, 1831, on October 22, amid
a great gathering of citizens and visitors, the first sill of
this pioneer railroad was laid, the ceremonies being in
charge of General Leslie Combs of Lexington. Accord-

---

[3]*Kentucky Reporter,* January 27, 1830.
[4]*Niles Weekly Register,* Vol. XL, p. 181, April, 1831.
[5]*Ibid.,* p. 194.

ing to the account of the day, "We have not witnessed for many years so imposing a pageant and never one more interesting."[6] Seven salutes were fired for the seven sections of the road then under contract for construction. All the church bells of the town were rung, prayer was said, and the Governor of the state "drove the nail attaching the first iron rail to the beginning of the stone sill," while "Hail Columbia" and "Yankee Doodle" were played by the band.

On the Lexington and Ohio railroad, the first cars were built on the model of the stage-coaches and drawn by horses. A later type of car was a two-story structure, for women and children below, and for men above. It was sometime after the first sill was laid before enough track was completed to run over, and, on August 15, 1832, at high noon the road was formally opened for transportation.[7] The first car left its "moorings" at the end of the lower market house with a number of railroad enthusiasts aboard, one of whom was Governor Thomas Metcalfe. This car was the marvel of the West, and the horse drew "a burden of forty passengers as easily as one horse could draw two passengers in a light gig along the highway."[8]

By March, 1833, the first six miles of the road were placed in successful operation; and horse-drawn cars began to make three daily trips with mail and passengers.[9]

[6]*Kentucky Reporter,* October 28, 1831.
[7]Although only a mile and a half of track was completed, citizens of Lexington delighted in riding the horse-drawn cars to the end of the line and return. *Lexington Observer & Reporter,* August 16, 1832.
[8]Muncy, *The First Railroad in the West,* p. 17 (pamphlet).
[9]*Lexington Observer & Reporter,* March 2, 1833.

At the end of this first division, six miles west of Lexington, the Villa House was established. It was the forerunner of our modern road house, and was described as "the most beautiful and pleasant on the line of the Rail Road, or anywhere in the vicinity of Lexington." A favorite diversion of Lexingtonians at this time was to ride the "cars" to this popular resort and partake of the refreshments of the well-stocked bar. In connection with this resort there was "a saloon for dancing parties erected in the Grove, and a handsome fishing boat for the use of the ladies." The Villa House was only a short distance from the Lexington-Frankfort stage road and travelers frequently broke the monotony of the journey by using the "cars" to the Villa and continuing to Frankfort by stage.

The cars had rattled along at the heels of equine power at a fair rate of speed for the time, and with just a fair amount of satisfaction, until the fall of 1832, when Bruen and Barlow decided that steam locomotion would be more desirable. These gentlemen[10] designed and constructed a small locomotive in Bruen's foundry.[11] It was strictly a home-grown product, and, at the same time, a mechanical curiosity. It had a boiler somewhere amidship which was encircled by a railroad fanguard. The engine had an overhead piston with a perpendicular stroke and

[10]Joseph Bruen and Thomas H. Barlow of Lexington.

[11]Bruen conducted a machine shop and foundry on Spring Street, Lexington, and it was here the locomotive was built along the plans of the inventor, Barlow. The *Lexington Observer & Reporter*, December 6, 1832, stated: "We yesterday had the pleasure of examining at the machine shop of Mr. Bruen, a new Locomotive Engine constructed for the Lexington & Ohio Rail Road Company. We understand the Engine will be in readiness for an experiment on the Rail Road some time next week."

two awkward rocker arms. There was no cab; the tender was an open box car, and in place of the cow-catcher or pilot, two beams projected in front "with hickory brooms attached for sweeping the track."[12] The entire engine was not over three or four feet high.

In appearance this contraption somewhat resembled a farm wagon which was capable of being navigated on nautical principles. Bruen and Barlow's tiny locomotive made its trial run, March 2, 1833, "from Lexington towards Frankfort"; but the experiment never advanced beyond the curiosity stage and consequently it was a gross failure. Then horses were again called into play as the motive power for the railroad, much to the satisfaction and delight of the jehus, stage owners, and farmers. "They can't get along without the horses" came the triumphant cry from many sides, and for the next two years passengers on the Lexington & Ohio railroad were conveyed in "cars" drawn by horse power.

In 1835, a splendid new locomotive was purchased in an eastern market and placed in operation on the road, just prior to its completion to Frankfort. It made the remarkable run from Lexington to the Villa House in eighteen and one-half minutes, which was "at the rapid rate of twenty miles an hour."[13] On Wednesday morning, January 28th, the new locomotive made its first trip to Frankfort, and "returned in gallant style in the evening with a long train consisting of five passenger cars . . . every seat was taken and we learn that the novelty of traveling by

[12]Kennedy—*Wonders and Curiosities of the Railway,* p. 63.
[13]*Lexington Intelligencer,* January 23, 1835.

steam was so enticing that as many others might have been filled . . . the locomotive, we presume, will hereafter make its regular trips."[14]

By the middle of the year 1835, regular trips to Frankfort were being made over this new railroad with steam locomotives; and the stage proprietors, seeing the folly of trying to compete with the "iron horse" and "steam cars," entered into agreements with the company to transport passengers the remainder of the trip, from Frankfort to Louisville, by stage. While stage-coach owners and operators were experiencing cut-throat competition and fare-reducing war, wrecks, and fights of the drivers, the newly organized Lexington & Ohio railroad was also having its worries. On March 16, 1836, a "most melancholy" accident occurred two miles this side of Frankfort, when the engine and cars left the rails and plunged down a thirty-foot embankment, killing three persons and seriously injuring a considerable number.[15] This "lamentable and distressing" accident tended somewhat to lessen the public's confidence in railroads, and for a while it stimulated the stage travel.

"It is a very remarkable invention," observed a citizen of Lexington with some degree of amazement in speaking of the railroad, "but a most dangerous and uncomfortable way to travel." Naturally the jehus and stage-coach owners looked with considerable jealousy and some disgust at the "puffing and snorting engines which scared the horses half out of their wits." Around the stage barns and on the stage routes, the drivers were heard to remark:

---

[14]*Lexington Intelligencer,* January 30, 1835.
[15]*Ibid.,* March 18, 1836.

"Twenty miles an hour it goes!" "I say no good will
come of people shooting around the country like sky-
rockets." "Give me horses!"

Several of the ladies riding in the open cars on the
road toward Frankfort had big holes burned in their
new silk dresses and parasols by the sparks from the
engine, and cinders got in the eyes of the children. Frequently grass and buildings along the route were set on
fire. There were many persons skeptical of the new-
fangled "steam cars" with the "hissing and puffing iron
horses," and they preferred the older and slower method
of conveyance—stage-coach travel.

But, as the editor of the *Intelligencer* remarked about
the recent mishap near Frankfort: "Such accidents are
not confined to railroads alone; every mode of conveyance
or traveling has the same or similar drawbacks. Whether
we travel by stage, by steamboat, in our private carriage,
on horse-back, or on Rail Road, we are exposed to danger
—indeed there is no situation exempt from it, and the hazard is by no means unequal as we may imagine."[16]

Notwithstanding the public's disfavor of the steam
travel for some time after the accident, and the loud cries
of negligence and mismanagement, the railroad continued to develop. Some of the stage-coach owners and
operators were farsighted enough to see that the railroad
had come to stay and that the days of the stage-coach were
numbered as the principal means of conveyance for the
people. The firm of Edward P. Johnson and Company,
the most powerful and best equipped stage company operating in central Kentucky, lost two of its members, Philip

---

[16]*Lexington Intelligencer*, March 22, 1836.

Swigert and John H. Hanna. These withdrew from their stage-coach associates, and under the name of Swigert and Company leased for a term of four years, beginning January 18, 1838, the Lexington and Ohio railroad, consisting of "twenty-seven miles of road, wing, abutments, the bridge over the Kentucky River, several lots in Lexington and Frankfort, houses and small tracts along the route, and the rolling stock including two locomotives, forty-four horses, and thirty-six sets of harness."

From the inventory of the rolling stock, it shows that horses were still considered necessary for the operation of a railroad. With Swigert and Company operating the railroad and Johnson and Company the stages, there was little chance for rival lines to gain much profit,[17] as they were practically the same firm, carrying passengers and freight over their combined facilities from Lexington to Louisville in eleven hours. Charles B. Lewis, who signed himself as "master of transportation" for the stage line of Johnson, Weisiger & Company, announced the new schedule[18] in connection with the railway travel:

RAILROAD REGULATIONS!
Car Hours
AT LEXINGTON AND FRANKFORT.
First Line
Leave Lexington every morning at 5 o'clock, and arrive at Frankfort at 9 A. M. before the departure

[17]"The railroad company turned out the old directors and elected five new ones in their places about the middle of last December. They promised that we should have the same privilege as any other stage company. Johnson has been paying the railroad fifty cents for each through passenger." John W. Weaver to Colonel McNair, Frankfort, January 20, 1838. Letter in author's collection.

[18]*Kentucky Gazette*, September 28, 1837.

of the *Accommodation Stages* for Louisville. Leave Frankfort at 4 o'clock P. M. after the arrival of the *Accommodation Stages* from Louisville, and to arrive at Lexington at 8 o'clock.

PASSENGERS from *Lexington* to *Louisville,* will by this arrangement be carried through *in daylight.*

Second Line.

Leave Lexington every day at 2 o'clock P. M., and arrive at *Frankfort* at 7 before the departure of the Mail Stage for *Louisville.* Returning from Frankfort every morning at 8 o'clock after the arrival of the Mail Stage from Louisville, and arrives at Lexington at 12 o'clock.

CHARLES B. LEWIS, Agent.

It was not long after the "old line" of stages, Johnson, Weisiger and Company, connected with the railway, that the rival line, or Good Intent Opposition Line, saw they were losing some of the stage and railway patronage, so they in turn formed the same kind of agreement, relative to this connection, and thus advertised:

RAILROAD AND STAGE NOTICE!

Traveling by the Railroad from Lexington to Louisville,

THROUGH IN 11 HOURS!

Cars leave at 5 A. M. and arrive at Frankfort at 9 o'clock. The Good Intent Opposition Line of Stages leaves Frankfort at 9 o'clock A. M. and arrives at Louisville at 4 o'clock P. M. Passengers entering at Lexington for Louisville *have the preference of seats in this line.* Baggage transferred from the cars to the Stages at the office in Frankfort.

PASSENGERS leave Louisville in the Good Intent Opposition Line at 5 o'clock A. M. and arrive in Frankfort to dinner, and in time for the 3 o'clock line of cars for Lexington.

H. McCONATHY, Agent.

This did not mean, however, that the stages had ceased operation from Lexington to Frankfort, but, on the contrary, they handled all the business possible over that part of the road. The additional patronage was cared for by filling out the railroad connection on the other end, so that a person going from Lexington to Louisville went by stage and steam, or all the way by stage.

Since Frankfort had a waterway to the Ohio River, the completion of this infant railroad, designated later as the Lexington and Frankfort railroad, marked an important event in the history of Lexington. Though its operation was attended with difficulties, it should have been a paying road. However, the management knew nothing about maintenance, and the track rapidly deteriorated. The flat iron rails, laid on stone sills,[19] along the main line had suffered much damage from the rails pulling loose at each end and bending up into "snake heads." This led to one or more serious accidents. The two locomotives, *Notta-*

---

[19] A section of this original track with stone sills is laid on the campus of the University of Kentucky, Lexington.

way and *Logan,* which Swigert and Company had received
from the railroad, were subject to frequent break-
downs.[20] The movements of the cars became sluggish
and decidedly more hazardous, because of the mishap
while going down the inclined plane at Frankfort.[21]

The old four-wheel locomotives had to be discarded as
they could not go around a curve without slowing down,
and often there was danger of breaking an axle. Business for the railroad during the year 1840 was small
in volume compared to what it had been. From the run-
down condition and the frequent accidents along the line,
the traveling public became dissatisfied with this new
means of travel, and "again sought safety in the stage-
coaches."[22]

Thus, at the end of the first ten years of this pioneer
railroad in the Bluegrass, the stage-coaches had not seriously felt the encroachment in their business. While it
had hardly passed the experimental stage, the "iron horse"
was rapidly coming into a place where it would drive the
old jehus and their coaches off the turnpikes that paral-
leled the routes of the railroads.

---

[20]There are two old bills in the papers of Governor Fletcher, in the
Kentucky State Historical Society files, presented by a "waggoner" for payment for transporting the locomotives of that road on two different
occasions from Frankfort to Lexington, in order that they might be
repaired.

[21]From the bluff overlooking the town of Frankfort, an inclined plane
was used to convey the passengers from the railroad into the town.
On January 31, 1839, one of the cars going down the incline plane
became disconnected and began a rapid descent. In their efforts to
save themselves many of the passengers attempted to jump out and were
seriously bruised and broken up. *Lexington Observer & Reporter,* February 5, 1839.

[22]Muncy—*The First Railroad in the West,* p. 28.

CHAPTER VIII

INCIDENTS OF STAGE TRAVEL

IN ORDER to gain an accurate idea of the pleasures and discomforts incidental to travel when the public stage and mail coaches constituted the only means of locomotion, it is necessary to read the diaries written by men at that time. Some found staging delightful, while others found it hateful and were miserable. This difference of opinion was usually traceable to their own characters, the state of the weather, and the nature of their traveling companions.

John Cleves Short, in a letter of October 25, 1829, to his brother, Dr. Charles Wilkins Short, professor of materia medica and medical botany at Transylvania University in Lexington, speaks of the discomforts of travel in going by stage from Lexington to Louisville: "We had not parted from you more than an hour or two I think in the morning of our leaving Frankfort, before the [Edw. P.] Johnson stage-coach broke down with us—a viler establishment than which never graced our country. A fence rail was substituted for a spring, and thus opprobriously and uncomfortably we had to ride for 33 miles to Middletown, annoyed moreover by an accession of dirty mechanics who crowded in at Shelbyville, and especially by the persevering impudence of a blackleg, who were all anxious to get on to the Louisville races."

After being subjected to this rough travel for thirty-three miles, the party reached Louisville, where the stage-coach was driven "to every tavern, boarding-house, and several private houses in town, where we sought lodging in vain—and finally had to go on board a steamboat to pass the night . . ."[1]

Ten years later, after the Lexington and Maysville Road had been macadamized and opened to the traveling public, we have the account of a Lexington merchant who in 1839 was returning from the purchase of goods in Philadelphia: "After traveling from Pittsburgh to Maysville in Kentucky, a distance of two hundred and seventy-five miles by stage, I was induced from want of rest to remain at the Goddard House for several days before pursuing my journey on to Lexington. This hotel from its widely-known hospitality was famous up and down the roads and all stages going and coming from Maysville made their headquarters at that place.

"While resting there I observed large piles of newspapers and mail bags thrown aside to make room for passengers in the crowded stages, and it is of no wonder people complain of the frequent delays in the nation's mail service. I saw one stage of Dickey, as it was leaving the Goddard House, refuse to wait for the mail stage while it was coming in sight on the other side of the Ohio River. This stage had the latest mail and newspapers from the east and it had to be ferried across the river and the mail transferred to the leaving stage, which would have been only a matter of minutes, but the driver

---

[1] Letter in the Filson Club library, Louisville.

wouldn't wait saying 'Dickey's stage waits for no man or mails.' Stage accommodations were numerous and the traveler had much to draw from. I bought a seat on the line of Johnson & Company as the taverns visited along the route were of a superior nature. Price of ticket for myself and trunk was $3.50 which was immediately entered on the way-bill by the stage agent, Mr. M. Stanley, who informed me the time of departure was four in the morning.

"At the appointed hour I presented myself and baggage, and the scene about a stage office at this early hour of departure was one of commotion and a study of character. Mr. Stanley was the busiest man I ever saw, running distractedly through the crowd in search of some lost baggage; anxious women dressed in their best bonnets and hoop-skirts wondering how they would manage them inside the stage; stern looking men anxious to be off to their destinations. The stage agent was head over heels in his duties, endeavoring to check the way-bill and weigh all the passengers' baggage, which in the case of extra pieces would be twenty-five cents per pound extra.

"Finally the mail and baggage was checked and loaded and the cry 'all aboard' was heard and with a crack of the driver's long whip the stage was off. Our first stop was at the village of Washington, only several miles from our starting point, and it was dark when we drove up to the post-office and discharged some mail. It rained for some time after we started so that our coach was buttoned up close, but when it faired, so that we could roll up the curtains and look out, it was really an imposing sight. Each town and village we passed through, men, women, and children were in the streets and at their doors to see us. At May's Lick we changed horses, the scene was both extraordinary and painful to me, to see the poor horses panting as if they had the thumps and all in a lather of sweat. Here we had a short breakfast and were on our journey again.

"There was much to see on the road, and we were meeting Concord and Troy coaches similar to the one we were in, each with the name of some famous general or statesman painted in golden letters on the side. The passengers and drivers waved and greeted each other as the swaying coaches clattered past. Several large droves of stock were passed on the road headed for an eastern market, in charge of a drover and his shepherd dog. There are on the road four rival or opposition lines of stages, and it is of some wonder how they make financial gains out of the business, with all the competition now going on between them.

"As each toll-house or toll-gate is reached, the stage draws to a stop and the toll-taker lifts the pole and counts the number of passengers riding in the coach, from which a settlement is made monthly with the stage owners. The toll fare is included when you purchase a seat on the stage. On this road [Lexington-Maysville] there are thirteen toll-houses, each about five miles apart, usually in charge of a man and his wife.

"Our next stop was for a change of horses at lower Blue Licks, where all the passengers got out to stretch their legs and to partake of some refreshments at the tavern bar. This hostelry under the charge of Major Ariss Throckmorton, is a well known watering place and draws crowds from all over the South who come here to avoid the sickly climate during the summer and fall. The place was thronged with visitors and an air of refinement permeated the atmosphere. With a fresh team of four prancing horses, our next stop was at James Bassell's in Millersburg. Hardly had the stage stopped before the hostlers were busy changing horses, taking the tired animals to rub, rest, and feed, bringing on fresh high-stepping spirited ones, champing their bits, apparently very anxious for a galloping start toward the next post.

"As the town of Paris was reached, the stage driver blew a long blast on his three-foot horn, to apprise the townsfolk of his coming, and with dash and flourish pulled up in front of Charles Talbutt's Hotel, where all unloaded to rest and refresh ourselves again. Several more passengers booked seats contributing no less comfort to the already crowded vehicle, and the stage proceeded on toward Lexington.

"William Moreland's tavern was reached about noon, where a sumptuous meal was enjoyed by the passengers, who sat at a long table with the popular driver at the head. After the meal was finished we all loaded in the coach, when the stable boy who was holding one of the lead horses by the bridle stepped aside, and with a flourish of the whip the horses leaped forward with a jerk and lurch of the coach, and we were on the last stretch of our trip. On reaching Lexington, our trip of sixty-five miles in the rumbling and lurching coach was at an end, and we pulled up in front of the stage office in Brennan's Hotel, once the Postlethwait's Tavern.

"We were all tired and dusty from the trip, which consumed nine hours without an accident or mishap. I was very thankful to be once more in the town of my birth and business. Mr. [J. H.] Penny, the stage agent, was on hand to meet us and to receive the way-bill from the driver. There was a large crowd milling around waiting to get the latest information and news from Washington and the East. The out-of-town newspapers were sold and read in front of the stage office and there was always a crowd to question the driver of what messages he had received at the other end of the line and along the way. The stage office was the hub of the town and the center of news distribution. The baggage was checked by Mr. Penny and distributed according to the way-bill. The majority of the stage travelers engaged quarters at Brennan's Hotel . . ."

Stage travelers and others coming to Lexington in the early thirties found places of refreshment and cheer scattered over Fayette County.[2]   At these taverns various

[2]List of tavern-keepers, 1832, Fayette Circuit Court, file 793.
"John B. Higbee, at his house in Fayette County, Curds Road [so. Elkhorn].
James B. Henderson, 4 miles from Lexington, Leestown Road.
James Eastham at his house, 8 miles from Lexington, Winchester Road.
William Goss and Wm. Harvy at Wright's Pond, 3 miles from Lexington.
Wm. Fitzpatrick at his house in Fayette County.
James Hutchinson, 6 miles from Lex, Georgetown Road [Donerail].
James Hainey at his house in Fayette County.
Thos. S. Graves, 6 miles from Lex, Versailles Road [Ft. Spring].
John West at his house near Lexington.
Jacob Embry at his house at Athens in Fayette County.
Jeremiah Rogers, 12 miles from Lex; Cleveland Road.
James Bibb at his house in Athens, Fayette County.
George Dunlap, 3 miles from Lex; Boonesboro Road.
Polly Pierson, 4 miles from Lex; Georgetown Road.
George Goreham, 4 miles from Lex; Henry's Mill Road [Newtown].
Richard Chiles, 8 miles from Lex; Strodes Road [Chilesburg].
Reuben Watts at his house in Fayette County."

degrees of accommodations were provided, but all were subject to the rates[3] as determined each year by the county board of magistrates. These rates as fixed by the magistrates each year varied to some extent as the traveler went through the Bluegrass counties, the prices of meals varying from 18¾ cents in Pendleton County[4] to 25 cents in Harrison County[5] and 31¼ cents in Bourbon County.[6] Judging from the rates fixed each year there was a good deal of travel by horse-back throughout the Bluegrass region of Kentucky, and special mention was always made for "stableage for twenty-four hours" or, for "horse at hay per night" and, if his owner was a good provider, the bill next morning would list this item "horse at oats and corn per night 25 cents." These prices varied also, but it was safe to estimate that a man traveling on horse-back could stop overnight and be taken care of as the taverns afforded from seventy-five cents to one dollar, including lodging, supper, breakfast, and keep of his horse.[7]

The subject and prices of drinks figured largely at the old taverns and were in a measure the chief source of revenue to the landlords. Different localities were partial to certain drinks, as in Harrison County at the tavern bars, "cider oil" at 12½ cents per quart was a favorite drink

---

[3]Fayette County Court, Order Book 9, p. 187, July, 1834.

"Dinner	25c
Supper	25c
Breakfast	25c
Lodging per night	12½c
Madeira wine per qt.	200c
Port, sherry, and other wines, do.	150c
Cyder and beer, per qt.	6¼c"

[4]Pendleton County Court, Order Book H, p. 217, April, 1834.
[5]Harrison County Court, Order Book G, p. 267, 1834.
[6]Bourbon County Court, Order Book L, p. 216, Sept. Term, 1836.
[7]Harrison County Court, Order Book G, p. 267, 1834.

with weary and thirsty travelers.[8] "Cherry bounce of whiskey" was a well known drink of Bourbon County, and sold for 12½ cents per half pint.[9]

As the stage-coaches approached the taverns, the passengers were only too glad for the opportunity to get out and refresh themselves at the tavern bar after a hot and dusty trip over ten or twelve miles of rough roads between relay stations or inns. Whiskey, apple jack, peach brandy, wine, and gin were cheap drinks and well liked by the most hardy traveler. Such a drink would be had for the small sum of six and one-fourth cents, and a half pint was the measure.[10] For the more aristocratic traveler in the stage, or in a private coach, a "toddy of foreign materials" was in keeping with his station, and commanded the price of 37 cents—but if concocted of "domestic materials" would lose some of its prestige, as well as 12 cents in price.[11]

Whiskey was the leading beverage, and it was plentiful and cheap. At the "waggon-stands" and "drovers stands" the price of a drink of whiskey was three cents, while at the stage houses, by reason of an assumption of aristocracy, the price was six and one-fourth cents. The current coins of the road were a big copper cent of the United States coinage and a Spanish coin of the value of six and one-fourth cents, known as the Spanish half réal. The Mexican or Spanish milled dollar was oftener seen than the United States dollar. The silver five-cent piece

[8]Harrison County Court, Order Book G, p. 267, May, 1834.
[9]Bourbon County Court, Order Book L, p. 216, 1836.
[10]Pendleton County Court, Order Book H, p. 217.
[11]Bourbon County Court, Order Book L, p. 216, September, 1836.

and the "dime" of the United States coinage were seen occasionally, but not as much as the half réal and the "levy."[12]

In some portions of Europe, travelers during this period were charged according to their rank, and the arrangements seemed quite right, "but," remarked a Kentuckian, "in this country where every man travels, whether rich or poor, the arrangement is not just, for it does not necessarily follow that a stage-coach passenger must be rich." Whether this arrangement was just or not, tavern-keepers were often accused of "charging the passengers of a stage-coach twice as much as they do for others."[13] Persons who traveled by stage were generally looked upon as being a little more prosperous and refined than those who journeyed by horse-back.

While this was a period of great drinking by all travelers, temperance societies became active and temperance taverns were frequently found by stage passengers. Those coming to Lexington who were adverse to slaking their thirsts with alcoholic beverages usually found lodging at the LaFayette Temperance Hotel, which enjoyed a fair amount of patronage based "entirely on temperance principles."[14] In times of stringency, the stage-coach com-

---

[12]Another term for the réal, a Spanish coin of twelve and one-half cents. Searight, p. 17. The Director of the U. S. Mint in his annual report, 1912, pp. 10–12 says: "The scarcity of money in the colonies of North America, except in the *Spanish* colonies in the Southwest, was a source of constant distress. No mint was established in the United States until 1792 and very little coinage was done for years afterwards. In the retail trade of the country, the Spanish, afterwards the Mexican, réal and half réal were in common use until the middle of the nineteenth century."

[13]*American Monthly Magazine*, Vol. III, p. 104, July, 1854.

[14]*Lexington Intelligencer*, February 13, 1835, John B. Higbee, proprietor.

panies, as well as taverns, inns, and hotels, along with turnpike companies, issued script which passed as readily as money. The script was similar to the national currency, lacking only in the artistic skill displayed in engraving the latter.

During the summer of 1834, a resident of Cincinnati, deciding that the city had no pleasures during the hot weather, started on a stage-coach journey through central Kentucky, and from his recollections we gain one of the best views of stage travel through this section during the days of its zenith. After boarding at a local hotel in Cincinnati during the month of June, 1834, he felt that "it is worth while to travel, if it be only to get something new to talk about." He experienced the truth of observation, for his adventures began with his journey.

As the stage-coach was the accepted means of travel through Kentucky, he decided to take the early morning stage from Cincinnati to Lexington and left word with the hotel porter to call him at the time of departure, in this case three o'clock in the morning. He was aroused at the appointed hour by a loud knocking at the door next to his, and heard a surly voice demand:

"What do you want?"

"Stage is ready, Sir."

"Well, what's that to me?" fiercely demanded his enraged neighbor.

"I was ordered to call No. 43 at three o'clock, Sir."

"Clear out, you black rascal!" Off went the porter grumbling "stage don't wait, I know better—I done call de gentleman—if he won't get up 'tain't my fault, I spec

nohow I' be dog gone if I pull de gentleman out of bed,
if he wants to lay dar."

"If the gentleman won't get up" reported our traveler,
as he opened the door, "you may light my candle and tell
the stage driver to wait for me."

"Is you 43, Sir? I beg de other gentleman's pardon."
In a few minutes the stage was loaded and then it
drove away rapidly, leaving the next door neighbor to
finish his broken nap and compose his disturbed temper.
With the picking up of passengers around the city and
other delays it "was five o'clock before we left Cincinnati," causing one of the passengers to remark that "a
mail stage is about as uncertain as a female temper" and
"more unaccommodating than anything else."

As the stage progressed along the route, it gathered
passengers. Already there were pocketed in the coach
eight adults and three children, with three persons on the
driver's seat and three more on top "making a sum total
of seventeen souls." Continuing on the trip the gentleman wrote: "Thus freighted we turned our backs on the
river and began to ascend the beautiful verdant hills of
Kentucky, over which the sun was just rising and pouring
a flood of joyous light. It was slow work—but we went,
dray, dray, dray—the horses sweating, the passengers nod-
ding, and the coach creaking under its heavy burden. Our
deck passengers soon increased to five, which with the addition of baggage stowed on top made the vehicle so top-
heavy that it swerved from side to side, rolling like a
ship in a storm with an awful inclination to capsize. Twice
we came within an ace of an upset, but did not quite go

over. Then one of the axletrees took fire, the proprietor's wheels not being sufficiently greased. People may say what they will but mail contractors must be very poorly paid when they cannot afford grease enough to keep their axles from ignition."

For the better part of the day nothing of unusual interest took place. Stage relays were passed, fresh horses were brought forth and changed, passengers, particularly the men, got out at the taverns and refreshed themselves with drinks, and the stage continued on its journey to Lexington. Late in the afternoon the next accident was occasioned by some country boys and girls. A large company had broken up and were riding home on horse-back as the stage passed. The young folks were gallantly prancing along and one of the boys thought it a good chance to show off a little before his sweetheart. So he flourished his whip and began "to cut up a few rusties." Away dashed the stage as fast as four animals could draw a heavy carriage, full of people, trunks, carpet-bags, band-boxes, and mail bags. "They made the dust fly" and the coach soon came to a hill and down that it went "faster than a streak of lightning." Suddenly the passengers felt a jolt and the stage tilted nearly over, running for some yards on two wheels and then righted itself again. The driver was thrown from his box, the wheels passed over his ankles, and the horses "streaked it" down the hill on their own responsibility. The women screamed, the children cried, the men swore, and the old coach creaked worse than ever.

Finally a passenger who sat on the box had the presence of mind to get on the foot-board and thence to the tongue, where he seized the reins of the wheel horses and brought the coach to a stop, thus becoming the hero of the trip. Finding their driver not much the worse for the scare, the stage continued on to Eagle Hills, which it reached sometime during the night. Becoming somewhat tired of the stage travel after his day's experience, our traveler hired a horse and "rode pleasantly by moonlight 14 miles to Georgetown" where he arrived before the stage-coach.

After registering at the Pratt Tavern in Georgetown, about midnight, the traveler inquired when the stage would leave for Lexington.

"At half-past seven, after breakfast in the morning," was the reply of the bartender.

Pleased with this answer, the traveler "went to bed under the delightful conviction that he should sleep until breakfast, and was just fairly nestled when in came the barkeeper."

"Sorry to disturb you, Sir."

"Well, what's the matter?"

"The stage has just come in, Sir, with a lady in it, and this is the only room in the house fit to put a lady in."

"Very good, the lady is heartily welcome."

"Show you to another room, if you please, Sir."

"Very well," said the disturbed guest, who bundled his clothes under his arm and marched off to another chamber where he crept into bed. Hardly had he dozed off to sleep, when in rushed the barkeeper again and exclaimed as before:

"Sorry to disturb you, Sir."

"Well, what now?"

"Stage is just going to start, Sir."

"How so, it is not one o'clock and the regular hour is half-past seven?"

"Can't help that, some of the passengers have bribed the driver with a five-dollar note, and he is going directly on."

Although the regular time for starting of the stage for Lexington was seven-thirty in the morning, two of the passengers had bribed the driver to continue that night. This he did, despite the remonstrations of others. The tired traveler went back to sleep and was ready at the scheduled time in the morning to start, having paid his fare from Cincinnati to Lexington, but he was neither carried by stage to Lexington nor had his money refunded. It then became necessary for him to pay another fare of seventy-five cents to be carried by stage from Georgetown to Lexington.

This was the period of stage-coach rivalry and competition, and as this traveler reported: "Scarcely a day passes in which an accident does not occur. Lives are lost and limbs broken; yet the law is silent. Scarcely any regulations to govern them but such as are suggested by the cupidity of the owners."

Approaching Lexington from the stage-coach, possibly riding on the box beside the driver, he saw "on every side the elegant residences of the wealthy, and productive fields upon which the art of agriculture has been practiced with almost unparalleled success. The finest equipages are seen dashing along the highway and the by-ways, the pastures are covered with the choicest domestic animals of foreign climate; with high bred horses, flocks of Saxony

and Merino sheep, and immense herds of noble cattle."
This traveler was somewhat amazed at "the number of
pleasure carriages [in Lexington] which are seen dashing
along the streets—gigs, barouches, coaches, and vehicles
of all sorts and sizes rattle about from morning till night,
but are generally numerous in the cool of the afternoon,
when they give to this place an appearance of great
gaiety."

Lexington, with its cultural and commercial interests,
greatly pleased the traveler who lodged "at the celebrated
old Postlethwait hotel which was crowded with strangers.
A considerable portion of these were wealthy gentlemen
from the South who spend a part of each summer traveling for health and pleasure." And of these visitors to
Lexington he says "on so long a journey from the South
most of them prefer the use of the public conveyances; as
the steamboats are very disagreeable in hot weather, and
the alarm of sickness often prevalent on our rivers, the
stage-coaches are liberally patronized." Also those coming up the river in the summer to Virginia and other
resorts further north "find it an agreeable change to leave
the steamboat at Louisville, pass round by stage-coach to
Frankfort and Lexington and to Maysville, where they
resume their voyage by water."[15]

Remaining in Lexington two or three days, the traveler wanted to stay longer. "But enough," he reported, "I
must be off." "Here is the Harrodsburg stage drawing up,
and an elegant affair it is—a new Troy coach[16] of the

[15]*The Monthly Magazine,* Cincinnati, November, 1834, pp. 534-536.
[16]Made by Orasmus Eaton and Uri Gilbert, in Troy, New York, and
"as late as 1850 Eaton & Gilbert boasted that they had made more than

latest construction, drawn by four fine horses. What a contrast is presented between the arrival and the departure of a stage! On one occasion, you see a handsome vehicle in complete order, the horses slick and shiny, the harness clean, the passengers decently clad, bustling full of excitement and all in high glee. The driver cracks his whip and off they dash at a canter.

"On the other, the same vehicle comes rolling heavily into town, weighted down by its cumbrous load and spattered with mud. The horses are covered with foam and dirt, wearied, panting, and with heads drooped. The passengers are all of one color and a monotonous gloom is seen on their visages; they are the saddest, sorriest, vilest-looking set that can be imagined. They are alike tumbled, angry, dirty, and silent. The gentlemen have not shaved lately and the ladies have had their dresses crushed out of shape. They are hungry, thirsty, sleepy, and covered with dust. They started a genteel, well dressed, affable company; but now they have arrived a silent, haggard, unhappy-looking set of creatures. One has lost his trunk—another his temper. One has forgotten her traveling basket, and they have all forgotten their good manners. They have been upset, perhaps, an arm has been broken, an umbrella fractured, and a new bonnet knocked into a cocked hat. A painter might study their faces as they crawl out of the vehicle, and would find depicted upon them all the varieties of impatience, peevishness, and discontent."

5000 coaches in use in N. America." It was this company "who first put a rail around the top of coaches to carry baggage, noted at that time a great improvement."

After visiting Harrodsburg, Olympian Springs, and Crab Orchard, the traveler rounded out his visit in the Bluegrass, and returned to Cincinnati toward the close of July, much the wiser from the viewpoint of stage-coach travel through central Kentucky.

During the half century from 1800 to 1850, a network of connected stage routes had rendered all parts of the Bluegrass easily accessible and had effected a great advance in the social, political, and industrial welfare of the country. This progress of travel was enjoyed and marveled at by many; one of whom remarked: "Where we now travel in a day, our fathers used to be on the road as many days as there are hours in a day. Or, in more direct terms, to live one *day* now [1850] is equal to having lived one *month* in 1810!"

Yet, with the seemingly common and well known method of travel, there were many who had not made trips by stage-coach. For those persons who contemplated a trip of some distance and duration, a resident of Cincinnati wrote, in the *American Monthly*,[17] July, 1854, the "Facts for Stage Travelers." He said in part: "Travelers ought to carry as few clothes as possible, these not of a valuable kind. A thin and a thick suit, an overcoat, and umbrella should be numbered among them. The traveler should provide himself with a small flask of good brandy, which he need not use unless occasion require it. He should have in his pocket a small piece of opium and a similar piece of gum camphor. These articles may be useful in case of [stage] sickness."

---

[17]*American Monthly Magazine*, Vol. II, pp. 102–105.

Commenting further on the pleasantness of the stage as a vehicle of romance and pleasure, he remarked: "For my part I have always loved the old stage-coach, and do yet, provided I am not in a hurry." There was something fascinating about the stage-coach, even if it was slow and a little crowded, and this experienced traveler of Cincinnati, who had traveled through central Kentucky on several occasions, compared it favorably with travel by the steam cars. "It is true," he said, "that when the weather is warm and the roads dusty one feels a little crowded with twelve in a nine-passenger coach. But it is a very sociable way for traveling, for the passengers are seated against each other, rubbing and being rubbed together until a degree of familiarity springs up between them by no means common on the rail car."

Some of the seats in the stage were more desirable than others, and, as one traveler advised: "It is better when we have to ride in the stage-coach to occupy the middle seat, for we thus escape the 'jolts.' The bodies of these coaches are generally hung on leather braces which give them a peculiar swinging motion most perceptible on the front and back seats, but more so on the back. Though this seat is usually occupied by the ladies, should there be any among the passengers, it is certainly the most unpleasant in the coach—for several reasons. First, on account of the motion of the coach; second, because it is difficult of access; and third, because it is very warm and more liable to injury from heavy baggage, in case of accident."

Many persons objected to riding on the front seat, because those occupying it must ride backwards, which induced nausea in many cases. But it was generally the rule that "if a gentleman is thus made sick, let him get out and ride a few miles on the box with the driver." And this was full compensation for his nausea, "for whoever in the stage-coach traveling neglects to ride occasionally with the driver will lose much valuable information he ought to know." And he too would find "the driver is generally well acquainted with the gossip of the entire line, as well as the country through which you are passing."

Another admonition to stage travelers was that "one ought to eat his meals as regularly as convenient, provided it is of a quality at all tolerable." The degree of sociability of stage travel as compared to rail travel is thus shown: "Travelers by this mode [stage-coach] of conveyance are less liable to sickness than any other, several causes conducing to this end. There is less care on the mind, more social intercourse, purer air, and more congenial exercise, as well as fewer persons collected together to generate disease."

The novice in stage traveling could get in the good graces of the "knight of the ribbons" by observing and complimenting his horses and in attending to the ladies, as "it was not handy for them to get in or out [of the stage] without assistance." Attention was called to those who traveled at night to remember that the driver sometimes got sleepy about two hours before day and "was likely to upset you." "If you find him silent," reported an old traveler, "and seldom speaking to his horses, you had, especially if your family is along and the weather is not too cool, better get out and keep him company."

This same traveler reported "that about the break of day you will get some fine notes from his bugle; and of all the sounds made by instruments of the horn kind none sound so pleasantly as the stage horn in the early morning. Many drivers perform with ease and beauty on these horns, and, strange to say, the horses seem to partake of the enlivening strains, for they move faster at the first notes of the horn."[18]

Not infrequently there were some good singers among the travelers and they would entertain the passengers with some of their choicest vocal pieces. At times they would be singing some sacred hymn, then again a change would be made to a comic or some lively patriotic song. Occasionally there were some good story-tellers among them, and they would entertain their companions with yarns and stories of their various experiences, or deliver to the "large and respectable" audience inside the coach a regular speech on politics, religion, or other suitable subject.

The ride through Kentucky in the stage-coach from Louisville by way of Bardstown to Nashville[19] was often the scene of many exciting events. To relieve the tedium of traveling, passengers often resorted to card playing, poker being the favorite diversion.[20] This field provided a good hunting ground for the professional gamblers from the river boats plying up and down the Mississippi River, as nowhere else were the merits of draw poker more readily appreciated.

---

[18]*American Monthly Magazine,* Cincinnati, Vol. II, pp. 102–105.

[19]Louisville to Nashville by stage in 1850—180 miles—33 hours—$12.00. Cassedy—*History of Louisville,* p. 253.

[20]Many exciting games of poker were played on the overland stage, crossing the plains to California, when "the 'ante' would be nothing less than a five-dollar greenback." Root and Connelley, p. 509.

One of the most notorious gamblers to travel by stage was Sam Austin, who despite his quiet and diffident manner was quick on the draw and skillful in the use of the bowie knife. There were many stories told of his deadly work on several occasions. On one of the trips south he sat in a game with two or three of the passengers, one of whom was a cotton planter returning home with a considerable sum of money. As usual Austin made a number of lucky draws and had won about fifteen hundred dollars, when one of the onlookers, observing him deal a card from the bottom of the deck, thrust an old-fashioned derringer pistol in his side.

"I've caught you at last, Sam Austin!" he exclaimed. "You killed a brother of mine in Cincinnati two years ago, and I swore if I ever caught you I'd get the drop on you. Now turn over that ace of diamonds you dealt from the bottom of the pack."

"You must be crazy," replied Austin, but, in a few seconds he exposed his whole hand, showing an "ace full" and a diamond ace.

"You have me foul," continued the gambler. "Give me a fair chance and I'll fight you when and where you like."

"Well," said the stranger, "I'll give you the fair chance; get off and I'll meet you, or, if the gentlemen will clear the coach, we will settle it now."

The stage driver, hearing the loud threats, left his seat, and, with the assistance of the other passengers, put the two men out on the road. By this time the stage had reached a point about ten miles north of Bardstown. Some of the passengers wanted to remain and see the end, but the driver complained that he had already lost too much time, and would not wait, remarking that it was "nobody's business if both of them are killed."

As the coach moved on, both contestants fell at the first fire. And before the stage was out of sight, both had arisen, loaded their pieces, and were firing again. The returning stage found both duelists seriously wounded. With the assistance of the passengers, the old stage driver converted his vehicle into an improvised ambulance and carefully conveyed them back to Louisville. There Austin died in a few days, but the stranger recovered.[21]

---

[21]Recollections of Dr. A. H. Merrifield, *Kentucky Standard,* Bardstown, July 26, 1906.

CHAPTER IX

EXPERIENCES OF TRAVELERS

TRAVELERS going by stage over the Bluegrass routes had little trouble with highway robberies and hold-ups, for such occurrences were rare. This may be attributed to several reasons. The country was too thickly populated, the principal stages carried the United States mail, and the penalty of highway robbery carried with it the death sentence.[1] Another reason was that most of the passengers in the stages carried letters of credit, checks, and bills of exchange, while those in other parts of the United States and later on in the West carried cash or gold dust.

Single travelers on horse-back or on foot afforded the best opportunities for the highway robbers. Those that escaped on the road were sometimes robbed in the taverns or inns at the end of the day's travel:[2]

"I was robbed at the tavern of John McCracken, in the town of Lexington, Ky., on the night of the 30th of December, 1830, by a villain who took lodgings for the night, of the sum of sixteen dollars, generously leaving me twelve and one-half cents to pursue a journey of four hundred miles by stage and steam. He reported himself at Wickliff's Tavern

[1]U. S. Statutes at Large, Vol. N, p. 232.
[2]*Cincinnati Daily Gazette,* January 8, 1831.

at 1 o'clock the same night for Louisville via Frankfort. His name is Ritchie, and he pretends to be a
patent cement mender of glass, china, and crockery
ware.

                                    "AARON TUFTS."

Travelers who were thus robbed took it upon themselves to publicly denounce the villain as a warning to
other less suspecting wayfarers. Rufus Lane, traveling on
foot near Bardstown, was met by two white men "who
laid hold of him, each by an arm and demanded his
money, having either dirks or knives drawn at the same
time," and after "a most prodigious scuffle tore off Lane's
coat pocket and took about $200 in money."[3]

While highway robbery was almost unknown on the
Bluegrass stage routes, numerous cases developed where
trunks of the passengers were stolen, robbed, and rifled
of their contents:

"On Tuesday morning last, just before day, the
Maysville stage was robbed of its baggage when
within a few miles of Blue Licks, on its way to Lexington. There were several passengers, all of whom
probably would have lost their trunks, but the driver
fortunately discovered what was going on, stopped
the stage, and pursued the villains. They succeeded
however, in carrying off one trunk, belonging to
a gentleman from Charleston, S. C., which contained
amongst other valuables, 100 dollars in specie."[4]

³*Lexington Intelligencer*, April 15, 1836.
⁴*Lexington Observer & Reporter*, October 25, 1836.

It was believed in several cases that there existed between some of the stage agents and drivers a secret understanding or connection, whereby the trunks would mysteriously disappear from the boots of the stage, between points along the line, after the trunks had been properly checked and entered on the way-bill.[5] One example of this:

"STAGE ROBBERY

"We learn from the Lexington Intelligencer that the boot of the mail stage between that city and Nicholasville was cut open on Thursday the 1st instant, and some trunks taken therefrom. The trunk of Mr. C. H. Wickliffe, the special agent of the post office department, containing all his papers and clothes was stolen."[6]

The loss of the trunks and other baggage led to a number of suits against the proprietors of the stage lines, who were entirely ignorant of how they had been robbed or how they were lost. The owners of the trunks easily recovered damages from the stage proprietors, but in most instances at a somewhat reduced value of their estimate. It was generally understood by stage patrons that no trunks could be sent over the roads without the owner or someone else going with them, but even that did not always guarantee the safe delivery of a passenger's luggage.[7]

---

[5]Henry B. Daly *vs.* Edw. P. Johnson & Co., Fayette Circuit Court, file 1088, May 10, 1839.

[6]*Western Citizen*, Paris, September 9, 1842.

[7]W. W. Justice *vs.* Irvine, Hawkins & Co., Clark Circuit Court, file 744, January 26, 1841, Dr. Justice's trunk disappeared from the Winchester-Mt. Sterling stage while he was a passenger en route.

Alex. M. Preston, who lost his "iron-bound trunk and buffalo cover," reported that he had paid the stage agent "three dollars which was the charge for carrying him and his trunk from Maysville to Lexington," and that the trunk "was stolen out of the boot of the said stage somewhere between Maysville and Lexington by reason of the negligence of the agents." He contended "his trunk and contents were easily worth $230.59." The jury decided for the plaintiff in the suit that followed, but granted him damages only "for a reasonable wardrobe," in the sum of one hundred and twenty-five dollars.[8]

On more than one occasion, the stage proprietors' attempts to solve the trunk robberies resulted in damage suits against themselves.[9] Another thing that harassed the stage owners was the indifference and negligence of stage agents in selling tickets to passengers, and properly entering their destinations on the way-bills. John F. West, an old man nearly eighty, took passage in midwinter in Irvine & Field's stage from Lexington to his home in Scott County, and purchased a ticket to "Jones' Tavern Stand." The ticket agent in Lexington, being busy about his duties in the office, carelessly entered the passenger's name on the way-bill to "Getty's Tavern Stand," another relay station and tavern along the same route. When the stage pulled up in front of this place,

[8] Preston *vs*. Edw. P. Johnson & Co., Fayette Circuit Court, file 1213, May 8, 1836.

[9] Thomas H. Irvine, the veteran stage owner, charged one of his agents "was in on the deal" and that "he stole trunks, money, checques, and is a thief of everything." This accusation was greatly resented by the stage agent who brought suit for ten thousand dollars, but the case was dismissed for lack of evidence. Hastings *vs*. Irvine & Scott, Scott Circuit Court, file 187, January 12, 1852.

the driver consulted the way-bill and called to West to get out—but West maintained his fare was paid to Jones' Tavern further along the route, and he was entitled to ride to that point.

After considerable argument between West and the stage driver, the latter "expelled him from the coach" some eight miles short of his paid destination, forcing him "to travel the eight miles on foot and by the fatigue and labor of walking through the snow greatly damaged and impaired his health." As a result, damages of two hundred and fifty dollars were awarded the old man for the carelessness of the stage agent in Lexington, and the rough handling received at the hands of the stage driver.[10]

Such occurrences as this were rare, as the stage drivers were, for the most part, the very exponents of civility and politeness toward the passengers, and fully capable of guarding the lives of those entrusted to their care. The driver was likely to be under forty years of age, though occasionally older men assumed the duties of piloting the coach. His complexion, tanned by the winds and weather, showed a ruddy hue, often heightened by the frequent visitations to the tavern bar. His dress was a flannel shirt, corduroy breeches stuffed into high boots, a well-worn hat or cap, a fur or leather coat, and a large buffalo robe to tuck around him. During the ante-bellum period, when stage-coaching attained its greatest vogue

[10]John F. West *vs.* Irvine & Field, Grant Circuit Court, file 85, April 10, 1855.

in this section, men universally wore whiskers,[11] and the important personage atop the old Troy or Concord coach was no exception in this particular.

Fair weather and foul were the same to the jehus, and they learned to read the road not only by day but by night. From the sky they interpreted the meaning of passing clouds or encircled moon, for the omens meant either comfort or discomfort to them and their horses in the hours ahead. Artists of a century ago pictured the horses of the stage-coach as prancing, fire-breathing steeds; but it is probable that much of this picturesqueness was highly imaginative. Practical teams were required to pull the coaches loaded with passengers and baggage, and the long, monotonous journeys conspired to produce conspicuous ribs, pronounced back-bones, and other indications of hard toil.

Harnesses were often adorned with ivory, or imitation, rings and trappings. These ornaments, especially ivory, were somewhat expensive and tempting to drivers of rival lines. More than one driver found his team with the harness stripped of its ornaments.[12] Changing of horses at relay stations demanded quick work, and, with fingers often numb from excessive cold, buckles and snaps were frequently manipulated with difficulty. The whole stage system was operated with the precision and punctuality of a railroad, in all kinds of weather, night and day.

---

[11]"I used to tuck my beard in under my vest to protect my throat and chest from the cold." Statement of an old stage driver, in author's collection.

[12]"$50.00 Reward for the harness and ivory trimmings worn by the off-horse." Advertisement of a stage driver. *Lexington Observer & Reporter,* August 10, 1837.

Along the routes and at the taverns, orders of the
stage drivers were obeyed without hesitation, and they
had little patience with those who were dilatory in carrying them out. This also applied to the passengers, regardless of their rank or station in life. There was much
suppressed excitement along the lines when Santa Anna
was being taken in a stage-coach through central Kentucky to Washington. Due to the massacre of the captured Texans in their struggle for independence, few
persons showed him but scant courtesy. General Santa
Anna stopped overnight at Colonel Throckmorton's Inn
near Millersburg, and the next morning when the stage
was ready to start the Mexican general had not arisen.

"Where's Santa Anna?" inquired the stage
driver Darby.

"The General is yet asleep," said one of the
Mexican attendants, "and he never permits anyone
to awaken him."

"Damn Santa Anna!" said Darby, "The United
States mail don't wait for anybody," and with that
he brushed past the attendants and kicked on the
General's door until Santa Anna arose from his
bed. He was then hurried into the stage without
an opportunity to eat his breakfast.

On another occasion, Henry Clay, James Harlan, and
several other distinguished Southerners were en route to
Washington. When the stage driven by George Pierce
pulled up in front of the Blue Licks Hotel to change
horses, the passengers got out to stretch their legs, and,

perhaps, went into the inn for some refreshments. They lingered a few minutes longer than pleased the driver, an irritable South Carolinian, and he drove off and left them. Mr. Clay and his friends hired a private carriage, and, by hard driving, overtook the stage as it entered May's Lick. They continued the remainder of the trip with Pierce, but, on other trips with him, they were a little more careful not to keep him waiting.

The stage driver had to go through foul weather as well as fair, in all seasons, day and night. Death sometimes rode beside the driver when the mercury descended to ten or twelve below zero. One cold morning the driver of the stage from Covington to Lexington left on time, perhaps four A. M. It was zero weather with blowing snow and large drifts on the road and, in places, over the fence tops, so that it was mid-afternoon when he reached Williamstown.

Despite the condition of the road and the weather, the stage passengers insisted on going on to Lexington. With a bottle of whiskey and a fresh team, the driver was on the road again. Inside the stage the passengers were warmed with "hot bricks,"[13] and sheltered from the wind and snow. Passing by several farm houses late in the afternoon, the "knight of the ribbons" shouted about the frigid temperature, and these were, perhaps, his last words, for when the stage dragged into Georgetown, and the horses stopped by habit at the post-office, he was found dead. How the animals negotiated the snow cov-

---

[13]These "hot bricks" were heated in an oven and rented to the stage passengers en route; ten cents for the first brick and five cents and the cold one for another heated brick. They lasted from three to four hours and were used by the passengers to warm their feet.

ered roads and hills before reaching Georgetown was a cause of wonderment; and to the passengers the thought of the driver freezing stiff in the cold air of the night was gruesome indeed.[14]

The ferries at the small rivers, the fords or creeks which sometimes got out of their banks, and the mud-holes and sinkholes were matters of no little worry to the stage drivers. Every stream of any depth had a ferry-boat, usually operated with a "wash-board" keel at the up-stream side, and slung at the quarters in harness that traveled on a stay rope fastened high above the boat to both shores. Many were not so good, and the driver of the stage often had to "sweep oars" with the ferryman.

Crossing the main ferries sometimes proved quite a hazardous undertaking, as related in the recollections of Charles E. Mooney:

> "My mother and I were going to Richmond [from Lexington] in the fall of 1837. When we got to Clay's ferry just after a storm, the Kentucky River was high on its banks and misbehaving, and was a sizable stream in those days. The boat on which the stage was to cross was a pendulum ferry. Some one shoved off before the bridle was set by the Negro ferryman, and the rushing water swept the boat out in the mid-stream, swinging free on one lead of the bridle, and then the line on a corner iron whipped and parted.

[14]Recollections of Thomas H. Irvine. The driver's name was Hall. Other cases of this kind are on record of the driver freezing to death, and, in one instance, the stage-coach overturned and killed two of the passengers. *Niles Weekly Register,* Vol. LVII, p. 28, September 7, 1839.

"The stage was full of people who had gotten
out on the deck for the crossing. The boat went
swinging down the river more than a mile amidst
a lot of driftwood and floating trees. One of the
men tore a piece of the side railing [of the boat]
loose and tried to stop the boat by sticking it in
the mud, but the slat stuck and when the man tried
to pull it out he went overboard and was drowned
in the presence of the party on board, who could
do nothing to help him. At last the ferry boat
stranded on a low shore, and a young man taking a
rope tried to go ashore, but he got stuck up to his
middle and the passengers pulled him out by drag-
ging him back to the boat. There we stayed from
about noon to nearly nightfall. The driver got his
horn and blew long blasts on it every little while.
At last a number of men came through the fields.
They had found the ferry boat gone. There was a
bend in the river so they could not see it stranded,
but heard the horn and figured it out that the stage
might be down there. They could not approach the
stranded boat because the mud was about one hundred feet to solid ground. The men on shore cut
down saplings and laid them crossways to form
a mat to stand on, and at last reached the boat.
By this time it was far into the night. A bright
moon came up and helped with the work. One at
a time they handed down the people from the boat,
and let them pick their way to the hard ground.

"The stage with the driver and team remained
on the stranded boat all night, and it was late the

next afternoon when the ferry boat and stage were landed back at the crossing at Clay's ferry."[15]

No matter how the breaks came, the driver had to be resourceful enough to get to his destination. Every driver who was a marked success gained that reputation by three accomplishments. First, by arriving regularly at the end of his run on schedule time, with only weather and road conditions allowed as reasonable variables. Second, by accounting for the safety of the passengers, the correct checking of cash, mail, and express manifests. Third, by winning the approval of the traveling public in taking care of the passengers' comfort, as well as the health and comfort of the teams driven by him.

Part of the driver's equipment consisted of a spade, pinch-bar, shovel, axe, hatchet, wedge to split rails, saws, ropes, tinder box, and "hoof pick," a little iron hook to extract rocks from the horses' hoofs. Nothing so retarded the progress of a stage team as for a horse to get a rock in his foot. Horse-shoe nails of the Keysville variety, in two sizes, were in each tool chest. Every driver had to know how to "set a shoe," use the rasp, and trim the hoof. They usually carried two or three light shoes that could be easily bent to the shape of the hoof, as they had to work on the runs without the aid of forge or anvil.

In addition to these, there was a simple home-made first-aid kit, and a large bottle of turpentine. The drivers

---

[15]Recollections of Charles E. Mooney, a native of Lexington and a veteran of the Mexican War. Clay's Ferry, once the site of General Cassius M. Clay's Mill, is on the Kentucky River at the crossing of the Lexington-Richmond turnpike.

were well qualified to do an emergency job of coach and harness repairing, clearing the roads of fallen trees, and rendering first aid to the passengers while en route. If a driver arrived behind schedule he lost caste with his fellow drivers; but to give up and wait for help "was a disgrace beyond repair," so they managed to get through somehow.

One early autumn afternoon in the ante-bellum days, the veteran stage driver, Thomas H. Irvine, drove his horses at a brisk gallop along the winding highway from Lexington to Maysville. Black, ominous clouds were piling up over the horizon north of the Licking River. Three passengers sat inside the dusty, swaying vehicle, a man, an elderly woman, and her daughter. About night-fall, near the Blue Licks, the storm broke with a deluge of rain, heavy gusts of wind, and terrific thunder and lightning.

For several hours Irvine's drenched horses plodded wearily along the rutted road, steadily losing time, utter-ly heedless of the shouts, muttered curses, and soggy whip with which he attempted to urge them forward. Suddenly a blinding bolt of lightning crashed through the inky darkness, and a large tree standing near the road-side reeled like a stricken giant and fell in two sections across the pike a short distance ahead. Irvine stopped the stage-coach immediately, dismounted from the box, and, with the man passenger, groped his way to the obstruc-tion, visible only by the intermittent flashes of lightning.

Suddenly a call came from the stage, and when Irvine returned to the vehicle the elderly woman informed him that her daughter's child was about to be born. Both women were almost frantic at this emergency, under the existing circumstances. No doctor, no light, none of the bare necessities which such an occasion required, and the storm was still raging.

But the old stage driver, a man of courage and action, was undaunted even in the presence of a situation never before encountered in all the years of his varied experience. In a moment he had produced from under one of the seats a battered, soot-stained lantern. The passenger's small leather-covered trunk was hastily removed from the rear boot of the coach and made available. Then Irvine mounted bareback one of the best horses in his team and dashed off in the darkness. About a mile down the road he halted at the farm house of an experienced pioneer woman whom he knew. In a short time he was splashing back over the rain-swept road, carrying a steaming cedar piggin, with the woman clinging on behind him. Her husband followed with some candles and a blanket wrapped in old newspapers to keep it dry.

Then, while the three men worked on the fallen tree, the "granny" woman, wise in the lore of her sex, with her crude obstetrical equipment, brought a new life into the world. Several hours later the sun shone brightly over the muddy Ohio, as the jaded stage horses slowly trotted down the hill to Maysville, carrying the United States mail, safely, but late, and an additional passenger for which the way-bill signed at Lexington did not provide.

CHAPTER X

OTHER USERS OF THE ROAD

A LL along the turnpikes and roads of central Kentucky travelers and passengers in the stage-coaches often saw great numbers of hogs, cattle, and sheep being driven to the eastern and southern markets. This was the only means of transportation by which farmers and stock-raisers of the Bluegrass region could dispose of their live-stock.[1] The men who drove the stock to market were called "drovers" and their social status was the same as the "waggoners" who piloted the heavy Conestoga or freight wagons over these roads.

An old letter, dated January 28, 1823, describes a scene familiar to Kentuckians of that period: "We have encountered immense droves of hogs going into your part of Virginia. At Squire Goodson's, there were two droves of seven or eight hundred each; and yesterday we met two others as numerous . . . We have a band of hog-drovers from Kentucky for our mess-mates tonight, bound eastwardly with I don't know how many hun-

[1]"Having one day [April 17, 1842] entered a stage-coach in our passage over these [Appalachian] mountains, I conversed with two Kentucky farmers returning in high spirits from Baltimore, where they had sold all their mules and cattle for good prices. They were carrying back their money in heavy bags of specie, paper dollars being no longer worthy of trust. They said their crops of grain had been so heavy for several seasons that it would cost too much to drag it over the hills to a market 400 miles distant, so they had 'given it legs by turning it into mules and cattle'." Lyell, Vol. II, p. 12.

dreds . . ."² Cumings, who traveled in Maryland in 1807, wrote that he passed "a drove of one hundred and thirty cows and oxen, which one Johnson was driving from the neighborhood of Lexington, in Kentucky, to Baltimore."³

For the year 1824, the toll-gate receipts showed that 4,005 horses and mules, 58,011 hogs, and 412 good beef steers passed the Cumberland Ford for an eastern market, and through the town of Frankfort, one resident observed, "numerous herds of sheep, containing altogether as many as five or six thousand a herd, have passed this fall."⁴

In consequence, many inns and taverns were needed to accommodate the travelers, for, not only were the inns small, but there had to be houses for all kinds of travelers from the aristocrat in post-chaise or coach, the "waggoner," or the humble teamster, to the "drover," and seldom did these different classes meet beneath the same roof. The tavern or inn which accommodated "drovers" would instantly lose caste with stage-coach patrons. It is related that one tavern-keeper when practically forced to shelter a "drover" one cold night, took him on condition that he leave early the next morning "before the coach guests should see him."

The "waggoners" were a rough and picturesque product of this early nineteenth century freight traffic, but mixed with them were folk of a gentler strain, whom poverty forced to seek the cheapest lodging on a journey to a new home. This class of travelers had to look to other such inns and establishments for their accommoda-

²*Atlantic Monthly,* Vol. 26, p. 170.
³Thwaites—*Early Western Travels,* Vol. IV, p. 228.
⁴*Niles Weekly Register,* Vol. XXXIII, p. 277, December, 1827.

tions. The houses of first class were known as "stage-stands" or "tavern-stands," and no "waggoner" or teamster ever thought of stopping there; but he must go to a "waggon-stand" such as the one kept by J. P. Johnson, on Main Street. He advertised: "My waggon-yard is now in complete order for the reception of waggoners and is one of the best in Lexington."[5] Another well known and much frequented "waggon-yard" was kept by Joel Wallingford on Main Cross Street and his hospitality was known far and wide. His notice read: "My yard recently improved as a waggon-yard is to be paved entire, which will render it one of the most desirable stands for WAGGONERS in town, to which they are respectfully invited to give a call."[6] As there were no public or city scales, some of the taverns gathered more patronage by keeping in their side yards "scales for weighing waggons and other produce." The tavern of E. Perkins advertised such a yard at the corner of Water and Mulberry streets, Lexington.

Drovers found accommodations at the "drovers-stands," or, as they were commonly called in this section, "regular stock-stands." Since so many travelers could not read, signboards which they could understand were displayed before each house. The "stage-stand" used a sign depicting a popular hero, or picturing something aristocratic, like the American eagle, the Indian Queen, a crown, or a ship.[7] The "waggon-stand" was apt to have a designation such as the Sorrel Horse or the Black

[5]*Kentucky Reporter*, September 17, 1825.
[6]*Ibid.*, July 11, 1822.
[7]Washington Inn, Harrodsburg; Indian Queen, Lexington; George Washington Tavern, Lexington; Spread Eagle Tavern, Maysville.

Horse,[8] while "drovers" stopped at stands whose signs were symbols of their professions, as a Bull's Head, Lamb or Ram's Head. John Brown notified the farmers and traders of central Kentucky that he was provided with "the best watered grass lots for horses and mules, and hog lots," and was "well prepared to accommodate drovers." As a further inducement to "drovers," he stated that, if "any drovers have tired or lame hogs, or who may have any drowned at my ferry, I will agree to take them, if large and fat, at five dollars per hundred."[9]

Michaux, a noted French traveler who visited Lexington early in the nineteenth century, made close observations on the live-stock industry of the Bluegrass, and stated that "those Kentuckians who deal in cattle purchase them lean, drive them in droves of from two to three hundred to Virginia, along the river Potomack, where they sell them to graziers, who fatten them in order to supply the markets of Baltimore and Philadelphia."[10]

The French visitor wrote further: "The southern states, and in particular South Carolina, are the principal places destined for the sale of the Kentucky horses. They are taken there in droves of fifteen, twenty, or thirty at a time, in the early part of the winter, an epoch when the most business is transacted at Carolina, and when the drivers are in no fear of the yellow fever of which the inhabitants of the interior have the greatest appre-

---

[8]Sign of Black Horse, four miles from Lexington on Frankfort Road, kept by James W. Henderson; sign of White Horse "waggon-stand" kept by M. Weedon, Maysville.

[9]*Kentucky Gazette*, September 12, 1836.

[10]Michaux, Vol. III, p. 245.

hension. They usually take eighteen or twenty days to go from Lexington to Charleston. This distance, which is about seven hundred miles, makes a difference of twenty-five or thirty per cent in the price of horses. A fine saddle-horse in Kentucky costs about a hundred and thirty to a hundred and forty dollars."

On several of the main roads leading out of Lexington were stock-stands, or "four-mile houses" which teamsters and "drovers" would try to make by nightfall, as it was both inconvenient and impracticable to stop in the city with their livestock. One stand where "drovers" stopped frequently on their way South was on the Nicholasville Road:

> REGULAR STOCK STAND—4 Miles South of Lexington. For the accommodation of drovers going South with mules or horses I am prepared to accommodate them in good shape and on better terms than can be done anywhere in Fayette County. My lots are supplied with good stock water and furnished with new troughs, sufficient at any time to accommodate 200 or 300 mules or horses. Terms; mules and horses at 10 to 12c per feed.
>
> F. C. McLEAR
> 4 Mile House—Nicholasville Pike.[11]

Such stock-stands had several large pastures alongside the sleeping quarters to take care of the herds of stock, and one proprietor boasted of having "cattle pens

---

[11]*Kentucky Gazette,* July 6, 1856. This "stock-stand" is also shown on Huitt's map of Fayette County, 1861, as "McLear's Four Mile House."

for the care of 1500 head of cattle at once." While "drovers"[12] along the route were dependent on the stand keepers for their provender, "waggoners" carried their supply with them. There were no relays of the wagon drivers. Each was responsible for the safe delivery of his cargo and the condition of his team.

Behind the shed at the "waggon-stands" was a large building with roof and open sides for the protection against rain and snow of the great number of loaded wagons. "Waggon-stands" did not profit generally from this class of travel, as most "waggoners" carried their own provender and food. Some of the drivers paid for a bed, some slept around the fire in the barroom, and in summer all slept out of doors. In spite of this economy, all spent money for drinks.

According to all accounts much whiskey was consumed during the period under consideration. It was generally believed that whiskey was a necessary and useful beverage. During harvest, laborers expected and were supplied with rations of strong drink, and a farmer refusing such an allowance was an exception. The numerous teamsters, "drovers," and travelers who frequented the roads at all hours and in all kinds of weather were generally afflicted with this prevailing thirst, thereby increasing the patronage of the taverns and stands and providing a good source of revenue to the landlords.

---

[12]"Notice to Drovers," advertised Richard M. Robinson, of Hoskins Cross Roads, Garrard County: "I have just completed a new set of Stocks and can shoe 100 head of horses or mules a day. Satisfaction given in all cases or no pay." *Lexington Observer & Reporter,* February 13, 1861.

Although the sale of strong drinks was usually regarded by the landlord as essential to financial success,
an abundant supply of pure water was perhaps the greatest asset of a tavern or stand. While teamsters and drivers
were not partial to water as a drink for themselves, they
were particular to stop at stands having a copious supply
to slake the thirst of their jaded animals. Landlords and
tavern-keepers fortunate in the possession of inexhausti-
ble wells or springs of good water made mention of the
fact in their advertisements. In some cases, the very
name of an inn indicated the treasure, as the Cool Spring
Tavern, in Elizabethtown.

Lexington merchants as well as those of central Kentucky often made one trip eastward each year to replenish
their stock of goods. This travel from Lexington eastward was by stage-coach and the route most used was by
Maysville, Zanesville, Wheeling, and on to Pittsburgh.
After buying the stock of goods, it was loaded into one or
more Conestoga wagons and started on the long trip to
the Bluegrass. These Conestoga wagons, famed in song
and story, first made their appearance in this region about
1805. A product of Pennsylvania Dutch ingenuity, they
were named after Conestoga district in that state.

The underbody of a wagon usually was painted blue
with the upper woodwork bright red, and each wagon
had a cover of cotton or linen cloth stretched over big
hoops and bleached white in the sun. Sometimes these
wagons traveled in groups of ten or fifteen. The driver
rode one of the horses, usually the near wheel horse, and,
on mountain roads, a man went ahead blowing a horn to
keep the road clear.

On the trips eastward, these wagons carried great loads of ginseng which was the only produce of central Kentucky profitable enough for hauling so long a distance.[13] On the return trips numerous articles of eastern manufacture were hauled to Lexington, and from there distributed overland throughout central Kentucky.[14] These large wagons carrying from two to three tons and drawn by six or eight horses traveled over roads which today would be considered impassable.

Early in this period a blast furnace was built a short distance from Owingsville on Slate Creek in Montgomery County, known as the "Bourbon Furnace" and being the first iron foundry west of the Alleghenies. The "iron works" were originally built for the purpose of casting ten-gallon kettles, to be used in boiling the sap of the maple trees upon which the early settlers were wholly dependent for their sugar. With the demand for other articles, however, there was the manufacture of nails, cooking utensils, "waggon tyres," axe blades, and "plow plates." Since there was no convenient waterway connection between the "iron works" and the Bluegrass region of central Kentucky, the "Ironworks Road" was constructed. This road began at Owingsville, passed between the towns of Mt. Sterling, Paris, Winchester, and Lexington, by way of Donerail and White Sulphur, and ended

---

[13]Michaux, Vol. III, p. 205.

[14]Speed said: "Citizens of Danville alive in 1894 could remember the passing through the town long lines of these [Conestoga] wagons, covered with canvas and drawn by horses with bells on their harness and hauling goods in great quantities to Crab Orchard and through the Cumberland Gap into the valleys of Tennessee and Alabama." Speed —*The Political Club*, p. 19.

at Frankfort.[15]   Great trains of Conestoga wagons were frequently seen on this road hauling castings to Frankfort where they were shipped by barge to Cincinnati and Louisville.   Large quantities of iron ore from the Slate Creek neighborhood were hauled to Lexington for use in Bruen's foundry.[16]

General Jackson, in anticipation of a British attack on New Orleans, placed an order with the owner of the Bourbon Furnace, Colonel Thomas Deye Owings, for supplies of cannon balls, canister and grape shot for the artillery corps of his newly-formed army. These were cast at Owings' foundry, and loaded on barges for the trip down the Mississippi River.   On January 8, 1815, with the aid of these munitions, General Jackson checked and routed the British veterans under Pakenham.   History gloriously relates the vital part the riflemen from Kentucky played at the battle of New Orleans; but few people know that hidden away in the hills of Bath County is a primitive foundry[17] where other Kentuckians toiled and sweated to make possible this greatest land victory of the entire struggle.

Another contribution of the Kentuckians to the victory at New Orleans was gunpowder.   The state of Kentucky was especially interested in having an adequate supply. In the early days her very existence depended upon the efficiency of the "long rifles," and, in the first years of the new century, approaching difficulties with England endowed

---

[15]A part of the Ironworks Road at present skirts the northern section of Fayette County from the Paris Road, through Donerail on the Georgetown Road, to the Scott County line.

[16]*Kentucky Gazette,* December 10, 1813.

[17]The ruins of this old foundry are still to be seen near Owingsville.

the subject with renewed importance. Lexington was one of North America's leading gunpowder manufacturing centers; six or more powder mills were located in this city.[18] Records of the early nineteenth century give every indication that American troops in the War of 1812 would have experienced a disastrous shortage of powder had it not been for the supply provided by Kentucky.

Kentucky's top rank was largely the result of rich deposits of niter found in caves in various sections of the state. Great Cave on Crooked Creek in Rockcastle County, as well as Mammoth Cave in Edmonson County, produced large quantities of niter several years before 1812 and during the war period. After preliminary processing in or near the caves, much of the niter in crystal form was hauled in the "road freighters" or Conestoga wagons to Lexington to be converted into gunpowder in the local mills. Neil McCoy[19] "was in Lexington as early as 1805 and set up as a manufacturer of gunpowder for the Government." The finished product of McCoy's and the other five powder mills in Lexington was hauled in covered wagons to the Kentucky River and transported by barges to New Orleans.

By 1812, Lexington was the center of America's greatest niter producing area. In that year Kentucky produced 301,937 pounds of niter,[20] a figure more than six times that of any other state. Virginia, with a production of 48,-

---

[18]Peter—*History of Fayette County,* p. 265.
[19]This mill and the McCoy property of fifty-two acres was just west of the Russell Cave Road, at the city limits, beyond the Belt Line bridge. Later in 1892, as the property of Judge James H. Mulligan, it was incorporated as a separate township, under the name of Granard. *Morning Herald,* Lexington, August 23, 1897.
[20]*Niles Weekly Register,* Vol. II, p. 227, June 6, 1812.

175 pounds, ranked next. After the War of 1812, there was a gradual decrease in the activity of Kentucky's niter or saltpeter industry. How long after that year Lexington held its place as one of America's leading gunpowder manufacturing centers is not known.

Coal was mined in the eastern mountains of Kentucky and floated on barges down the Kentucky River to Clay's Ferry.[21] Here it was transferred to the heavy road wagons and hauled by six and eight horse or oxen teams to Lexington for use and distribution throughout central Kentucky.

John Gorin, in his book *The Times of Long Ago*,[22] describes a wagon team of the early twenties that hauled produce and freight from Lexington to Glasgow, in Barren County:

> "It was a six-horse team, the leader a gray, as proud as Lucifer; his mate a bay. The fourth leader was a black, black as ebony; his mate a sorrel chestnut. The saddle horse a steady bay; his mate a roan. The horses were equally powerful, all without a blemish, and valued from $1,000 to $1,200. Large bear skins covered the shoulders [in the winter]; all had a crescent of bells, except the saddle horse, above the hames, and tassels of ribbons hanging down from the head. The music of the bells was delightful, and they were the admiration of all . . ."

---

[21]Thomas, Cowperthwait & Co.'s map of Kentucky for 1850 shows three important warehouses in this vicinity; one of the largest being Thompson's, at the mouth of lower Howard's Creek and the Kentucky River.

[22]Gorin—*The Times of Long Ago*, p. 68.

Many of the "waggoners" hung bells very similar to dinner bells on a thin iron arch over the hames of the harness. Often the number of bells indicated the prowess of a teamster's team. The custom prevailed, in certain parts, that when a team became fast or was unable to make the grade, the "waggoner" rendering the necessary assistance appropriated all the bells of the luckless team.[23]

These Conestoga wagons were the highest type of freight carriers by horse-power. The body was boat-shaped with curved canoe bottom which was especially good for the trips over the mountains; for in them freight remained firmly in place at whatever angle the body might be. The rear end could be lifted from its sockets, as on it hung the feed trough for the horses, a tool box on the side, and, under the axle, a tar bucket and water pail.

Is was truly an American product, evolved and multiplied to fit perfectly any existing road conditions. After their days of usefulness were over in central Kentucky, the wagons gradually moved westward and were renamed "prairie schooners," figuring prominently in the gold rush of 1849 and the carriage of passengers to the Golden Gate. The coming of the railroads in the Bluegrass a decade or two before the opening of the war between the states sounded the death knell for these turnpike freighters, or "scoop wagons."[24]

---

[23]The practice of having bells on the harness continued for many years, until the Legislature of 1851 passed the following act: "Bells of no kind, unless their clappers be so secured as to prevent their making a noise, shall be carried on any animal or animals drawing any vehicle." A violation of this act carried a fine of from two to five dollars for every day so used.

[24]The use of these wagons by both contenders during the Civil War brought back their popularity and clearly demonstrated their stability and strength as army wagons.

No story about staging would be complete without mention of the stage-coach dogs. In the palmy days, every driver had his own dog, whose duty was watching the rear boot and its contents. The driver and the team were at the front of the vehicle, with the mail under the driver's seat. As the driver could not see the rear boot, the coach dog was trained to consider this as his property, and to guard it with his life. This dog, the Dalmatian coach dog,[25] was endowed with a generous amount of "road sense," taking the keenest enjoyment in following the stage-coach, the protection of his master's property, and the companionship of his great friend, the horse. They either rode in the rear boot, trotted directly under the coach or within easy sight of it.

These coach dogs always wore big leather collars with two rows of spikes which protected them from the shepherd dogs of the "drovers." The "drovers" had to "open up" to let the stages through, as that vehicle had the right of way over everything excepting funerals. "Opening up" meant that the "drovers" would ride ahead of the stage with their shepherd dogs to drive the stock out of the way. The shepherd dogs and the coach dogs often engaged in fights, but due to the heavy armor of the latter they usually emerged victorious.

When two big droves of stock met, it required some skill to "make the pass." If a stage-coach happened to be mixed up with the "pass," there was nothing that irritated the jehus more. These frequent droves of steers and

_____
[25]The coach dog was of medium build, white with black spots and originally came from the Province of Dalmatia, in the southern part of Austria, from which province it derives its name.

sheep encountered on the roads reduced the time of the stage-coaches more than twenty-five per cent. On account of the objectionable clouds of dust occasioned by these droves of stock, many passengers who were experienced travelers preferred the night coaches, when available, as all the tired stock were driven off the road to graze and rest up for the morrow's trip.

The record run in a four-horse stage, from Maysville to Lexington, was made at night by Thomas H. Irvine in four hours and fifty minutes. There was a clear road without any obstruction other than meeting the stage running opposite him and a few farmers' rigs that cleared at his horn. He had only through passengers, light express, and mail. In the daytime, it required eight hours or more to make the same run.

Rolly Hazelwood often made the Lexington-Versailles run with a four-horse team in sixty minutes, provided he didn't have to "wade through a drove," which required fifteen or twenty minutes longer. He was running on schedule when he made the run in an hour and a half. To maintain an average speed of eight miles an hour on a run of sixty to seventy miles it was necessary to make more than twelve miles an hour when running free, to allow for relays, "walk ups" on many of the hills, passengers getting on and off, and "wading through droves of stock" on the roads.

Eight miles per hour on the best turnpikes of central Kentucky called for a great deal of skill, resourcefulness, organization, and substantial investments of money. The speed often fell off to six miles an hour and, sometimes, as low as four miles in winter and rainy seasons, or over unimproved roads.

All kinds of vehicles plied back and forth over the turnpikes of the Bluegrass region in the ante-bellum days. It was not unusual to see coaches, landaus, coachees, rockaway coaches, droskies, britskas, chariotees, barouches, sulkies, cabriolets, phaetons, tilburies, gigs, Prince Alberts, trotting wagons, single buggies, and York wagons—each having its proportionate amount of toll to pay at the "gate" or toll-house.

CHAPTER XI

TAVERNS OF A LATER TIME

THERE has been nothing yet contrived by man, asserted Dr. Johnson,[1] "by which so much happiness is produced as by a good tavern or inn." Surely this must have been the sentiment of every traveler who dared the long, tedious, and many times monotonous journeys through Kentucky during the stage-coach era.

It is to be doubted that if at any time there were inns and taverns anywhere that could compare with those of the thirties, forties, and fifties, the three middle decades, when the pioneer had passed, when the stage-coach was the acme of travel, and when inventions had not standardized life. There were in central Kentucky during that period more than a dozen taverns and "watering places" of national importance and reputation, and numerous others locally popular.

During that period the pleasure of a stage-coach journey or a trip in a private coach in Kentucky depended in a considerable degree on the entertainment provided at the taverns along the route.

"Postlethwait's in less than an hour, ladies and gentlemen!" How those words must have gladdened the heart of every traveler. Some had journeyed far and long, from Pittsburgh, Washington, or Zanesville; others had started

---

[1] James Boswell—*Life of Samuel Johnson*, Vol. II, p. 281.

from Maysville and had been cold and tired and uncomfortable for six or seven unending and weary hours. And now, in less than sixty minutes, they would reach their destination. Evenings at the taverns were the happiest moments of the long stage-coach trips. After the evening meal, all gathered about the great fireplace in the assembly room. What richness, what abundance of good cheer, crowned those gatherings! How glad, how strong were the warm handclasps filled with good fellowship! "The muffins had been hot, the steak tender, the butter and eggs fresh, and the coffee divine." There had been peach brandy and honey; jokes had passed with much laughter. News had been related from Washington, New York, and New Orleans. Celebrities had stopped the week before, dined at that very table, and the magnificence of their talk and dress was lived over again.

An evening at the tavern! Than this, there was no finer luxury, no brighter share of that far-off day before the romantic blast of the stage-coach horn was drowned by the shrill shriek of the "iron horse." During the evening a crowd of merry youngsters would burst into the big room of the tavern bringing with them gusts of the cold winter night. They were a laughing, singing, and rosy-cheeked crowd. They had come for a dance and brought their fiddler with them. The shout went up: "Clear the floor and choose your partner!" The crowd sang. All the guests were included in the merriment. The fiddler scraped out the tune and patted heartily with his foot. They sang:

"I came to town the other night,
I heard the noise and saw the sight,
The watchman he was running round,
Crying old Dan Tucker's come to town."

The crowd shouted the chorus, and with a stamp of leather boot and swish of calico skirt the tune was brought to its gay ending:

"Then get out of the way for old Dan Tucker,
He's too late to get his supper."

The misadventures of old Dan Tucker were over. Then, above the groan of the fiddler's tunes and the rhythmic shuffle of the dancers' feet, boomed the voice of the caller of the square dance: "Balance all and swing your partner." The hours passed swiftly and, at length, the Virginia reel announced the sudden termination of the evening's gaiety. Soon all had sought their beds. The fire in the great open fireplace died to covered embers. A peaceful stillness was over the tavern and another day's journey completed.

By sun-up the travelers had dressed, ready again for the stage-coach. They had washed their faces in cold water, had enjoyed their breakfast of buckwheat cakes, hominy, and sausages. They faced another day's trip at the rate of seven or eight miles an hour through the beautiful Bluegrass region of central Kentucky. And when it too was finished, there was another evening at the tavern farther on, other faces, other friends to gladden a traveler's heart.

The more famous inns and taverns were along the stage routes that stretched from Maysville to Lexington, to Nashville, and from Lexington to Louisville, and southward from the Falls City by way of Bardstown to Nashville. Much of the local history centered about the old taverns, some of them figuring in outstanding episodes in the history of the state, while within their walls many a political intrigue was evolved.

Perhaps the best known and most popular tavern in central Kentucky was the old Postlethwait's Tavern, situated on the southeast corner of Main and Limestone streets in Lexington. This inn, later to become the well known Phoenix Hotel of today, is surely the oldest hotel site in the state and probably in the West. On the eleventh of August in 1796, Adam Steele purchased from the town fathers of Lexington the original site of the Phoenix Hotel. It was part of "out" lot No. 16 lying on the Boone Station Road. The tavern came into prominence in 1800, when Captain John Postlethwait, a native of Carlisle, Pennsylvania, assumed control of the resort.

Captain Postlethwait was a prosperous, public-spirited citizen, serving the city as treasurer and banker as well as tavern-keeper. Later his organization, "Captain Postlethwait's Light Infantry Company," was an important unit of all public functions. For a time the Captain allowed the post-office to be conducted in his tavern, which was a long, rambling, log building with its principal entrance on Mulberry Street. Much of the furniture was made by local cabinet makers, and built from "native cherry and walnut which was fine and glossy." The comfort of the

Captain's corded four-post beds, the beauty of his Windsor chairs, and hospitality to all were mentioned by more than one writer of the times. The rag carpets were as fashionable then as now, and while the guests had to be "lighted to bed by tallow candles," there was a small army of faithful slaves to render this gracious service.

Captain Postlethwait conducted the tavern at various intervals, until his death in 1833, during the cholera plague in Lexington. The tavern soon after its establishment was managed by Joshua Wilson, who had the honor of entertaining Aaron Burr. Wilson's management was followed by that of Sanford Keen, and later by Mrs. Keen. It was Keen who was conducting the tavern when the great fire occurred; and it was he, who, seeing it rise from its ashes like the fabled Phoenix bird of old, conferred upon it the name it now bears.[2] He caused the sign of the Phoenix to be placed on the walls above the Main and Mulberry Street entrances.

The first disastrous fire came on the third of March, 1820, and, despite the heroic efforts of the "Property Guards" and the "Leather Bucket Brigade," it reduced the building to blackened ruins. The following fifty-nine years saw many changes in management and style of the old hotel. Then again, on May 14, 1879, it was destroyed by fire. At this time the Lexington races were on and the

---

[2]It is not clear just when the old tavern was first called Phoenix, but in the opinion of the author it was shortly after the fire of 1820. The editor of the *Lexington Public Advertiser,* March 4, 1820, in reporting the fire, said: "We hope, however, it may soon rise, like the *Phoenix* from its ashes." And several years later, the *Kentucky Reporter,* July 11, 1825, carried this announcement: "Commencement Ball—Tickets for Gentlemen may be obtained from any of the managers, or at the bar of the *Phoenix Inn.*"

inn was filled to capacity. Evidently no one was injured, for, according to one authority, the rescue of the hotel's favorite cat, "Tabby," held everyone's attention. When the building was almost in ruins, "Tabby" was seen in one of the front windows. "Her destruction seemed inevitable, when a man seized a ladder, ran up to the window, and brought her down, amid the shouts of the multitude."

Another cornerstone was laid in October, 1879, and, when the spring races again brought another filled house, a new front repeated the story told and retold in those early days—old Postlethwait's had again risen from the ashes. During the Keen management the famous hostelry sheltered two of Lexington's distinguished guests, President Monroe in 1819 and General LaFayette in 1825. Among other famed travelers who stopped at Postlethwait's were: Isaac Shelby, General Andrew Jackson, William Henry Harrison, Henry Clay, Amos Kendall, Daniel Webster, Generals Grant, Bragg, Kirby Smith, and John W. Daniel.

"The tavern in Kentucky," wrote N. Parker Willis in 1852, "is not only the resort, but the respectable resort of the male inhabitants of the village at all leisure hours. You seldom drive up to one without alighting amid a group—oftener a crowd—and the titles flying from mouth to mouth soon inform you that all the judges, generals, and colonels possible to the size of the population are among the company. The stranger is received with some show of courtesy—a chair is given him, remarks are addressed to him, and he is asked if he will take anything to drink. If he requires any other information or civility, it is abundantly ready for him. But they require something in return. Who and what is he, and where is he going, and what for? If it does not all ooze out in his conversation, it is specifically asked about in the course of the evening."[3]

Travelers coming from Maysville to Lexington enjoyed not less than half a dozen timely and interesting stops at hospitable inns. In Maysville, they stopped at the old Goddard House on Front Street,[4] the Hill House,[5] or the old January Tavern. The journey was short to Blue Licks Springs Tavern, or, as it was popularly known, Blue Licks Hotel. To this renowned resort came guests from the North and wealthy planters with their families from the South to escape the "sickly climate" and to drink the health-giving waters for which the springs were famous.

The "Springs" hotel was a large three-story frame building, 670 feet in length, with 1800 feet of gallery; a large dining room 100 by 36 feet, and a spacious ballroom 26 by 80 feet. During the height of the social season from four to six hundred guests were frequently registered at this hotel. On April 7, 1862, the main building was destroyed by fire, and, although it was later replaced by a smaller one, much of the prestige of the old resort died with the failure of the springs in the middle eighties.

---

[3]Randolph—*Mammoth Cave & the Cave Region of Kentucky*, p. 57.

[4]The old Goddard House is still standing on Front Street, near Market. Between 1835 and 1865 it ranked as one of Maysville's best hotels and it was here that all stages from out of town stopped. It contained the stage-coach office.

[5]The Hill House, built by Peter Lee in 1840, still stands on the northwest corner of Sutton and Front streets. It was the aristocratic place of town and crowded in summer by southern tourists on their way to spend the "watering season" at Blue Licks Springs.

Horses of the stage-coaches were changed at Forrest Retreat, another well known tavern-stand on the Maysville-Lexington Road, at the junction of the Carlisle Pike. This hostelry was long known for its lavish and traditional Kentucky hospitality. The house and grounds adjoined the home of Governor Thomas Metcalfe, and many were the noted visitors who stopped here to accept the favors of its genial host. In addition to its claim as a tavern, it was one of the principal post-offices on the Zanesville-Florence stage-coach mail route through Lexington to Nashville. Presidents Jackson and Harrison stopped on several occasions for "refreshments" at Forrest Retreat, as did Henry Clay, who was a warm personal friend of "Old Stone Hammer," as Metcalfe was familiarly known.

On through Millersburg, where Captains Waller and Edward Martin operated their respective taverns, lies Paris. Here the stage stopped at the Bourbon House, host to every important statesman of the ante-bellum days. First known as the Indian Queen, this inn was long famous as the high-light of the Maysville-Lexington stage-coach journey. During the existence of the old Bourbon Fair, which ran continuously for sixty-five years, the dances given during the fair were attended here by society belles and beaux from all parts of Kentucky and surrounding states. The first Bourbon County tavern, built of course of logs, was kept by Thomas West.

Another important tavern on the road to Lexington was Johnson's Inn, located in Bourbon County, five miles west of Paris. Filson's map of Kentucky, 1784, listed this time-honored inn as "Cap'n Johnson's," and gives it antiquity as one feature. This well known inn and "waggon-yard" was on the original road from Lexington to Limestone [Maysville] at Clay's Cross Roads, on the middle fork of Cooper's Run, and was the one stopping place for all travelers. One old resident stated that he had seen as many as fifty covered [Conestoga] wagons in the front yard at one time. The land on which it was built was a part of a pre-emption of John Craig and Robert Johnson, both settlers of Bryan's Station. The land subsequently passed into the hands of Captain William Johnson.[6]

Cumings, in the *Early Western Travels* in 1807, mentions stopping at this inn:

> "Traveled seven miles from Millersburg, then left the main road and went to Baylor's Mills. Two miles on the way came to Colonel Garrard's fine stone house. After leaving Baylor's crossed Stoner Creek toward Lexington, leaving Paris four miles to the left. Came to Johnson's Inn. Captain Johnson had a son and daughter living near him, a fine farm, a quantity of last year's produce, wheat and corn . . ."

Johnson's Inn still stands, in an excellent state of preservation, and undoubtedly is the oldest inn and tavern standing in central Kentucky.[7] The interior woodwork of the old inn is solid walnut; doors on the lower floor

<hr>

[6]Bourbon County Court, Deed Book E, p. 129.

[7]"From thence [Paris] I proceeded to Mr. Ferguson's plantation and hotel at Johnson's stand, about five miles from Paris. The landlord there is very wealthy, and has a large improved farm and good cattle and horses. I had a beautiful ride this morning from Mr. Ferguson's farm, eleven miles to Georgetown, through a rich country, well cultivated. . ." This is an account of a stage-coach trip through Kentucky by James Stuart, in May, 1830. Stuart, Vol. II, p. 272.

are of six panels, while those on the upper floor are bat-ten. There are eleven rooms including the bar, which has six cupboards. The dining room, adjacent to the bar, is thirty by eighteen feet and was the scene of many brilliant social functions and dances.

Captain Johnson and his wife, Rachel, moved to Missouri in 1827. Later when Captain Johnson died, his body was brought back to the old farm and buried in the orchard at the rear of the house. In 1832, the farm and old inn were purchased by Joseph Henry Clay, who changed the name to "Rosedale," which it has carried to the present, with the fourth generation of the Clay family now occupying the house.

Beyond Lexington, the center of the Bluegrass, on the many turnpikes leading to and from the central portion of Kentucky were numerous other taverns and inns, each famed as a host to Kentucky's early visitors.

On the old Zane's Trace leading south from Lexington and near the settlement of Bryantsville, is still standing what was once a well known tavern-stand and relay station, commonly referred to as "Burnt Tavern." The old farm here was owned by the Reverend James Smith, a Virginian, and the hotel was given its name after the buildings on the ground had burned twice. It was a famous old road house in the stage-coach days and one wing, saved during the second fire, is now more than a hundred years old. The son of landlord Smith of "Burnt Tavern" after leaving Kentucky moved to Texas where he was one of the first governors of the Lone Star State.

Bright's Inn, one mile and a half from the town of Stanford, in Lincoln County on the famous old Wilderness Road, was familiarly known as Bright's Stage Inn. This well known hostelry was built in 1816 by John Bright, son of the Revolutionary soldier Henry Bright. The structure was of logs, and soon additional rooms were added to accommodate stage travel from Lexington to Cumberland Gap. This inn was often visited by Isaac Shelby, who lived only a few miles away, and by Henry Clay, George Rogers Clark, and many others of fame in the pioneer and ante-bellum days. Bright's reputation was known throughout the Carolinas and the Virginias; and it was here the great bulk of the stage-coach travelers stopped and refreshed themselves on their long journeys.

Chiles' Tavern, at Harrodsburg, was another favorite stopping place for horse-back as well as stage travelers. Known later as the Morgan House, a long two-story building extending from the corner of Chiles and Office streets on the west to about half way of the square, its life has known variety and splendor. The building consists of four sections, with three fire walls between, running up about one and one-half feet above the roof. The wall, during a fire which destroyed a great section of the corner, saved the old tavern from destruction. The date of its construction is uncertain, but tradition places it at 1807.

The building was first called "Chiles' Hotel" when John G. Chiles purchased the inn from Squire Joseph Morgan. The older hotel was a popular rendezvous for all the leading lawyers and visitors to Harrodsburg. Too, it was a popular gambling resort, and until the burned section was replaced the old watch-hole was easily detected with its nicely fitted slot for opening or refusing admittance to the many who sought entrance.[8]

Also popular among Harrodsburg inns was the Allin House, on Lexington Street. Atop the old house was a small belfry with its keen-toned bell long used to call the guests to dinner. It is certain that this tavern was open in 1858. One traveler tells of a man who rode his white horse through the main lobby, up to the bar, ordered his drink, and nonchalantly rode out. During the first period of the Civil War, John Hale was the proprietor of the Allin House, which was one of the main gathering places for officers and soldiers.

Not to be considered lightly is the fact that while the old taverns and inns were usually the very center of fun-making and gaiety, tragedy often stalked into their history. The "Ellis House" in Bardstown is a notable example. Known successively as the "Old Kentucky Home Hotel," and the "Central Hotel," this inn witnessed the deaths of not less than six men, mortally wounded within the luxurious confines of its lobby and rooms.

"Stone Tavern," the best known of Bardstown's two taverns, enjoyed a more tranquil reign. One of the most popular proprietors was the Reverend G. W. Robertson, who, because of the large number of beautiful locust shade trees in the east front yard of the house, gave it the name of "Shady Bower Hotel." Strangers coming to town so frequently asked for the "Shady Bower" that the Reverend Robertson acquired the name and carried it until his death. Another step in the hotel's quiet history

---

[8]Hutton, Mrs. G. S.—*Old Taverns,* Pamphlet, 12 pp. Harrodsburg, 1926.

came when George Talbott bought the inn and caused the saloon, an indispensable adornment, to be removed.

An unusual contest gave rise to one of the most frequented and popular taverns in the eastern part of the Bluegrass region, on the first stage-coach route out of Lexington. When Owingsville was selected as the county seat of Bath, in 1811, Colonels Richard Menefee and Thomas Deye Owings owned most of the land upon which the city of Owingsville was to stand. Each landlord claimed the right to bestow upon the unborn town his name. The debate was settled finally when it was decided the village should be named for the man who erected the finest residence in the shortest time. Colonel Owings won with his masterpiece, the old Owings' mansion. The War of 1812 was in progress at the time the mansion was built, and, in view of possible invasions by the British or Indians, Colonel Owings had it so constructed that, should the people of the Bluegrass again be put on the defensive, it could be used as a fortress. The building is still standing, with its walls three to four feet thick. The windows formerly were provided with heavy wooden shutters.

Upon the Colonel's death, the mansion passed into the possession of another family, who converted it into a tavern and inn. The "Owings House" was situated on the stage-coach route from Lexington to Washington, D. C., and was the center of social life in this part of Kentucky during the first half of the nineteenth century. About the fine old colonial fireplace in the living room met famous men of that time, to enjoy together a stimulating round of apple toddy, an evening over their pipes of Burley, and often to indulge in a friendly game of poker. A grand ball was given in 1826 to Henry Clay when he was Secretary of State, and on numerous occasions the youth of the neighborhood attended the magnificent balls to dance the Virginia reel beneath Latrobe's winding stairway.[9]

Bell's Tavern, at the "Three Forks," later Glasgow Junction, was another tavern long regarded as one of the best in the Bluegrass region of Kentucky. It was advantageously located where the stage roads leading from Louisville and Lexington to Nashville united. It was here the stage travelers disembarked from the regular travel and journeyed to the greatest of Kentucky's wonders—Mammoth Cave. Stages often left the Galt House in Louisville at five in the morning; reached the Eagle Tavern or the Hill House at Elizabethtown at noon for dinner; and by nine that night drove up in front of Bell's Tavern, covering ninety miles of travel. After spending the night at Bell's Tavern, the stage passengers reached Nashville the following night at nine, making one hundred and eighty miles in two days. This old tavern was considered the half-way house between Louisville and Nashville, and was one hundred and twenty miles from Lexington.

This famous old tavern constructed by slave labor burned in the early sixties. The old Gibson House of Cincinnati was selected as the model for the new hotel, and the new Bell's Tavern was half completed at the beginning of the war between the states. Then the project

[9]*Kentucky Magazine*, Vol. I, No. IV, September, 1917.

The Monticello-Burnside stage, at Mill Springs, Wayne County. Courtesy of the J. Winston Coleman Collection, University of Kentucky Libraries.

The Lexington-Versailles stage, 1882. Courtesy of the J. Winston Coleman Photographic Collection, Transylvania University Library.

As roads improved and the popularity of stage-coach travel grew, taverns and inns became colorful parts of the stage travel experience. Above, Johnson's Inn, near Centerville, in Bourbon County. Below, Cross-Keys Tavern on the Lexington-Louisville Road, five miles east of Shelbyville. Courtesy of the J. Winston Coleman Photographic Collection, Transylvania University Library.

At first crude and uncomfortable, by mid-century taverns were
lively watering-holes offering sustenance and merriment. Above,
Forest Retreat, Lexington-Maysville Road, Nicholas County.
Courtesy of the J. Winston Coleman Collection, University of
Kentucky Libraries. Below, Burnt Tavern, near Bryantsville.
Courtesy of the J. Winston Coleman Photographic Collection,
Transylvania University Library.

STAGE OFFICE

AT THE GALT HOUSE,
E. M. MUNFORD, · · · · · · Agent.

NASHVILLE via BOWLINGGREEN,

Leaves every other day at 4 o'clock, A. M., and

FOR BOWLINGGREEN

every other day at 4 o'clock, A. M., forming a DAILY LINE to Bowinggreen and Mammoth Cave. This line connects at Bowlinggreen with Stages for

Russelville, Clarksville,
Elkton, Hopkinsville,
Smithland, etc., etc.

NASHVILLE
Via BARDSTOWN AND GLASGOW,

Every other day at 4 o'clock, A. M.

FOR BARDSTOWN

Every other day at 4 o'clock, A. M., making a Daily Line to Bardstown, and connecting at that place with Davison & Co.'s Lines for Springfield, Lebanon, Campblesville, Greensburg to Glasgow, and also to Perrysville, Harrodsburg and Danville.

FOR FRANKFORT, DANVILLE,
HARRODSBURG, SALVISA, LAWRENCEBURG & SHELBYVILLE,

Leaves every day, except Sundays, at 4 o'clock, A. M.

ACCOMMODATION FOR SHELBYVILLE,

Leaves every Monday, Wednesday and Friday at 2 o'clock, P. M.

FOR BLOOMFIELD

Every Tuesday, Thursday and Saturday at 9 A. M.

For Taylorsville and Chaplin

Every Tuesday, Thursday and Saturday at half past 9 o'clock, A. M.

The schedule of E.M. Munford & Co., Louisville, 1855. Courtesy of the J. Winston Coleman Photographic Collection, Transylvania University Library.

Mile posts from stage-coach days: above left, on the Shelbyville-Louisville Road; above right, on the Frankfort-Shelbyville Road; below left, on the Lexington-Maysville Road; below right, on the Louisville-Bardstown Road. Courtesy of the J. Winston Coleman Photographic Collection, Transylvania University Library.

A stage-coach making a river crossing by ferry. Courtesy of the J. Winston Coleman Collection, University of Kentucky Libraries.

A toll-gate on the Harrodsburg Road, near Lexington. Courtesy of the J. Winston Coleman Photographic Collection, Transylvania University Library.

A slate bulletin board that posted stage schedules in a Harrodsburg tavern. Courtesy of the J. Winston Coleman Collection, University of Kentucky Libraries.

The last stage-coach in Kentucky, driven by Charles H. Burton, at Monticello-Burnside. Courtesy of the J. Winston Coleman Collection, Transylvania University Library.

was abandoned. Today, its vine covered walls and arched windows, its moss covered steps, with stately forest trees growing from the center of its roofless rooms, provide an interesting sight for tourists. Bell's Tavern was the rendezvous for folks from miles around and many a traveler has ridden or driven far into the night to reach its hospitable surroundings, or stopped his journey at midday, because he knew he had found a place of unparalleled entertainment.

Old Jimmy Bell, keeper of the tavern, was a regular boniface with "an ideal rosy-cozy phiz, and a real rotund waist." He had the regular jolly laugh; always in a good humor and ready to take a drink with any of his guests. It is said that he left a note in his will for peach brandy and honey to be served to stage passengers free of charge as long as his "stand" continued a public house.

In 1851, Jenny Lind, after giving a concert in Nashville, traveled by stage-coach over the Louisville-Nashville road to Mammoth Cave, stopping at Bell's Tavern en route. Many were the pleasant stories connected with her brief stay at the old tavern with Old Jimmy. The year before the Civil War, Rhoda Hite King stopped at Bell's Tavern and there she met General Leslie Combs, of Lexington, Thomas Marshall, and Lovell Rousseau, later General Rousseau of the Federal army. Bell's Tavern had its local celebrities. First there was Uncle Jim, the colored centenarian, who had received a "quarter" from Washington, and held Jefferson's horse upon one occasion. Here too was Shad, the "blackest little girl with the whitest teeth" anyone had ever seen.

"Years after," wrote Rhoda King, "I went back to the old place. Bell's Tavern lay in ruins, the victim of a destructive fire. I wandered into the garden. The tangled roses bloomed in fragrance and beauty. Down in the orchard the apple-trees were pink and white with bloom. Under the spreading boughs of one, Uncle Jimmy lay sleeping peacefully. By his side a tiny mound covered the dead body of Shad. The little tireless feet were asleep forever. I was not ashamed of the tears that fell on the flower-petals covering these graves. Bell's Tavern has arisen from the ashes—but it is not my tavern, with its memories bright and now sacred . . ."[10]

Toward Frankfort, six miles from Versailles, stood a two-story frame house with an ell that was very popular in the early days with both the traveling public and the dwellers of the community. This hostelry was known as Dorsey's Tavern. Watkins' Tavern, in Versailles, was operated by Henry Clay's stepfather, and it was here General LaFayette was entertained in 1825 on his way to Lexington. Several years ago the old landmark burned, being at the time over a hundred years old.

Beyond Frankfort, near Shelbyville on the Lexington-Louisville stage-coach road, was the popular Cross-Keys Tavern. This inn was built in 1800 by Adam Middleton, a blacksmith of Virginia, who settled near by and for a time plied his trade. The stream of travelers who poured down the old dirt "state road" suggested to young Middleton the idea of a tavern, and, because the road forked there, he hung up two immense brass

[10]Rhoda Hite King—*Bell's Tavern; A Reminiscence of Ante-Bellum Days in Kentucky,* Appleton's Journal, October 3, 1874.

keys on a tree at the roadside and called his inn the "Cross-Keys" Tavern. The tavern was run by two brothers, Adam and Robert Middleton, who married sisters and for many years[11] successfully operated one of the most enjoyable inns along this historic route.

Cross-Keys Tavern was the old-time stopping place for all who journeyed over the turnpike from the Bluegrass to the Ohio River, and for all those who "staged it" from the East. It was the "half-way house" between Lexington and Louisville, and, between the years 1800 and 1825, it is estimated to have sheltered ten thousand travelers. One of the claims to popularity of this well known hostelry was that it never had a tragedy or supported a tavern ghost.

The original structure built of stone became the center when a wing of logs was added in 1813, and the front with the great white columns in 1851. To this stopping place came many distinguished guests, including Henry Clay, Andrew Jackson, and General LaFayette. Until it burned,[12] this fine old Corinthian-columned hostelry attracted every traveler and visitor who passed or lingered to partake of its well known hospitality. Certainly, in Cross-Keys Tavern, Shelby County had a venerable landmark that linked the present with the delightful ante-bellum days.

This list of old hostelries could be extended, as there were many worthy of every attention, many whose important roles in the scenes of tragedy and romance and his-

---

[11]This old inn and grounds remained in the Middleton family until 1919 when it was sold at public auction.
[12]May 21, 1934.

torical episodes were closely interwoven into the life of the community and state. Yet, with but a word concerning one more phase of ante-bellum tavern life, we must conclude our visit with yesterday's glamour and romantic adventure.

Not unimportant in the stage-coach days were the well known springs or "watering places" to which great crowds flocked. The visitors came in stage-coaches and private carriages during the summer and fall to enjoy the healing qualities of the waters, and the gay whirl of the social life. These resorts were most successful before the patent medicine craze swept the country. Dr. Joseph C. Chinn, an old physician of Lexington, recommended that every person ought to spend at least ten days every summer at one of these springs "to tune up the digestive system."

The spring, summer, and fall seasons at Olympian Springs, Blue Licks, and Crab Orchard were brilliant social affairs for wealthier people before the Civil War, and even afterward. Guests chartered stage-coaches to take their parties to these springs, while there were no less than fifty private traveling carriages in Fayette County that ordered "post-horses" at the stage barns, or went on short stretches with their own horses.

The best known springs were: Graham Springs or the old Greenville, at Harrodsburg; Crab Orchard Springs in Lincoln County, which rivaled Graham as the Saratoga of the South; Paroquet Springs in Bullitt County with accommodations for eight hundred guests; Grayson Springs in Grayson County; Cerulean Springs in Trigg County; Drennon Springs in Henry County; Blue Licks

Springs in Nicholas County; Estill Springs, Aden Springs, and the well known and historic resort—Olympian Springs—in Bath County.

Wise tavern-keepers of this period armed themselves with a copy of the "Western Counterfeit Detector," a monthly publication containing "a full and complete report of all broken, uncurrent, and counterfeit notes in circulation in the western country."[18]   Without it, the proprietors were made recipients of money quite worthless, and the slicker, even in that day of ease and plenty, enjoyed a very profitable field.

Many institutions have passed with the old stage-coach and tavern days. Two stand out in the memory of many. One was the aged Negro major-domo with a "biled" shirt and correct dresscoat with large brass buttons, who in his bearing toward the guests was the paragon of civility and politeness. The other was the custom of sitting out in front of the hostelry. Rows of chairs and benches were provided and even part of the street was pre-empted by the community loungers, who made the old tavern or inn their headquarters. To them, the arrival and departure of the stage was the one big event of the day, and many were the hours and rich the conversation that passed while they awaited those rare moments.

Receded into the dim regions of legend are the traditions of the taverns and the old boniface, who drank your health from a foaming tankard and wished you "a pleasant journey and a soon return" as he doffed his cap, while the stage driver gathered his reins and cracked his long whip . . .

[18]*Louisville Daily Journal*, March 29, 1842.

CHAPTER XII

ANTE-BELLUM DAYS

A S the old stages swayed and bumped along the dusty turnpikes of the slave-holding Bluegrass region, it is not at all surprising that passengers often found themselves in a turmoil with abolitionists, who "reprobated slavery as the great bane of this fine country." On several occasions it is related that the timely assistance of the driver averted serious consequences.

On February 2, 1833, the Legislature of Kentucky passed an act prohibiting the importation of slaves for the purposes of sale, with severe penalties for its violation, which dealt a heavy blow to the slave trade. Its passage was a signal victory for the friends of gradual emancipation,[1] and there began a constant stream of fugitives headed for the northern states and freedom.[2]

Slave owners of central Kentucky were experiencing considerable trouble, for their slaves availed themselves of the facilities offered by the stage-coaches to escape

---

[1]Slavery was not legally abolished in Kentucky until December 18, 1865, when 27 of the 36 states ratified the Thirteenth Amendment. Blaine—*Twenty Years of Congress*, Vol. I, p. 538.

[2]Levi Coffin and his wife, Catherine, conducted the celebrated and mysterious "underground railroad" which carried hundreds of men, women, and children from slavery to freedom, and which gave rise to many dramas and tragedies. This couple lived in Cincinnati, and under cover of a country store provided a haven of refuge for the fugitive slaves from Kentucky and the South on their way to Canada. Mr. and Mrs. Coffin were the Simeon and Rachel Halliday of Mrs. Harriet Beecher Stowe's *Uncle Tom's Cabin*.

from their masters. The "rapidity with which they were carried" by those conveyances as well as the mode of traveling enabled them to elude pursuit and detection. The practice was growing as stage lines were increasing and improvements advancing. Public attention was directed to the growing evil, which resulted in the passage of this act:[3]

> "That it shall be unlawful for the owner and proprietor of any mail stage or other stage-coach to suffer or permit any slave or slaves to go as passengers therein, without a written request of their owners, under the penalty of one hundred dollars for each slave taken contrary thereto, and also being liable to the owners for the full value of all slaves which may thereby escape from their owners, with such additional costs and damages as the owners may incur in attempting to recover such slave."

On the morning of May 3, 1841, as William S. Bryant opened up his harness and saddle shop on Main Street, Paris, he noticed his slave, Peter, was absent. Upon inquiry, it was found that he had the evening before made some repairs to the harness of Edward P. Johnson and Company's stage, shortly after it had discharged some mail and passengers at the old Bourbon House. Further inquiry proved that it was about nine o'clock when the stage started, and Peter got aboard and rode beside the driver all through the night, reaching Maysville sometime during the early morning. Here at the end of the

[3]*Acts, General Assembly,* 1838.

run, the slave quietly climbed down off the stage-coach and slipped off into the darkness, toward the Ohio River.

Bryant promptly entered suit against the stage-coach proprietors for the loss of his slave, Peter, who was described as being "about six feet high, proportional, active, intelligent, and a harness maker by trade, and of the value of twelve to fourteen hundred dollars."[4] Notices of the runaway slave were posted in the barrooms along the road from the Bourbon House to the Goddard House in Maysville, offering the customary reward of ten dollars if taken in Bourbon County, twenty dollars in another county, and in the state of Ohio one hundred dollars; but Peter undoubtedly by that time was well within the interior of Ohio and assured of his liberty.

Charles T. Garrard, foreman of the jury, brought in a verdict in favor of Bryant in the sum of $1,332.25, which allowed twelve hundred dollars for the lost slave and one hundred thirty-two dollars and twenty-five cents for expenses and advertising paid in searching for the slave, who was never recovered.[5]

Not only were the stage-coaches used in aiding slaves to escape, but various other vehicles of the road, such as hacks, gigs, and barouches. One such case relates that three Negroes were conveyed by hack from Lexington to Maysville, late in the month of September, 1844, under the care of Delia A. Webster and Calvin Fairbank, aboli-

---

[4]Bryant *vs.* Edw. P. Johnson & Co., Bourbon Circuit Court, file 953, September 16, 1841.

[5]This is one of a number of cases in which the courts held the agents or drivers of the owners liable for "suffering and permitting slaves to be taken on their coaches without passes." A similar case occurred in Fayette County. Barnam *vs.* Scott & Irvine, Fayette Circuit Court, file 1182, October 12, 1847.

tionists from the North, who feigned an elopement to detract attention. When Maysville was reached, the slaves were set across the Ohio River and to freedom. Upon their return from this trip, the abolitionists were arrested, tried, and convicted in the Fayette Circuit Court for "aiding and enticing slaves to escape" from their masters.[6] Fairbank served in all seventeen years and four months for his abolition activities in Kentucky, and his partner, Delia Webster, the New England school teacher, after serving six weeks in the state penitentiary on her two-year sentence, was pardoned by Governor Owsley, February 24, 1845.[7]

Stage travel in 1844 was beginning to be more of a pleasure than peril, and this year saw another reduction in the price of tickets upon the line of Edward P. Johnson and Company. They agreed to take passengers from Lexington to Cincinnati for four dollars each, and from Danville to Louisville in one day for four dollars and fifty cents.[8] They stated as before: "Our coaches are good and substantial; our stock fleet and true." Johnson and Company's teams of four horses were carefully selected and changed every ten or twelve miles. As the sound of the horn announced the approach of the stage to the "stage stable" or relay stations, the fresh horses were brought out, each with his own harness and in charge of a groom or hostler. The change was effected and the

---

[6]Commonwealth of Kentucky *vs.* Fairbank and Webster, Fayette Circuit Court, file 1102, October 17, 1844.

[7]Executive Journal, 1845, Vol. I, p. 73. Miss Webster was the first woman to serve in the state penitentiary at Frankfort, and as there were no quarters at that time for women, a special frame house was constructed for her in the center of the large enclosure.

[8]*Kentucky Tribune,* Danville, May 24, 1844.

coach rolled away before the passengers hardly realized what was being done.

These relay stations were located at frequent intervals and consisted of a stable, granary, and a room for one or two stock tenders. They were sometimes placed near and in conjunction with taverns and inns, where travelers could rest and refresh themselves while the horses were being exchanged. Grain and provender were usually obtained from the farmers in the vicinity of the relay stations. When this could not be done, it was hauled from distant points. Oftentimes, in case of drought or crop shortage, this was a serious problem for the stage owners, as is shown in the following letter: "This has been a very hard and dry summer I assure you. Oats is very high, they pay on the Lexington and Louisville roads 75 cents per bushel, but I can get none at any price. I don't know what I will do for feed . . ."[9]

In addition to the relay stations, the owners had to maintain at the headquarters of each division, or terminus of the run, coach repair shops or "coach repositories," blacksmith shops, stables, and pasturage, as well as harness shops. There was considerable expense attached to owning and operating a stage-coach business in the late thirties and early forties, when competition demanded the best of everything—horses, equipment, and accommodations along the route.

Dickey and Company's equipment for operation on the road between Lexington and Maysville consisted of

[9]Letter of W. A. Moyston, stage agent of McNair & Weaver, Maysville, to the president of the company, Colonel Dunning R. McNair, October 22, 1838. Letter in author's collection.

"one hundred horses, fifty sets of harness, and ten coaches."[10] Probably four or five coaches would ordinarily suffice on this route, but when there was an unexpected rush of patronage at some point along the line, as at Blue Licks, additional coaches had to be maintained at these stations. There were also extra stages at both ends to provide for the emergency of more passengers being "booked" than one coach could accommodate.

With the above equipment of Dickey and Company, it is interesting to show the amount of business this stage line transacted over the Lexington and Maysville road. During the month of October, 1838, the revenue derived from stage passengers was $3,690.68, while for November the receipts were $1,719.75, and as winter came on the fares dwindled down to $438.75 for the month of December.[11] Stage travel dropped off to almost nothing over some of the Bluegrass routes during the extreme winter months of that period.[12]

September was considered the ideal month for stage travel, as related by Reverend Robert Baird, who passed through Lexington in 1832: "September is the best time to travel by stage in Kentucky and there is scarcely any important place in the state which cannot be reached by stage, especially between March and October." And

---

[10]Dickey to Thompson, mortgage, Fayette County Court, Deed Book 15, p. 223, July 8, 1838. These coaches, Concord and Troy, cost from $2,000 to $2,500 each, and stage horses ranged in price from one hundred to one hundred and fifty dollars.

[11]Dickey's Admrs. *vs.* Johnson & Co., Fayette Circuit Court, file 1105, July 18, 1840.

[12]Col. McNair wrote his partner from Lexington, January 29, 1838: "There is very little travel on the Lexington-Maysville road at this time of the year, and three daily lines operating. I expect that in about six weeks travel will commence and then it will be good until next fall." Letter in author's collection.

further added: "Numerous stage lines run in the summer from Lexington, as a center, in every direction, to Nashville, Cumberland Gap, and the Southern States; to Louisville, Cincinnati, and Maysville. The facilities for traveling are abundant."[13]

The baggage of this period was quite as unique as the mode of travel. There were queer carpetbags of brilliant coloring and fantastic flower designs, strange hair-covered trunks, curious boxes from foreign lands, and other nondescript pieces. Then too, fair ones brought from abroad the coach bandboxes of various kinds, some more or less attractive. In these feminine contrivances[14] were the personal possessions of the owner, not only headgear of various styles created through the passing years, but calashes, muskmelon hoods, and poke bonnets sufficiently large to hide pretty faces.

These boxes, of various hues and frequently elaborately decorated with pictures of Faneuil Hall, the New York post-office, or the Erie Canal, contributed not a little to the picturesqueness of the outfit. Military scenes were popular—Napoleon, Washington, or General Jackson being shown. There were also infantry and cavalry drills, ships of all patterns, some in storms and some in calm, all with canvas set. Another important piece of hand baggage was the tall leather or suede hat boxes of the

[13]Baird, p. 135.

[14]They were first designed for gentlemen, who during the eighteenth century wore powdered wigs, ruffled shirts, buckled shoes, and knee breeches. Doubtless their wives, intrigued by the charming possibilities of the bandbox, appropriated them for their use. The early specimens were made of wood covered with paper, pasteboard coming into general use about 1850. They ranged in size from a two-gallon measure to mammoth ones large enough to hold a bushel.

gentlemen, used to carry and protect their "stove-pipe" hats. All large pieces of baggage, carpetbags, and trunks were carried in the rear boot and strapped in with a waterproof curtain, while those of lesser proportions were carried on the passenger's lap, or under the seat.

All travelers wore a buff or gray "linen duster," a baggy coverall to protect their clothes from the clouds of dust on the turnpikes, while the women removed their best hats and bonnets and wore "duster caps." These items were a part of every traveler's equipment and went into the carpetbag along with the necessary articles of toilet. During the staging period, the carpetbag was the most important piece of hand baggage. This was made from a piece of Brussels carpet with a pair of metal jaws that closed on hinges. Many travelers were known to have carried all their earthly belongings in one of these spacious and clumsy pieces of baggage.

There was another feature of the stage-coach travel that left a lasting memory with passengers and drivers of the stage days. It was the "postilion." A groom, usually a young boy, with two horses stationed at the foot of some of the long hills, added to the ordinary team of four horses in making the ascent. The summit gained, the extra horses were quickly detached and returned to await and aid the next stage. On the Bluegrass stage routes the "postilions" were stationed at the foot of the steep hill at Clay's ferry on the Kentucky River, and on the hill coming out of Maysville toward Lexington, where valuable service was rendered. It was generally understood that when the Clay's ferry hill was reached, it was the signal for the men passengers to get out of the stage and walk up the hill beside the coach, and, in cases of need, to assist the driver in whatever way possible.

For a good many years the stage-coach industry of the Bluegrass was under the control of Edward P. Johnson, whose lines extended in every direction with Lexington as a center. Associated with him in this business were the two Swigert brothers, Philip and Jacob of Franklin County, John G. Chiles of Mercer County, and John H. Hanna of Franklin County.[15] To Edward P. Johnson was due much of the credit for building up the efficiency of the stage-coach system—better coaches and teams, with more favorable connections and lower rates of travel.

In the late spring of 1836 there came to Lexington a young man, Thomas H. Irvine, who was destined to succeed Johnson and become the stage-coach king of the Bluegrass. He happened to be in the stage office at Zanesville, Ohio, one day as Henry Clay and a party of politicians in a privately chartered stage on their way to the Lexington races stopped to exchange drivers. None being available, Irvine consented to drive the stage all the way to Lexington. This he did, and his first visit to the Bluegrass so impressed him that he definitely decided to settle in Lexington.

Irvine, despite his youthful appearance, was a veteran driver, having driven the United States mail from Hagerstown to Frederick, Maryland, and over the dangerous

---

[15]Preston West to Edw. P. Johnson, et al., Fayette County Court, Deed Book 20, p. 400, July 14, 1842.

mountain stretch from Hagerstown to Wheeling, West Virginia.

Shortly after he came to Lexington, Irvine[16] began "driving stage" for Johnson and Company, and after several years became superintendent for all their lines. He continued in this capacity for a long period. In 1850, Johnson retired from the stage-coach business and moved to Mississippi,[17] his interests being taken over by Irvine, who, the next year, added a partner, Cary A. Hawkins, of Richmond.[18] This new firm, Irvine, Hawkins & Co., the largest and best equipped in central Kentucky, was a little later known as the "Kentucky Stage Company" with principal offices in Maysville, Lexington, and Louisville. It also retained the familiar name of "old line," which gave it added prestige as the successor to Edward P. Johnson & Co., the oldest and best known stage line in Kentucky.

Thomas Irvine was successful in securing the mail-carrying contracts throughout central Kentucky, and these contracts he divided or sublet to various individuals. Thus, there were numerous partnerships and companies, as Irvine and Berry, who operated between Paris, Carlisle, Sharpsburg, and Maysville.[19] David J. Field and Silas P. Scott were other partners of Irvine. As soon as there

[16]Born in Aberdeenshire, Scotland, August 6, 1810—died in Lexington, Kentucky, June 16, 1892.

[17]Edward P. Johnson was born in Scott County, Kentucky, September 5, 1797, and died in Washington County, Mississippi, April 4, 1866. His body was later removed to Kentucky and buried in the family lot in the Lexington Cemetery. Thomas L. Johnson—*Genealogy of the Johnson Family*, pp. 39–40.

[18]C. A. Hawkins Admrs. *vs.* Thos. H. Irvine, Madison Circuit Court, file 208, June 3, 1869.

[19]Samuel Berry—see Irvine & Berry *vs.* Redmon, et al., Bourbon Circuit Court, file 1467, July 17, 1856.

was a threat of a rival line, Irvine would form a partnership for the line in question with the man who intended to go into opposition. Then he would lengthen
the route by getting the mail contract to the point further
out. Later he would sell the outlying half of it to that
partner, and keep the line into Lexington. By this
method, in a large degree, Irvine was able to keep down
opposition, and it was the key to his remarkable success.

Before Irvine rose to the control of the stage industry, the three principal owners and operators were
Edward P. Johnson, Milus W. Dickey, and Augustus
W. Gaines, who were at times rivals—then again partners. By 1852, all of them were out of the stage business. Yet, with an almost clear field and without opposition, the opportunities of the Kentucky Stage Company were not nearly so great as the two decades before
had been. Lexington and Louisville were this year for
the first time linked together with the "iron horse," seriously threatening the life and usefulness of the stage-
coach as a means of public conveyance.

The great revival of railroads began to be effective
in Kentucky in 1851. The Louisville and Nashville and
the Lexington and Maysville railroads, as well as the
Covington and Lexington and others, were aided by the
state and local subscriptions in large sums. The general
development of the railroad system of the state seems
to have been outward from Lexington, just as the stage-
coach system had been several decades before.[20]

This linking of the Lexington and Frankfort and the
Louisville and Frankfort railroad in 1852, making a

---

[20]*DeBow's Commercial Review*, Vol. X, p. 340.

through service from Lexington to Louisville by "steam cars" was, perhaps, the greatest blow the stage-coach industry had felt up to this time. It may be regarded as the beginning of the decline of that form of travel in the Bluegrass. Various stage lines nevertheless fought hard and well to retain a vestige of their former glory, but their day as a factor in the upbuilding of the country and movement of population was practically over. From this time, the stages on the Bluegrass routes operated to an advantage only in the directions and routes not opposed by the railroads, such as from Lexington to Richmond, to Crab Orchard, and Stanford, Harrodsburg, Versailles, and on the smaller lines and out-of-the-way towns and villages.

Suitable offices for the stage lines were usually located in the barrooms of the best hotel or tavern in the town. For a long period the Phoenix Hotel, Lexington; the Galt House, Louisville; Mansion House, Frankfort; Bakes' Hotel, Covington; Gibson House, Cincinnati; and the Goddard House in Maysville served as stage offices. Incoming stages would deposit their baggage in the stage offices, generally at one end of the barroom, and there it remained until placed on another stage for various towns and villages. This transfer and method of handling baggage by the stage agents often resulted in lost trunks, valises, portmanteaux, carpetbags, and other small articles and packages. There were no check rooms. Baggage was simply thrown in one end of the barroom and trusted to luck to get on the right stage at the proper time.[21]

Way-bills played a very important part in the operation of the stage lines. They were the daily as well as the permanent records of the business transacted, of fares collected, names and number of passengers transported. Way-bills[22] for passengers were on white paper, mail on yellow, and express on pink. These bills were often produced in court as the principal factors in settling suits growing out of contracts, and they furnished the basis upon which stage lines were bought and sold, being then considered the only true means of ascertaining the worth and income of any line.

Among other things of major importance to the stage-coach owners was the health and condition of the horses. This sometimes proved a serious problem, often involving great expense. In 1855, there broke out an epidemic of "glanders" among the horses of Thomas H. Irvine, on the Lexington-Cincinnati route, at Williamstown. This was one of the most dreaded and fatal diseases of the stage horses, and drastic measures were taken to prevent its spreading. In the words of Irvine: "There were fourteen good long-legged horses there and they had to be shot and the barn with all the contents destroyed by fire to stamp out the disease. Mules you know

---

[21]Dean *vs.* Irvine & Field, Fayette Circuit Court, file 1260, February 12, 1854.

[22]These bills also served as a means of transmitting messages between agent and agent, or persons along the stage lines. On one of the bills in the author's collection is this message: "Mr. Herndon please send back my stone hammer by the next stage," signed H. Sayres, Cincinnati, November 1, 1841. Another reads: "One pair of venison hams for Mr. B. Morrison, Lexington, Ky., which the agent will please send to him and oblige," signed A. D. B., Cincinnati, December 3, 1841.

don't get the glanders, so I rode up there [from Lexington] on a mule with a horse pistol to do the shooting. We had to wait for three days until there was no wind to spread a fire. Then I had a Negro hostler lead the horses one at a time to the center of the barn and shoot them through the heart, so that they all died together. Then we pulled a great pile of dry hay out of the loft to cover up the carcasses, stuffing the hay around them. A big crowd of people had congregated because of the shooting. Then I set fire to the barn . . . I was working two hundred head of horses at the time, and we had to get rid of the glanders. All the other horses on that route were taken to my farm on the Versailles Pike and turned out to graze for twelve weeks. None of them developed the glanders . . ."[23]

Stage-coaches had by 1855 given up the idea of competing with the "iron horse" as the main public conveyance, and now served only as feeders from the railroad and as connecting links to distant points in the Bluegrass. The railroads throughout central Kentucky were appealing to the traveling public to use their cars "and avoid the disagreeable night travel by stage," stressing the fact that the trips could be made in daylight.[24]

The Lexington & Frankfort and the Louisville & Frankfort railways in their time-table for November 11, 1856, announced:[25]

---

[23]Irvine's farm was about four miles west of Lexington, on the Versailles Road, the present site of the Calumet Stock Farm.
[24]*Kentucky Statesman,* May 25, 1855.
[25]*Ibid.,* November 11, 1856.

"Passengers by this train connect at Eminence with stages for New Castle, Drennon Springs, and Shelbyville; at Frankfort with stages for Versailles, Hardinsburg, Lawrenceburg, Harrodsburg, and Danville; at Payne's Depot with stage for Georgetown; and at Lexington with stages for Winchester, Mt. Sterling, Owingsville, Richmond, Irvine, Nicholasville, Danville, Lancaster, Crab Orchard, Stanford, London, Barbourville, and all points South; by railroad for Paris, Falmouth, Covington, and Maysville."

Notwithstanding the fact that in 1860 there were one hundred and seventy-five miles of railroad tracks in the Bluegrass region of Kentucky,[26] there were many places that could not be reached by this means of travel. The spring announcement of Irvine and Hawkins in 1860 enumerated the places their stages reached:[27]

"KENTUCKY STAGE COMPANY—
DAILY LINES

"Lexington to Harrodsburg—leaves daily after the arrival of the Covington & Louisville cars—passing through Shakertown and arriving at Harrodsburg at 6 o'clock P. M., thence with Robinson & Thomas line for all southern and western points.

"Lexington to Glasgow—connecting with lines to Louisville, Nashville, and other southern points.

[26]Davis—*Geography of the Bluegrass Region*, p. 141.
[27]*Kentucky Statesman*, April 9, 1860.

"Leaving Lexington daily after the arrival of the Covington & Louisville cars, passing through Nicholasville, Bryantsville, Danville, Perryville, Lebanon, New Market, Saloma, Campbellsville, Greensburg, Monroe, Blue Springs Grove to Glasgow. This line passes within a short distance of Mammoth Cave and is the best route for that point. It also connects at Bryantsville with a line which passes through Lancaster, Crab Orchard, Stanford, and Somerset, and returns in time to connect with the Louisville & Covington trains for all eastern and western cities.

"*From Lexington*—stages to Richmond, Rogersville, Kingston, London, Barbourville, Cumberland Gap, Tazewell, Bean Station, there connecting with lines through Virginia, North and South Carolina, Georgia, and other southern states.

"*Lexington to Mt. Sterling*—via Winchester, 6 hours.

"Stage Office in Lexington—Phoenix Hotel.

"IRVINE, HAWKINS, & CO."

Such were the schedules and routes of the stage-coaches in the 1860's when the war clouds were gathering, threatening to disrupt so many things, North and South, and which was to usher in the last, yet not the least, interesting phase of the old stage's history in central Kentucky.

CHAPTER XIII

THE STAGE AS A MAIL CARRIER

WITH the passing of the post-rider, the stage-coach became the principal conveyance of the United States mail. This service was inaugurated in the Bluegrass region of Kentucky in the late spring of 1816. Improvements were slow for the next fifteen or twenty years until the "artificial" or hard-surfaced roads were introduced, which made it possible for the stage-coaches to maintain longer runs and schedules at seven or eight miles per hour.

The main trunk for all the mails from the East was the great National Road,[1] sometimes called the "Cumberland Road," leading from Pittsburgh, Baltimore, and Cumberland, Maryland, through the states of Ohio and Indiana, and terminating at St. Louis. This road (now U. S. 40) was built by the Federal Government. It was the great military road to the Mississippi River and the backbone of the western mail service.

In 1829, President Andrew Jackson appointed William T. Barry, a citizen of Lexington, to the office of Postmaster General. Barry planned the great mail stage route from Zanesville on the "National Pike" to Mays-

---

[1]This road, conceived by Albert Gallatin, took its inception in 1806 when commissioners were appointed to report on the project. In 1811, the first contract was let for ten miles of the road west of Cumberland, Maryland, which was the eastern terminus. The road was completed to Wheeling in December, 1820, and to the Mississippi River in the early thirties.

ville, through Lexington, Nashville, to Florence, Alabama, and on to New Orleans. General Jackson lived on this road at Nashville, and he traveled this route in his private carriage to the capital. It was also the route of Henry Clay, a member of the Senate post-office committee, who was in charge of the "Cumberland Road and all the mail extension in the West." The improvement of this great highway through the heart of the country contributed to the popularity of Henry Clay, who was identified with it from its beginning to its completion. The southern terminus of this mail route through Kentucky was marked with a statue of Clay located in the middle of Canal Street, New Orleans, near the custom house.[2]

It was well known that General Jackson had unlimited faith in Barry and backed him without question, which enabled him to accomplish so much in such a short time. His work consisted in getting the trails and roads improved so that the mail stages could get over them at the rate of eight miles per hour. There is no question that the post-office developed the country as much as any other factor. These stage owners were actually building the nation without knowing it, when they caused highways to be opened and improved in order to get the mail delivered more easily. Thus, the natural routes were opened over which travel could always flow with the least resistance and lowest cost.

---

[2]This statue of Henry Clay, erected by the citizens of New Orleans as a token of their appreciation of his efforts in internal improvements, was removed to Tulane Park, when traffic crowded it on Canal Street.

During the period of the great mail development, three Postmasters General were from Lexington—William T. Barry, Amos Kendall, and Charles A. Wickliffe. To these men belong the credit of making Lexington the mail center of the West in the early days of the stage-coach, when it required twelve days to get a letter from Washington to New Orleans, by way of Lexington, Nashville, and Florence, Alabama.

Early in the nineteenth century, Lexington was the distributing post-office for the states of Kentucky and Tennessee.[3] The link between Zanesville on the "National Pike" and the distributing post-office at Lexington came by way of the ferry at Maysville, and this was considered the "feeder" route from Washington City and the East. All the mail from the East came directly by stage-coach to Lexington, where it was distributed and carried over the various "star routes" of central Kentucky to the outlying post-offices and villages.

In connection with the exploits of Postmaster General Barry,[4] mention may be here made of the work of the car-

[3]According to the Postmaster General's report of 1832, distributing post-offices (D.P.O.) were located "only in populous cities and towns where travel concentrated" and "where mails and passengers have a temporary rest."

[4]William Taylor Barry was born in Lunenburg County, Virginia, February 15, 1784, and after graduating from William and Mary located in Lexington in 1805 to practice law. He served various political positions: U. S. Senator, 1820–1824; Postmaster General 1829–1835; appointed Minister to Spain and died on his way to that post in Liverpool, England, August 30, 1835. The remains of Barry, after reposing nearly nineteen years in a foreign land, were brought back to Kentucky by an act of the Legislature, and reinterred with honors in the state cemetery at Frankfort, November 8, 1854. A plain and unpretentious monument was erected by Lexington citizens to Barry's memory in the southeast corner of the court-house yard. On the west side facing Cheapside, was inscribed: "His fame lives in the history of his county, and is as Immortal as America's Liberty and Glory." After the court-house burned, May 17, 1897, the monument mysteriously disappeared while the site was being cleared for the new court-house.

rier pigeon, an important feature of American life previous to the introduction of the telegraph system. It was likewise a valuable branch of stage-coach transportation. As soon as the first stage-coach routes were established in this country, carrier or "homing" pigeons were imported. They were bred and used by the post-office, army, and navy to transmit important messages from place to place. The peculiar characteristics of this bird have been known in Europe for centuries. After they have become accustomed to one home or "loft," they can be taken several hundred miles and released, always flying straight back with their best possible speed.

Not only were these pigeons used by the government, but stage-coach owners derived a steady income from them; and for many years the largest pigeon "loft" in the country was located in the top of the old stage barn on Limestone Street, in Lexington. In this "loft" were rows of cages marked "Washington," "Knoxville," "Zanesville," Cincinnati," "Nashville," and other cities, indicating the "loft" to which the bird would return when released, and likewise in Washington and other cities would be cages for the birds marked "Lexington." Thus when a pigeon was released it would return immediately to his home "loft." The charges for transmitting a message by pigeon were greatly in excess of the present-day telegraph rates, and this, with the breeding and raising of the birds, was an additional source of revenue to the owners of the stage-coach lines.

Among stage owners and drivers there was no charge for the exchange and transportation of the pigeons. The stage-coaches were the only method of transporting the birds to a foreign "loft." Little wicker cages large enough for one bird were used in transporting them, and these were suspended on a little iron rail that ran through the top of each cage, just in back of the driver's seat. In a large measure, the success of the carrier pigeon was due to the network of stage-coaches in operation throughout the country.

It is related that carrier pigeons brought the news of the battle of Buena Vista to Lexington, word of the death of Colonels McKee and Henry Clay, Jr., and of the capture of Cassius M. Clay.[5] The birds attached to General Taylor's army belonged to the New Orleans "loft," and the report came by pigeon to Lexington, where it was relayed to Washington by the same method. It was a scientific and practical way of transmitting information and messages, and the entire nation depended upon that service as we do upon the telegraph.

The great mails of a hundred years ago were operated on very much the same principle as are our mails today. The post-office department at Washington negotiated with the leading stage lines for the transmission of the mails by yearly contract. These contracts were usually determined by advertisements for bids in the local papers and acceptance of the lowest offered. Mail contractors were under bond to transport the mail in their stages "with celerity, certainty, and security" and for every trip lost, the fine was equal to the value of that trip, whatever may have been the cause. Another

---

[5]Recollections of Charles E. Mooney, a veteran of the Mexican War and a native of Lexington.

thing that subjected the stage operators to a severe fine and possible loss of contract was "transporting commercial intelligence by express or stage more rapidly than the mail."[6]

Possibly the most important mail stage route in Kentucky was the "Zanesville-Florence star route." The stage-coaches of Johnson and Company and associated companies got the mail at Zanesville as it came over the National Road from the East. Then the route followed to the ferry at Maysville, thence to Lexington, Harrodsburg, Perryville, Lebanon, Campbellsville, Glasgow, Gallatin, Nashville, Columbia, to Florence, Alabama, where the mail was transferred to a steamboat "star route" for New Orleans, another distributing post-office.

The reason for the existence of the "Zanesville-Florence" route was that the steamboats could not compete with the schedules of the stage-coaches. It was approximately five hundred miles from Zanesville to Florence by stage, while the distance by river was over two thousand miles. Both the stage and the steamboat had about the average speed of eight miles per hour running time. If the steamboats picked up the mail at Wheeling on the National Road, it took them over a week longer to deliver it in New Orleans than for the stages to get the same mail at Zanesville, ninety miles further west from Washington. The difference in time was more than doubled on the north-bound trip, due to the current in the rivers and the delay at the falls of the Ohio, at Louisville. The few remaining iron road markers

[6]*Kentucky Gazette*, June 18, 1835.

on the Lexington-Maysville turnpike near May's Lick
are silent reminders of the Zanesville-Florence route.
It held full sway until the middle fifties when the railroads were extended to the gulf ports, causing the aban-
donment of this great mail stage route through Kentucky.

Lexington, as the distributing post-office for Kentucky,
had various "star routes" stretching outward to all parts
of the state and beyond. The Richmond "star route" out
of this city extended to Knoxville, and the Harrodsburg
route continued south to Corinth, Mississippi, across the
state of Tennessee.

On the Zanesville-Florence mail route which passed
through Lexington and central Kentucky, one driver
came out of Zanesville to the ferry at Aberdeen, Ohio,
opposite Maysville. The mail, passengers, and baggage
were transferred to another stage-coach that went through
to Florence;[7] but the drivers changed at Lexington, Perryville, Glasgow, Nashville, Columbia, and doubled back on
the north-bound stage to their respective starting places.
This called for standard and identical equipment to be
used on the route. Four days and two nights were usually
about the schedule, or about seventy-five hours running
time to make the five hundred miles. Some of the roads
were rather primitive and the condition of the bridges
poor.

The pay of the stage drivers was arranged according
to the terms of the mail contract more than anything else.

[7] A well appointed Concord or Troy coach, rigidly inspected, was good
at any time for a thousand-mile run with regular grease and oil attention. They cost from $2,000 to $2,500 according to the trim and
size. A set of stage harness for a four-horse team cost $150 to $200
and a six-horse set about $50 additional.

The Covington-Lexington route was about eighty-two miles. One coach and driver made the trip in eleven hours, with seven changes of horses. The south-bound stage returned all the teams that the north-bound stage took out of their respective barns, and the driver would spend one night in Covington and one night in Lexington. Ten hours on the "box" was always considered a day's work for the stage driver, and five cents per mile the established pay, some more or less, but the differences were not great. The jehu who came from Maysville to Lexington received three dollars and twenty-five cents for the run, and would make two round trips per week, with a day's lay-off after each trip.

On the turnpike from Maysville to Lexington, which was a part of the Zanesville-Florence mail route, the following post-offices were established: Maysville, Washington, Lower Blue Licks, Forrest Retreat, Millersburg, Paris, and Moreland. At each of these places seven minutes were allowed the stage-coaches for opening and closing the mails, while at Lexington, the distributing post-office, one hour was allowed for this service.[8]

Drivers of the stages carrying the mail felt that the road was theirs and that they should be given the right of way over all vehicles. This feeling of superiority was not confined to the drivers alone. Milus W. Dickey, the mail stage contractor from Maysville to Lexington in 1836, refused to pay the turnpike company the customary tolls at the toll-houses for the passage of his stages. He

[8]*Kentucky Gazette,* June 18, 1835.

claimed that as carrier of the United States mail he was not subject to the charges.[9]

When Dickey refused to pay the toll, his stages were halted at the toll-gates. This led to several suits against the turnpike company[10] which later reached the higher court. In all probability, Dickey tried to make this a parallel case with the "National Pike," a government-built and owned road over which mail stages passed free from toll. But it was clearly shown by Judge George Robertson that the Lexington and Maysville turnpike had received no aid from the government and was a private corporation. The verdict was that Dickey "was not entitled to wear out private property without compensating the owners, and that he be, justly and constitutionally, compelled to pay the prescribed toll."[11] This case attracted wide attention, and the opinion rendered by Judge Robertson set the precedent for mail-carrying stages throughout Kentucky using the private turnpike roads.

From the Postmaster General's report for 1836, Kentucky was shown to have 5,968 miles of stage routes over which mail was carried at a cost of 10.2 cents per mile, as compared with 8.4 per mile for the United States in general.[12] Changes in the mail routes were continually being made consistent with the improvement of the turn-

---

[9]This practice had been going on for some time in other parts of Kentucky. Stage owners would throw a mail sack in their stage and claim exemption "as a stage having within it the United States mail." One well known case was in Lincoln County. Proctor *vs.* Crozer & Marshall, Kentucky Reports, B. Monroe VI, p. 268.

[10]Dickey *vs.* Maysville, Washington, Paris & Lexington Turnpike Co., file 264, Mason Circuit Court, June 12, 1836.

[11]Maysville, etc. *vs.* Dickey, Kentucky Reports, Dana VII, p. 113.

[12]U. S. Executive Documents, 24th Congress, 2nd Session, 1836.

pikes, one of which is typical of the times: "Route from Bean Station, Tennessee, to Lexington, Kentucky, changed from semi-weekly to tri-weekly line of post-coaches."[13] Thus, at that early date, Lexington was provided with a tri-weekly mail service to the South. The little settlement of Bean Station was quite an important stand in the stage-coach days when the United States mail was carried by this conveyance. It was the crossing point of the Baltimore to Nashville stage route and the road from Kentucky to the Carolinas and Virginias. Bean Station Inn, built in 1814, was the largest tavern and stopping place for stage travelers between Washington, D. C., and New Orleans.

The old stage maps of that period (1830-1850) give the distance from "Lexington, Kentucky, to Bean Station, Tennessee," as 172 miles, the route being through Stanford, Crab Orchard, Barbourville, Cumberland Ford, and Tazewell, Tennessee. Here at Bean Station, the mail that was carried south from the distributing post-office at Lexington was reassigned to stage-coaches for various places in the South, and the bulk of the New Orleans mail and express was assembled at this point.

Augustus W. Gaines, a well known stage operator, held the mail contract from Lexington to Cincinnati from 1838 to 1842 at an annual salary of $5,500 on route known as No. 3212:[14]

---

[13]*Ibid.*, The settlement of Bean Station, Tennessee, is about 35 miles south of the Kentucky line, and 11 miles north of Morristown. Here the highways U. S. 11 and U. S. 25 cross.

[14]U. S. Executive Documents, 26th Congress, 2nd Session, 1838.

> "Lexington, Kentucky, to Cincinnati, Ohio, via
> Delphton, Georgetown, Big Eagle, Williamstown,
> Dry Ridge, Crittenden, Gaines Cross Roads, New
> Lancaster, Florence, Dry Creek, and Covington—84
> miles and back daily in 4 horse post-coaches."

There were numerous smaller routes that paid fairly
well, one of which was from "Burnt Tavern, Kentucky, to
Danville" eight miles and back daily which netted John
G. Chiles the annual sum of $466.00. Overton P. Hogan,
who held the contract from Georgetown to Cynthiana, was
allowed "horse service 6 months in the year" on account
of the roads, and this lowered the value of his contract to
$575.00 annually.

Many of these old contracts are interesting, not only
for the mail phase but for the routes and stations. In
1842, William Elder was the successful bidder on the
"white line"[15] at an annual contract of $1,998:

> "Route No. 4816 from Lexington by Childsburg,
> Colbyville, Winchester, Mount Sterling to Owings-
> ville—50 miles and back, three times a week in two-
> horse coaches."

In the late thirties and early forties, the "old line" of
Edward P. Johnson held the principal mail routes; Lexington-Louisville, $4,500; Cincinnati-Lexington, $4,000;
and Maysville-Lexington, $3,400.[16]

---

[15]This line, the oldest stage route in Kentucky, was known as the
"white line" from the stage-coaches so painted on that route.
[16]U. S. Executive Documents, 26th Congress, 1st Session, 1838.

"Maysville to Lexington—via Washington, May's Lick, Lower Blue Licks, Forrest Retreat, Millersburg, Paris, Hallocksburg, Moreland—61 miles and back daily, in 4 horse coaches."

Another important stage mail route in the northern part of the state was from Maysville, by way of North Ford, Flemingsburg, Sherbourne, Sharpsburg, to Mt. Sterling. This line intersected the tri-weekly line of stages at Mt. Sterling running from Lexington to Owingsville.[17]

By 1850, the mileage of the mail stage contracts had been greatly reduced, and the main stage operator in central Kentucky was the firm of Thomas H. Irvine & Company. This firm held the Lexington-Cincinnati contract at $4,275; Lexington-Maysville $3,970; and the Lexington-Harrodsburg route at $1,174.[18]

While the stage-coaches held full sway until this time as the mail carriers, it was now necessary for a showdown with the Lexington and Frankfort railroad. For the first time the stamina of the horse had been challenged and that meant much to Kentuckians of that day. The post-office department proposed a month's test from Lexington to Frankfort to show the comparative speed and reliability of the stage versus the railroad as a mail carrier. The holder of the best record of sixteen days or more would be considered the winner. The course was a round trip from the Lexington post-office to the Frankfort post-office.

Interest and excitement ran high, and there was an immense amount of betting on the daily runs, as well as

[17]Octavius M. Weedon held this route at $1,499 annually. *Western Star*, Maysville, May 2, 1843.

[18]U. S. Executive Documents, 32nd Congress, 2nd Session, 1852.

the final result. Both contestants had their equipment in the best of order. The stage teams were picked from the finest stock of the road and the celebrated driver, Hiram Lawrence, was on the box. A big crowd of people assembled at the old stage stable on Limestone Street and at the railroad terminal to see the start, which was early in the month of April, 1851. A few minutes before seven in the morning, Lawrence with his spirited team drove up in front of the post-office to receive the test mail pouch. Also at the post-office there was a man on horseback to take another test pouch to the waiting train. In a few minutes the clock on the old brick courthouse struck seven times, and, by agreement, on the seventh stroke they were off. By the time the mail pouch reached the the train and was safely in the conductor's possession, Lawrence's horn had already been heard at the crossing west of the city. Spectators placed themselves at favorable points along the turnpike and railroad tracks to witness this unique trial of speed. Many avowed the "iron horse" would never surpass the Kentucky horse and for the next few hours everybody was in a state of suspense waiting for the result of the race.

About eleven, a carrier pigeon from the Frankfort "loft," brought the news that the train had won the lap by ten minutes. The stage had changed horses one time, and the passengers remained seated. This was done in the record time of one minute.

On the return trip that afternoon, the same thing was repeated with both the stage and the railroad reducing their time a couple of minutes. Betters on the railroad were now giving odds with few takers. A heavy rain began around eight that night, which gave added courage to the stage backers, and a drizzling rain next morning greeted the spectators. Lawrence was on the job with a fresh team, and on the stroke of seven gave two blasts on his horn and was off for Frankfort. The locomotive screeched and whistled, and the race was on again. After a couple of hours a bird from the Midway "loft" brought the news that the train was about one minute ahead of the stage-coach. The rain continued intermittently and the engineer had trouble with wet wood. News came in from Frankfort claiming a dead heat, as both mail pouches had arrived at the post-office at the same time, and all bets on that lap were withdrawn.

On the return trip the stage-coach arrived in Lexington three or four minutes before the train, which was delayed near Midway by water running over the track. The "iron horse" did its best work in the first week of the contest, while the machinery, equipment, and supplies of every kind were in the best condition. The solid iron straps threw the locomotive off the track nearly every time when running fast—twenty miles per hour! Then, also, the culverts were inadequate to dispose of the storm waters or even a heavy rain, which caused the ballast to wash out of the road bed and stall the locomotive. Due to the small boilers of the *Logan* and *Nottaway* and the green and wet wood gathered along the line, the fires lagged and the steam went down so that the engines often had to "stop and take breath." With the cry of the engineer, "out all," it was necessary for the able-bodied passengers to alight and help push the train over the numerous grades along the line.[19]

After the first week's run the stage-coach had the better of the railroad and at the end of the month had scored a momentous victory. But it was only temporary. Several months later, Samuel Gill, a professional engineer, was placed in charge of the railroad and he had the embankments carefully drained and the road completely rebuilt. The old flat iron rails were junked, and the new model "T" type substituted, with cedar ties in place of the stone strips.[20] A new and improved type of locomotive was purchased and put in operation under the name of William R. McKee, it being the only one of the three wood burners which could "make all the grades with a full load." With these improvements, the railroad passed the experimental stage and came into its own as a reliable conveyance of the mail and express.

By the spring of 1852, the mail-carrying contract passed from the stage-coach into the hands of the Lexington & Frankfort and the Louisville & Frankfort railroads at an annual sum of $6,500.[21] The Lexington & Maysville railroad was next in importance in the Bluegrass, and caused the abandonment of the stage lines in that direction. It was the shortest connection between the capital of the Bluegrass and the Ohio River.[22] The line

[19]Manuscript—Samuel D. McCullough, 1803–1873. Lexington Public Library.

[20]The road as originally built was completely worn out, and although repaired at various times it was not until 1852 that it was completely rebuilt.

[21]U. S. Executive Documents, 33rd Congress, 2nd Session, 1852.

[22]There was never much of a stage-coach line between Louisville and Cincinnati, as the steamboat service between those cities always was popular and generally carried the mail.

of this railroad left out Blue Licks Springs, which at that time was the most attractive social and health resort of the entire West. The stage line became the owners and managers of that popular resort and improved its facilities. Soon their stage lines were running again, first as a summertime proposition, but afterwards it was resumed for all the year and continued to operate for years even without the through mail contract. This is an exceptional case of a stage line coming back with renewed strength after once being put out of business by a railroad.

By 1860, the Kentucky Central and other railroads mentioned held the principal mail-carrying contracts of central Kentucky, leaving Irvine and Hawkins only such contracts as Lexington-Richmond-Irvine, and Lexington south by way of Stanford, Crab Orchard, and London. Upon the outbreak of the Civil War, stage owners and contractors of the mails were removed from the service for siding with the Confederacy, and their contracts were forfeited.[23] Shortly after the first Federal troops, the Fourteenth Ohio, arrived and camped in Lexington, Hawkins joined the Southern army and "left for the territory under the control of the so-called Confederate States."[24] This resulted in the forfeiture of Irvine and Hawkins' mail contracts, but the Government agreed to make a partial payment to Irvine because of his loyalty. He formed a partnership with Silas Wolverton and continued the mail stage routes, with William Purnell as stage agent at the

---

[23]U. S. Postmaster General's annual report, 1861.
[24]Hawkins *vs.* Irvine, Fayette Circuit Court, file 1487, January 8, 1866.

office at the northeast corner of Main and Limestone streets, Lexington.

For the greater part of the war, Lexington was under Federal control, and the Kentucky Stage Company ran their mail-carrying stages "except such times as the Rebels were in the country, which prevented their doing so for a considerable portion of the time."[25] The Confederates, in 1863, after a small skirmish at Clay's ferry, burned the ferry, so that "for a long time there was no boat at the ferry by which the mail stages could cross the Kentucky River." It was not until several months later when Colonel Hill of the Fourteenth U. S. Cavalry occupied the ferry and built a new boat "that stage travel and mail service was resumed to Richmond and beyond, and then only with very irregular schedules and service."

During the movements of armies, the stage horses were in such demand[26] that it was never known if a stage would reach its destination. Thomas H. Irvine, the veteran stager and principal owner of the Kentucky Stage Company, gives this account of the perils confronting stage travelers at this time:

"Alvin Brown drove out of Stanford [to Lexington] in June, 1863, with a big stage loaded with passengers and they crowded the top of the stage as well as the inside. The rear boot was heavily loaded

---

[25]Hacker *vs.* T. H. Irvine & Co., Fayette Circuit Court, file 1471, May 17, 1866.

[26]"The stock was pretty well run down on all the stage lines out of Lexington during the war owing to the very unsafe condition of the road by soldiers." Deposition of John L. B. Alberta, French *vs.* Kentucky Stage Company, Montgomery Circuit Court, file 19, March 18, 1866.

with hams and bacon. It was a big hitch of six horses. There were several regiments of soldiers in training at Camp Nelson in Jessamine County on the Kentucky River. They needed artillery horses, so the stage horses were commandeered by an officer who gave Brown some kind of paper. The soldiers began to help themselves to the hams and bacon. That was too much for Brown, and he pitched in to lick the whole Union army single handed. He made good progress for a few minutes, but was soon beaten up. The stage was pushed over to the side of the road and left there, and the passengers had to foot it all the way into Nicholasville."

The practice of seizing horses became so common among "stragglers, followers, and cavalrymen" that the stage proprietors were left with old worn-out horses which the soldiers derisively called "crow baits." At various intervals, a stage bearing the mail flag would be allowed to go through the lines with letters for the South, but this service was often very irregular and most uncertain. Following the termination of the war between the states, the stage-coaches had ceased to figure prominently in the mail-carrying contracts, and served only as feeders to the railroads and to localities and sections of the state not served by the "steam cars."

CHAPTER XIV

TURNPIKES AND TOLL-GATES

SHORTLY after Kentucky had been admitted into the Union, there came into existence a sentiment for the improvement of the trails and roads. Economic upheaval following the Revolutionary War delayed internal improvements. Roads and bridges were constructed only in a few necessary cases. Stout logs were placed across streams for the sake of foot passengers.

When the great Kentucky migration began, all roads and trails became the subject of animated conversation. Around the fireside of cabins and in taprooms in the Tidewater country bits of information concerning the mountain passes, points where ambuscades were likely to occur, location of springs and camping places, grazing for the pack horses, and other general information necessary to the travelers of that period were passed and repassed. One route about which information was sought was the "Wilderness Trail." Afterwards this trail became in turn known as the "Wilderness Road," the "Kentucky Road," and the "great waggon-road." Starting in the valleys of Virginia, it passed through Cumberland Gap, down the banks of the Cumberland River and by the Hazel Patch to Crab Orchard in Lincoln County. From this "trunk line" were built many of the roads which led to different parts of the state.

In 1793, the Legislature of Kentucky passed an act
providing for the clearing of a "waggon-road from Frankfort to Cincinnati."[1] This improved road became of
great importance to the people of Kentucky. Over it
traveled immigrants from the East. Over this same
road the militia of the Bluegrass marched to participate in
the campaigns under General Wayne against the Ohio and
Indiana Indians.

Until well into the nineteenth century each village was
an independent community, having its own church, blacksmith, shoemaker, gristmill, grog shop, and country store.
Clothing and bed covering were spun and woven by the
women of the frontier family from wool of their own
sheep. Grain was harvested into barns on the same premises, or ground into meal or flour at the mill, usually but
a few miles distant. From their cattle they stored away
their winter's supply of meat; and the hides, dressed near
by, were made into shoes by the local artisan, who usually
boarded with his patrons while doing this work.

Little need was there then for many roads. The one
fixed journey was the weekly trip to church, and the road
provided generally led to the gristmill and the country
store. Here were kept the few imported articles the
farmers needed in daily life but could not produce, and
here also he could dispose of the surplus which his farm
might yield. Roads were generally established along
certain well defined trails. Rivers afforded the early
means of travel, but in order to develop the country and

[1]Littell, Vol. I, p. 185.

carry on trade it was necessary to build roads to the market centers and court houses.

During the last quarter of the eighteenth century and the first half of the nineteenth, when this country was emerging from the wilderness, public funds were lacking for the construction of the much-needed roads and bridges. These improvements were often financed with private capital, by the issuance of stocks and bonds. Single individuals or groups were empowered by the State Legislature to raise money through subscriptions. The payment of interest and dividends and the retirement of bonds were accomplished by funds derived from toll charged those who traveled the roads. This method of financing served a most useful purpose, and no doubt contributed greatly to the material development of the state.

The first private turnpike companies incorporated in Kentucky "for the purpose of forming artificial roads" were the Lexington and Louisville Turnpike Road Company and the Maysville and Lexington Turnpike Road Company, both of which were chartered February 4, 1817.[2] Nothing, however, was done in the way of road building until the Lexington and Maysville road was incorporated anew in 1827, as the "Maysville, Washington, Paris, and Lexington Turnpike Company" with capital stock of three hundred and twenty thousand dollars.[3] The early need for hard-surfaced roads in central Kentucky was easily recognized by a traveler who passed through Lexington in 1829: "It appears to me that not only in order that the towns, on the road from Maysville to Lou-

[2]Littell, Vol. I, p. 510; p. 535.
[3]*Acts, General Assembly,* 1827.

isville by Lexington, should prosper, but even that they should hold what improvements they have gained, *the road must be turnpiked*."[4]

In May, 1830, a bill passed Congress authorizing the United States Government to subscribe one hundred and fifty thousand dollars to the stock of the Maysville-Lexington road, but, to the consternation of all friends of internal improvement, the bill was vetoed by Andrew Jackson. However, this paralyzing blow was but temporary in its effect. Friends along the route seemed to gather new vitality and impetus, and most liberal private subscriptions were made. Besides the stock taken in this road by the counties and cities through which it passed,[5] the State Legislature appropriated the sum of $213,200 toward the building of the road, one-half of the total cost.

The first stretch of this road, from Maysville to Washington, a distance of four miles, was completed November 7, 1830, and was the first macadamized road in Kentucky and the country west of the Alleghenies. The entire road from Maysville to Lexington was completed and opened to travel in 1835, a distance of sixty-four miles, at a cost of $426,400 including thirteen toll-houses and six covered bridges.

Often the state took stock in the private turnpike companies, upon the condition that the private stockholders would subscribe three times the amount of the state stock. Between 1835 and 1850, by means of state

---

[4]Draper MSS. 17CC90–91, August 22, 1829. Wisconsin Historical Society, Madison.

[5]Fayette County agreed to take $15,000 in stock, and the city of Paris $8,000. *Western Citizen*, Paris, February 9, 1831.

aid, there was a network of macadamized roads operating successfully in central Kentucky equal to any in the United States. The chief nuclei of the system were Maysville, Lexington, and Louisville. It was not long after the era of turnpike building began that Lexington became the macadamized road hub of central Kentucky. An enthusiastic Lexingtonian declared: "We have seven turnpike roads terminating at this city. A greater number, we believe, than in any city in the world . . . We defy the earth to exceed us in the variety and pleasantness of travel from Lexington . . ."[6]

By 1837, three hundred and forty-three miles of these roads had been completed in central Kentucky, and two hundred and thirty-six more were under way.[7] Roads built upon the MacAdam plan varied in cost from $5,000 to $7,300 per mile, including bridges and culverts.[8] When a route or road was thought profitable, a number of citizens would meet at some inn or tavern on a designated day and open the books for a new turnpike road company, having first secured their charter from the State Legislature.[9] When sufficient stock had been sold, the road would be laid out and constructed "on the general macadamized plan—the stone broken, usually so as not to exceed six ounces in weight, and laid upon the road,

[6]*Kentucky Gazette,* April 4, 1839.

[7]Smith—*History of Kentucky,* p. 522.

[8]The contract for the Lexington and Richmond turnpike was let (1836) from the city limits of Lexington to the Kentucky River for $5,628 per mile.

[9]Meeting was held in John Keiser's Tavern, May 3, 1836, in Lexington, to open the books of the Frankfort, Lexington, and Versailles Turnpike Road Company. Numerous other accounts of similar meetings can be found in the files of the *Kentucky Gazette* for this period.

according to the probable wear, nine or ten inches deep, and one to three inches deeper in the center."

The leading feature of this kind of road, which derived its name from a Scotchman—Loudon Mac-Adam[10]—was setting a limit in size and weight of the stones to be used on the road, the weight itself being six ounces, or rocks that would pass through a certain size ring. Whenever as much as five miles of the new road had been completed, the turnpike company was permitted to acquire one-quarter acre of land and to erect a toll-house thereon, and charge the users of the road according to the kind of vehicle and the distance traveled. Originally the word turnpike meant a "turnpike or toll-bar" and *not* a road, but around 1830 it signified a road surfaced with some hard material, and has since been applied to all macadamized roads in Kentucky.

The introduction of the "artificial" or macadamized road into Kentucky formed a new era in road building and paved the way for the successful operation of the stage-coaches. With the coming of the "metalled" or hard-surfaced roads, the stage-coaches profited greatly, increasing their average speeds from three and four miles an hour, to seven and eight, counting time lost for stoppages. The journey in a stage from Lexington to Cincinnati, which required two days before the "artificial" roads, was now reduced to twelve hours. The average speed including stoppages over the hard-surfaced roads during the zenith of the stages in 1838 was 8.2 miles per hour

---

[10]John Loudon MacAdam, 1756–1836, a famous builder of broken stone roads. The broken stone is often called "macadam" and the work of construction "macadamizing." Turnpike roads are often called "pikes."

from Louisville to Lexington, and 8 miles per hour on the Maysville-Lexington route.

A schedule of the toll to be collected was generally specified in the charter granted by the Legislature to the private or toll road companies and was often subject to revision when it was found that the rates of return were too large or too small. Rates were generally in keeping with the services rendered, and investors in these road companies did not get more than a fair return on their money.[11] Toll-gates, or toll-houses, were set up every five miles on all privately-owned turnpikes, and the rates varied with the company and the distance traveled. Perhaps the rates[12] for the Lexington-Maysville road, one of the model roads in the thirties, strikes a fair average of the charges. There were thirteen toll-gates on this road. These rates carried the following exemptions: "Persons passing from one point on his farm to another; to and from any place of worship or funeral; militiamen on days of training or attending court-martial; grand jurors or electors on days of general elections."

[11]*Kentucky Statesman,* December 11, 1857, announced that the Lexington & Winchester Turnpike Company had declared its annual 3 per cent dividend.

[12]For every 20 head of sheep, hogs, or other small stock................$6\frac{1}{4}$c
For every 10 head of cattle..$6\frac{1}{4}$c
For every horse, mule, ass, or other four footed animal of
    the larger kind, except cattle 4c
For every two wheel pleasure carriage...8c
    (exclusive of the beasts by which it is drawn and the
    persons transported by it)
For every four wheel pleasure carriage 16c
    (same exceptions as to beasts and passengers)
For every cart, wagon, or other carriage of burden whose
    wheels do not exceed three inches in width........................25c
For every person 2c

Companies were authorized to open and operate "dirt turnpikes" but charges could be only half the regular toll, until the road was completely hard-surfaced. All moneys and revenue taken in could not be paid out but had to be used in finishing the road. Toll-gate keepers, or "toll-gatherers" saw that there was no mistake about the fares collected, for a large board "having the appearance of a mock window" was firmly set in the wall of every toll-house, displaying in plain figures the rates in force, and which could lawfully be demanded from every traveler.[13] Any toll-gate keeper found guilty of demanding more than the legal rate from the users of the road, was subject to a fine of ten dollars. The managers of the turnpike companies were required by law to declare semi-annual dividends of the net profits of the road among the stockholders, and in the event of these being over ten per cent, a reduction of the tolls would be necessary to keep within that limit, under forfeiture of the charter. Whenever a section of road on a turnpike was out of repair, no toll could be charged the traveler within five miles. The owners were subjected to a forfeiture of their charter if the road was not repaired within thirty days after due notice had been given.

Tolls of the Danville, Lancaster, and Nicholasville road company for the year 1847 amounted to $12,772.39, while the net proceeds for the year before were $7,-600.92.[14] The counties were empowered by the State Leg-

---

[13]Due to various kinds of money used in Kentucky in the early days, there was always much confusion and often heated discussion at the toll-gates over the tolls, until in 1844 the Legislature passed an act: "To regulate money for the tolls to make them conform to the Federal Standard of coin in the United States."

[14]*Lexington Observer & Reporter,* March 14, 1848.

islature to purchase stock in the turnpike companies which greatly improved the finances. In 1851, the State Legislature fixed the rates of all turnpike companies in which the state was a stockholder, and these rates[15] were generally accepted as the standard for all turnpike companies throughout central Kentucky.

Rates of toll were determined by the wear on the road. Tolls were charged to keep the road in repair, and, consequently, each animal or vehicle was taxed in proportion as it damaged the roadbed. Cattle were taxed eight times as heavily as sheep and according to the tariff of 1851, hogs were taxed twice as much as sheep. Wagons and carts with narrow tires cut grooves in the macadamized roads, so most of the turnpike companies passed rules allowing a much lower rate for vehicles with a broad tread. These broad tires rolled the road and were actually a benefit to the turnpike.

It is to be understood that tolls were to be paid at each toll-gate or toll-house, and these were usually stationed five miles apart, with one just outside the city

---

[15]For every horse, mule, and rider 5c
For a horse, mule, jack, led or driven 3c
For each head of cattle 2c
For each head of hogs ....½c
For each head of sheep ....¼c
For each vehicle, drawn by one horse or mule 10c
For each vehicle, drawn by two horses, mules, or oxen 20c
For each pleasure carriage or hackney coach, two horses 25c
For same with four horses or mules 30c
For each sleigh, drawn by one or two horses, or mules 15c
For each wagon, drawn by three horses, mules, or oxen 30c
For same drawn by four animals 50c
For same drawn by five animals 60c
For same drawn by six animals 75c
For each stage-coach having seats within for six 35c
For same for nine passengers 55c
For same with twelve passengers 75c
For each additional passenger over four 2c

limits of each town or village. As for example, a man living seven miles from a town or city would travel one and one-half miles to the first "gate," where his toll would be prorated on the distance he had traveled,[16] being a part of the distance between the two "gates." Then at the next "gate" he would have to pay the full amount of toll, and on the return trip the same procedure followed which made traveling over the turnpikes an expensive item.

An individual traveling on any of the turnpikes or roads in the Bluegrass was not liable for toll so long as he did not pass a "gate" or toll-house.[17] Families living in the country often had an arrangement with the managers of the toll-gates or officials of the turnpike companies to pay their tolls at the end of each month, or some other stated period. Damaging the toll-house or sign board, failure to pay toll, or going around the toll-gate subjected the user of the road to a ten-dollar fine. Unfamiliar persons going through the toll-gate[18] were required by the keeper to state on oath the distance traveled on the road, the number contained in any drove of stock or whatever else was necessary to obtain the correct amount of toll, and the failure to comply resulted in a ten-dollar fine before any magistrate.

[16]Joseph How *vs.* Maysville & Lexington Turnpike Co., Kentucky Reports, B. Monroe, Vol. 14, p. 427, Summer, 1854.
[17]Lexington & Georgetown Turnpike Co. *vs.* W. B. Redd, Fayette Circuit Court, file 1840, April 7, 1840.
[18]The job of toll-gate keeper was often looked upon as a sinecure, with comfortable homes and a fair income. Here at the "gate" was collected the news and gossip of the road; news of lost stock; accounts of strangers passing, and other bits of information. Many a fat hen, bushel of apples, or choice basket of vegetables passed the friends of the gate-keeper, and this, to some extent, accounted for many of the turnpike companies declaring little or no dividends.

The turnpike companies, as owners of the roads and toll-houses, or "gates," often leased these annually for a stated amount of money, and all that the "toll-gatherer" collected belonged to him.[19]   On the other hand, a man and wife would be employed to tend "gate."   When the toll-house was leased, the pole or "pike" was kept down all night, but when the gate-keepers were employed, the pole was raised about ten-thirty and "was free the rest of the night."   Usually an Irish couple tended "gate"— the "old lady" keeping the "gate" while the "old man" worked the road, using his dump cart to keep sections of the road in repair, by hauling loose rock[20] and dumping in the holes.

When the "gate" was tended by employees of a company the free period lasted from ten-thirty in the evening until five or five-thirty the next morning, except in the tobacco-hauling season or during some holiday, court day, or circus. At other times, the poles or "pikes" were kept down, and only raised during the passing of a vehicle or horse and rider. Some accounts relate attempts to rush the "gate" while the pole was raised and the successful results, but in many cases a person would have

[19]Toll-house No. 5 at the Kentucky River, on the Lexington-Harrodsburg & Perryville Turnpike was leased to Thomas L. Cogar for $500 annually, and the ferry at the same place for $400 a year, in 1855. Thomas L. Cogar *vs.* Irvine & Hawkins, Fayette Circuit Court, file 1302, June 15, 1856.

[20]The specifications called for "all rocks to be knapped fine so as to pass through a ring 3 inches in diameter." This was done by means of the "knapping hammer," a simple contrivance of steel, round as an apple, weighing about a pound and with a hole through the center for the insertion of a hickory handle. Laborers were paid by the "perch" or "rod" for knapping the rock, which was piled in long narrow rows by the side of the turnpike.

"the pole pulled down on him, taking the top of a buggy off" or "knocking a man from his horse."

One story is related of a wealthy Fayette County land owner, noted for his miserliness, who would ride his horse almost to town, where the first toll-gate was reached, then he would dismount, hitch his horse, and walk the remainder of the distance into town. After attending to his customary business, he would walk back to the toll-house, mount his horse, and ride home feeling delighted that he had saved the "dogged toll fare." Other instances were common where attempts were made to dodge or "shun" the toll-gate, by taking a detour over an unimproved road or a private lane.[21] When the Lexington and Lancaster turnpike was macadamized and toll-gates erected, there were some who refused to pay toll, and opened a parallel route nearby, which was as free as it was rough. It became known as the "Shun Road," which name it bears today.

There were various exemptions on the turnpikes, according to the will and pleasure of the president and directors of the company owning the road, but most of them permitted preachers and funerals[22] to pass and repass free of charge. One road had this rule in force: "All wagons and carts whose wheels shall exceed eight

---

[21]Rev. H. W. Pierson, one time president of Cumberland College, Princeton, Kentucky, recites instances of these roads he encountered while traveling through central Kentucky: "At various points along the 'pike' as it was universally called, I saw tracks leading off into the woods, and was told that they were known as 'shunpikes,' and that some people in traveling would take these and go through the woods around the toll-gates, in order to avoid paying toll." Pierson, p. 27.

[22]Many instances are related of farmers and travelers, who, seeing a funeral, would whip up their horse and fall in with the procession, and pass nonchalantly through the "gate" free of toll.

inches in breadth shall pass and repass the gates free of toll, and no tolls shall be collected from any person or persons passing or repassing from one part of his farm to another, or to and from a mill, or to and from any place of worship, funeral, military training, elections, or from any student or child going to and from any school or seminary of learning, or from persons and witnesses going to and returning from courts, or any wagon or carriage loaded with the property of the United States, or military stores belonging to the United States."

Some of the turnpike companies exempted a man from tolls when he hauled coal for his own consumption, or would make a reduced price for a team and wagon when it returned empty from market. Plank roads were not used to much extent in Kentucky, because of the abundance of rock in every locality. The plank roads[23] in use were "at least eight feet broad, and covered with plank not less than two and one-half inches thick, with suitable turnouts at convenient places."

While the toll-gate system was largely responsible for the excellent turnpikes in the Bluegrass, there were many who thought the rates entirely too high for the service rendered. "It is a luxury to drive, and also an expense, as one will discover before he passes through many toll-gates," reported James Lane Allen in his *Bluegrass Region of Kentucky.*

Tollage was not uniform on all the roads, and the people complained and grew dissatisfied in many sections. Stirring editorials began to appear in the Blue-

---

[23]Being alternately wet and dry, the plank rotted rapidly, and at best did not last more than five years and sometimes only two.

grass papers demanding that tolls be charged according to the condition of the road.[24] In the early eighties, the feeling grew more intense against the "hated toll-gatherers." "Of all the clogging relics of old fogyism which stops the wheels of progress in Kentucky today—the turnpike toll is perhaps the most glaring." "Free roads, free markets" were the demands of the people and these to be maintained by the public tax.

The editor of the *Lexington Daily Transcript,* February 24, 1882, well expressed the sentiment of a large number of the people: "Such absurd restrictions as the toll-roads are utterly too medieval for a rejuvenated Kentucky." The agitation for free roads began in 1890 by the people and through the press. The majority of the people, or "free turnpikers," favored free roads, while a number opposed the roads being free because the purchasing and upkeep would increase taxation.

During Governor Bradley's administration, beginning in 1896, a certain element of people rebelled against the toll-gates on the public roads. This lawless element, or, as they styled themselves, "turnpike regulators," issued warnings to the toll-gate keepers to collect no more tolls. When these warnings were not heeded, the toll-gate houses were raided and burned, the "gates" cut down, and occasional horsewhippings administered the toll-takers. Notwithstanding the efforts of the Governor and other officials of the state, the lawlessness continued

---

[24]The "free turnpikers" charged that the toll roads were managed "solely with references to securing returns upon the capital invested and without regard to the interests of the people."

and the fear of the "night riders" was felt in many sections of the Bluegrass.

Groups gathered in communities and formed themselves into clans under a leader. These armed bands rode around the country under cover of darkness with the war cries "Free roads" and "Down with the toll-gates!" The most serious outbreaks occurred in Washington, Anderson, Marion, Mercer, Franklin, Woodford, and Jessamine counties, where nearly all the toll-houses were burned and the "gates" cut into pieces and pitched over on the side of the road. Whole sections of some turnpikes were abandoned by their owners, with no one to look after them or collect toll.

The spirit of the "toll-gate raiders," or night riders, was reflected in the note which William Mattingly, of Mercer County, found tacked on the front door of his toll-house early one morning in December, 1896:

"TOLE GATE RAIDERS NOTICE

"We ask you Not to collect no more tole, you must Not collect one cent if you do we are a Going to Destroy your House with fire are Denamite so you must Not collect No more tole at all. We Don't want to do this but we want a Free Road and are agoing to have it, if we have to Kill and Burn up everything. Collect No more Tole we mean what we say, so fair warning to you."

Other similar or stronger warnings appeared on the doors of many of the toll-houses throughout the Bluegrass, threatening to take the lives of the president and directors of the turnpike companies and to burn and dynamite their personal property. Roland Curd, the keeper of a "gate" on the Harrodsburg-Perryville turnpike, was aroused from his bed at the point of a pistol and forced "to get his axe and cut the pole in three pieces," the raiders curtly telling him to "cook his breakfast with the wood!"

In another instance, the "turnpike regulators" captured Thomas Hunter, the keeper of the "gate" on the Frankfort-Owenton road, and moved Hunter and his family, with their furniture, outside and set fire to the toll-house and watched it burn. Hunter was so frightened, he would not testify against any of the raiders or help identify them. This was the case in many other instances.

In Mercer County, feelings reached a high pitch when two of the toll-gate keepers lost their lives in defending the rights of the people and property of the stockholders. The condition of affairs was very much the same as in the days of the Ku Klux outrages throughout Kentucky. This reign of lawless violence continued well into 1897, when it seemed the "night riders were determined to make way with all the toll-gates in this part of the state."

To Anderson County goes the credit of bringing in the first arrests and indictments against six of the raiders.[25] Other counties soon followed with similar steps, and this lawlessness was finally suppressed by the

---

[25] *Morning Herald*, Lexington, April 19, 1897.

strong arm of the law. To settle matters, the counties purchased the stockholders' interests in the turnpikes within their borders, at greatly reduced prices.[26] By 1900 practically all the "gates" in central Kentucky were abolished, and the roads made free to travelers.

To the present generation, to whom toll-gates are almost unknown, a study of this archaic system affords novel entertainment, helping one to realize something of one of the serious questions of public economies of four and five decades ago.

---

[26]The prices paid for the principal turnpikes of Fayette County varied from fifteen hundred to two thousand dollars per mile, exclusive of the toll-houses. One of the prominent roads—the Maysville & Lexington Turnpike Company, through its president, W. W. Baldwin, sold to Fayette County its road, 8.19 miles for $15,555. Fayette County Court, Deed Book 115, p. 226, November 27, 1897.

CHAPTER XV

LAST DAYS OF THE STAGE

BY the middle of the summer of 1865, the attention of travelers was directed to the announcement of the Kentucky Stage Company: "We are happy to inform the traveling public that we are again running regular stages, and will make all connections as per schedule." This resumption of regular coach travel was welcomed with much satisfaction by the users of the stage lines after the years of irregular service caused by the war. Soldiers of both armies were still returning home and the stages were convenient conveyances to interior towns and remote rural sections.

But the stages, like everything else, had suffered the inevitable deterioration of the great struggle. Poor equipment, bad roads, and the recklessness of drivers resulted in accidents and suits for damages.

On the morning of October 12, 1865, Joseph Smith, driver of the coach of the Kentucky Stage Company on the Mt. Sterling-Lexington route, stopped the stage, near the New Zion Meeting House in Montgomery County, to fix the rubber block which had slipped out of the brake. While doing so, the horses became frightened and ran away, carrying the only passenger, Mrs. Louisa French, in the lurching vehicle. The team, generally regarded by other drivers as "very wild," galloped down the hill at full speed. After repeated screams for help, Mrs. French "jumped out while the horses were running like thunder"[1] and sustained many bruises and a "concussion of the spinal cord." A mile and a half down the road, the team stopped after knocking down a telegraph pole and smashing the vehicle against a rock fence.

Mrs. French sued the Kentucky Stage Company for ten thousand dollars and the record of this litigation sheds certain light upon the operation of the stage-coach business. There was evidence that the stage proprietors "have a competent mechanic in Lexington whose business it is to examine every day the stage-coaches running on the road and to keep them in good running order." This "wood workman of the stage lines" testified he had inspected the particular vehicle involved in the accident before it left on the run and found the shoe block or brake in good order. "The brake or rubber blocks, the axle points, and thorough braces," said he, "are the most important and difficult parts of a stage to keep in repair."[2]

Mrs. French charged negligence in the use of a "wild and untractable team," and the coach, which was in a worn-out condition, dangerous to travelers, and, as she told the jury, "a very shacklin' affair." After hearing the evidence, a verdict was returned in favor of the plaintiff in the sum of five hundred dollars against Silas

[1]French *vs.* Kentucky Stage Company, Montgomery Circuit Court, file 19, December 10, 1865.
[2]Deposition of William H. Lankart, of Lexington. French *vs.* Kentucky Stage Company, Montgomery Circuit Court, file 19, December 10, 1865.

Wolverton, Thomas H. Irvine, and William H. Winn, the owners of the Kentucky Stage Company.

On November 23, 1870, a stage was overturned near Greensburg and a man by the name of Roach, of the firm of Grove, Roach & Co. of Louisville, was instantly killed and five other passengers were injured.[3]

One morning the Crab Orchard-Lexington stage, while descending the treacherous hill near the ferry below Shakertown to meet the river packet Blue Wing, crashed over a cliff. As related by one who remembered this accident: "At one of the dangerous passes, where the head grew dizzy in looking on the river beneath— the descent very precipitous and the road narrow, the stage came upon a short curve which it was difficult to pass with safety. Just as the driver had brought his lead horses as close into the hill as possible, to carry the coach clear of the chasm of the curve, the horses took fright and dashing furiously to the opposite side plunged headlong over the precipice, carrying coach, driver, and the passengers with them. Down, down they went through the air and tree tops, until the coach came to a sort of natural bench on the side of the hill; the wheels were broken to pieces and flew off in different directions; the coach bed crushed; the passengers stunned to insensibility; the wheel horses killed, and the driver thrown with violence from his box."

The coach, divested of its wheels, rolled over and over and over until it was stopped by some obstruction, and was reduced to a complete wreck. All the passengers

---

[3]*Kentucky Advocate*, Danville, November 25, 1870.

were injured, but all recovered; most of them were able
to proceed on their journey the next day—but the wonder
was that any should have escaped death. Bob White,
the driver, was not seriously injured; but as a result of
the accident "his hair was entirely gray, though it was
black when he left Crab Orchard."

During this period, however, a problem suddenly confronted operators of public vehicles which was far more
vexatious than accidents or lawsuits. The terrifying men-
ace of robbery and violence hovered for the first time
over the stage-coaches of the Bluegrass state. The wide-
spread lawlessness of war days had not wholly subsided.
Some of the guerrilla bands that had galloped over the
highways for four long, tempestuous years were not
yet ready to resume the pursuits of peace and the habits
of good citizenship. Armed men of sinister appearance
still prowled the forests and held rendezvous in old,
familiar hiding places.

As the Louisville-Taylorsville stage rumbled along
between Elk Creek and Taylorsville on the afternoon of
December 1, 1870, two men darted from the woods beside the road and with cocked pistols commanded the
mail stage to halt. James Mudd, the driver, hardly realized their object, but upon the "earnest solicitation of the
great revolvers," the horses were checked. The coach
contained Dr. Allen of Louisville, Mr. Hoagland of
Taylorsville, and John Martin, stage contractor. The
bandits immediately disarmed the driver, and after rifling
his pockets of about two hundred dollars, began a search
of the passengers and each of them was compelled to

wait his turn to be robbed. After their deed had been accomplished, "the daring daylight robbers" mounted their horses and disappeared through the woods, "with their booty, amounting to about $800 in money and watches."[4]

Encouraged, no doubt, by the success of this hold-up, the robbery of stage-coaches during the next decade or more became a favorite activity of the criminal element. Finally, the newspapers announced that America's most famous outlaw and highwayman—Jesse James—was at work in Kentucky, and it was not long before tourists to Mammoth Cave[5] were able to verify this rumor.

On the afternoon of Friday, September 3, 1880, the stage-coach left the Cave for Cave City, loaded with sightseers who, at this season of the year, came from all parts of the country to view the great national wonder. The road ran through a lonely rocky region with dense woods skirting much of the way, and just as the coach reached the most desolate point about dusk two men, mounted but unmasked, emerged from the forest and covered the driver and passengers, seven men and one woman, with their pistols. When the coach[6] came to a halt, the highwaymen curtly ordered the passengers to "Come out of the stage." And, looking through the open windows into the muzzles of the long, black revolvers,

---

[4]*Kentucky Advocate,* Danville, December 9, 1870.

[5]One of the routes to the Cave, and the one used by a large majority of the visitors, was by way of the Louisville & Nashville railroad to Cave City, and thence by stage-coach to the Cave, ten miles distant. There were two lines of stages. Andy McCoy operated the "old line" and D. L. Graves, proprietor of the cave hotel, operated the "opposition line."

[6]This coach was the old favorite "John A. Bell" of the "old line," and had formerly been in service between Lexington and Georgetown.

they lost no time in obeying the command, as a harsh, impatient voice urged them to "hurry up." Miss Lizzie Rountree, daughter of Judge R. H. Rountree of Lebanon, however, was permitted to remain in the stage,[7] but the seven men were quickly lined up along the side of the road. Then, talking pleasantly as he worked, one of the bandits proceeded to empty their pockets, reaping a rich harvest of valuables—Judge Rountree gave up a handsome gold watch worth $200.00 and $55.00 in cash; J. E. Craig, Jr., of Lawrenceville, Ga., $670.00; S. W. Shelton of Calhoun, Tenn., $50.00; S. H. Frohlechstein of Mobile, Ala., $23.00; George M. Paisley of Pittsburgh, $33.00; W. G. Welsh of Pittsburgh, $5.00 in cash and a fine gold watch; and Miss Rountree lost several valuable diamond rings. The only passenger who escaped the general loot was Phil Rountree, a relative of the judge, who slipped his wallet and watch under the seat as he left the stage.

When every pocket had been emptied, the bandit ordered his victims to re-enter the coach and move on. Then in parting, he astonished them by apologizing for his rudeness, saying "his business demanded it," wished them better luck next time,[8] and in an effort at consolation informed them that he and his accomplice had robbed the out-going stage to the Cave, taking upwards of $700.00 from Mr. Croghan, one of its owners.[9]

---

[7]There are several conflicting accounts of this robbery, and one has it that Judge Rountree, at that time of advanced age, was allowed to remain in the coach. Letter from Judge Rountree's grandson, R. Harry Ray, to the author, April 16, 1934.

[8]Recollections of Dr. A. H. Merrifield—*Kentucky Standard*, Bardstown, July 19, 1906.

[9]Buel—pp. 390–397.

Judge Rountree immediately published descriptions of the highwaymen and, with Governor Luke Blackburn, offered rewards for their capture and conviction. Several weeks later, a man named T. J. Hunt was arrested in Ohio County and brought back to Cave City. He was held in the Glasgow jail eighteen months under indictment of the Barren Circuit Court for "robbing the stage which runs and conveys passengers from Cave City in the County of Barren to the Mammoth Cave in the County of Edmonson, and that he and another man whose name is unknown to this jury, with force of arms, did unlawfully, wilfully, and feloniously with drawn pistols rob the passengers of the stage against their will of about one thousand dollars in money, several gold watches, and two diamond rings . . ."[10]

On this trial, Hunt vehemently denied any knowledge of the robbery, but the stage driver and several passengers testified that he resembled one of the highwaymen, and the jury returned a verdict of guilty and fixed his punishment "at three years confinement in the State Penitentiary." Then, while Hunt awaited sentence in the Barren County jail, Bob Ford, in St. Joseph, Missouri, sent a bullet crashing through the brain of his old companion in crime, the notorious Jesse James, and news came that on his lifeless body was found the gold watch[11] of Judge Rountree, with the presentation inscription from Hon. J. Proctor Knott, member of Congress from the

---

[10]Commonwealth of Kentucky *vs.* T. J. Hunt, Barren Circuit Court, March Term, 1882.

[11]This watch and key were recovered by the Rountree family, and are worn daily by R. Harry Ray, of Owensboro, a grandson of Judge Rountree.

fourth district of Kentucky, and the diamond rings of Miss Lizzie Rountree.

A picture of the dead outlaw bore a striking resemblance to the prisoner, Hunt. From affidavits submitted to Governor Blackburn, it was shown that Jesse James and Bill Ryan, then serving a twenty-five year sentence in the Missouri penitentiary for train robbery, were the outlaws who robbed the Mammoth Cave stage, and on May 1, 1882, the Governor pardoned Hunt,[12] after he had been imprisoned nearly two years in jail. His case is still one of the most remarkable instances of mistaken identity on record; yet his conviction was, at least partly, the result of his refusal to disclose his whereabouts on the day of the robbery. The theory was that "he was in a scrape somewhere else," but it is certain that he had nothing to do with the crime for which he was convicted.[13]

The Jesse James exploit and other holdups throughout the country greatly unnerved the people and threw them into a state of uneasiness and provoked sharp criticism in local newspapers. "If sheriffs throughout the country would promptly and fearlessly arrest bad men who have violated the laws; if judges would promptly and fearlessly prosecute them," said the *Lexington Observer & Reporter*,[14] "*then* fifty per cent of the lawlessness

[12]Executive Journal, 1882, p. 85. Kentucky State Historical Society, Frankfort.

[13]Recollections of Judge Harry Gorin, who defended Hunt at Glasgow. *Courier-Journal*, Louisville, March 29, 1914.

[14]February 16, 1881. For several years previous, Kentucky newspapers carried proclamations offering rewards to break up this unbridled crime. The *Kentucky Yoeman*, March 17, 1871, carried notices of rewards totaling $3,800 for persons guilty of robbery, murder, rape, and lynchings.

that is now disgracing our land would come to a sudden and effective halt."

Close on to the robbery of the Mammoth Cave stage came the robbery of the Columbia-Campbellsville stage-coach on November 20, 1882, as the stage was passing a thick wood, some two or three miles from Campbellsville. Robert Borders was on the seat manipulating the reins. Inside the coach were three passengers—Hon. Moses H. Rhorer, member of the Legislature, Joe Edwards of Moulton, Iowa, and Mrs. Dodds of Columbia, Indiana. As the stage came rumbling along the dusty road just at daybreak, a man wearing a black leather mask over his face suddenly emerged from the woods, pistol in hand, and commanded the driver to stop. The order was obeyed, and the robber threw open the door of the coach and ordered the men to get out, which they did, but Edwards found the opportunity to thrust his pocketbook under the seat of the coach. "Your money or your life!" commanded the highwayman to Edwards, who replied that he had no money. "How do you travel without money?" inquired the bandit.

Edwards replied that he had paid his fare already to the next town and it was none of his business, to which the highwayman demanded, "Are you telling the truth?" and with that, rudely jerked out his valuable watch and chain. The other male passenger was then robbed of his watch and wallet, which contained only a small amount of money and some valuable personal papers. Rhorer pleaded with the bandit to give him back his papers, but the man behind the leather vizor refused, saying, "There

isn't a damn bit of accommodation about a highway robber." After robbing the woman passenger, the mail
sacks were next rifled. Then, lining the passengers up
against the stage, he forced the driver to unscrew the
tap on the front wheel, and, putting this in his pocket,
suddenly darted into the dense woods. The stage-coach
was unable to proceed, and the victims of the robbery
were forced to walk to Campbellsville, where the news
of the holdup was spread and alarm given, but no trace
of the highwayman was ever found.[15]

However, as one reads the records, it will appear
that personal hazards had little or nothing to do with the
gradual, though steady, decline of the stage-coaches following the Civil War. The real cause was the coming
of a new, more rapid, and more comfortable means of
transportation—the railroads. Stage-coach lines in the
Bluegrass and the central portions of the state were the
first to feel the effect of this new competition.

The Louisville & Nashville railroad, one of the three
principal lines of the Bluegrass today, was chartered
under the laws of Kentucky, March 4, 1850,[16] but the
main stem from Louisville to Geddes was not opened to
traffic until November 5, 1859, and the Bluegrass lines
were of still later construction. In similar manner, the
lines of the Chesapeake & Ohio and Southern railroads,
including both those which are owned and those which
are operated by these systems today, were relatively unimportant prior to 1865.[17] The period between 1865

---

[15]*Lebanon News & Standard*, November 23, 1882.
[16]Clark—*The Beginning of the L. & N.*, p. 22.
[17]Poor—*Manual of Railroads*, p. 665.

and 1885 witnessed the construction of many miles of track in the Bluegrass.

But for a long time the stage lines fought hard for their share of the travel, calling attention to the fact that "forty-five railroad accidents have taken place in this country since the commencement of the year, in which sixty-one persons have been killed."[18] Henceforth the main source of usefulness of the stage-coaches lay in serving the towns in the interior of Kentucky, running as feeders from the towns through which the "iron horse" passed. One notable example of this was the stage connection which met the trains at Nicholasville and then conveyed the train passengers by stage-coach to "Danville, Crab Orchard, Somerset, Mt. Sterling, and all other interior towns."[19]

The railroads of this period advertised as part of their schedules service to points off the railroad, by the use of stage travel, and through tickets on the railroad and stages could be purchased at the railroad office. The Louisville & Frankfort and the Lexington & Frankfort railroads, the year following the war, informed the traveling public of the connection "at Lexington by rail and stage for Nicholasville, Danville, Harrodsburg, Lancaster, Stanford, Richmond, and all interior towns" and also a stage "connecting at Payne's Depot for Georgetown; at Midway for Versailles; and at Christianburg for Shelbyville."[20]

---

[18]*Lexington Observer & Reporter*, March 8, 1865.
[19]*Ibid.*, February 15, 1866.
[20]*Union Standard*, Lexington, April 6, 1866.

With the extension of the railroad lines throughout central Kentucky, one stage-coach route after another was abandoned.[21] Even as late as 1875, some of the stage roads were pretty bad, judging from the account related in the *Interior Journal*, Stanford:[22]

> "Larkin Edge says a man can't drive a stage from this place to Somerset and be a Christian. The mud is so deep and the road so long that a Christian man would lose all patience with himself, his horses, and his coach before he got to Waynesburg. After he reached that point, Job himself would get out of heart before he reached his destination."

The year 1885 saw only two stage-coach routes centering at Lexington. These were under the ownership of the veteran stager, Thomas H. Irvine, and extended to Richmond and Irvine, and to Versailles and Lawrenceburg. When the Kentucky Central Railroad announced in the local papers that effective "January 1, 1889, train No. 4 will run to Richmond, Ky.," the death knell of stage-coaching was sounded in the Bluegrass region of central Kentucky, and the last stage ran out of Lexington a short time after the Richmond train started—January 1, 1889.

Thus closed the golden era of stage-coach travel in the Bluegrass.[23] With it passed the usefulness of the old

---

[21]The last stage-coach ran from Lexington to Harrodsburg, July 22, 1877.

[22]*Interior Journal*, Stanford, February 5, 1875.

[23]There were several smaller lines, however, that continued to operate in Kentucky for some years; the Lebanon-Springfield two-horse stage owned and operated by Charlie Moore, ran with some degree of success until 1910, and the Monticello-Burnside, owned and operated by Charles

stage-coaches, those vehicles of romance, anecdote, and color which had served the people of Kentucky for almost three generations, and were looked upon as indispensable to the growth and progress of the country.

With the passing of the stage-coaches—drivers, hostlers, owners, and those connected with this means of travel, were thrown out of work, which is invariably the price of progress. Nearly every driver seemed more or less fascinated with his chosen profession, sitting on the "box," and, when once in the business, it appeared as if he could never retire from it. There was evidently some sort of charm about staging that could not be resisted. All of the old stage drivers have long since passed to their reward, but they have left behind them many descendants to perpetuate their names and deeds.

And now—the old Concord or Troy coach, painted in brilliant colors perhaps, bearing the name of some prominent personage, drawn by four prancing horses, with its proud and arrogant driver is gone and forgotten. The old stage-coach! Had it a tongue to speak—what forgotten tales it could tell—what secrets, social, political, and commercial, it could divulge. What recollections it could revive—what a strange and eventful past it could relate.

But the old stage-coach has ended its career—made its last trip. What remains of this relic of bygone days stands beneath some old shed or wayside inn—weather-beaten, storm-broken, and forlorn. One who loved the good old days sadly wrote:

H. Burton ran as late as April, 1912, being the last stage-coach in Kentucky.

"We hear no more the clanging hoof,
  And the stage-coach rattling by;
  For the steam king rules the traveled world,
  And the old pike's left to die."

. . . And so, the old stage-coach, the "mercury" of
its day, through heat, cold, rain, snow, and mud served
the people of Kentucky as an adequate means of conveyance, until it was superseded by the "iron horse," and,
not being able to compete with this swifter and more
commodious means of travel, is now only a fading memory.

ADDENDA

APPENDIX A

TAVERNS AND INNS OF CENTRAL KENTUCKY, 1800–1820

Postlethwait's Tavern—John Postlethwait, Lexington.
Bell's Tavern—Jos. W. Hendrick, Glasgow.
Buckhanon's Tavern—Henry Buckhanon, Paris.
Columbian Inn—Asa Wilgus, Lexington.
Travellers Hall—Robert Bradley, Lexington.
Watkins' Inn—Henry Watkins, Versailles.
Indian Queen Tavern—Richard Davenport, Danville.
Milner's Tavern—Benjamin Milner, Richmond.
Lebanon Inn—D. Jennings, Lebanon.
Sign of Globe Inn—Thos. J. Crawford, Perryville.
Sign of Green Tree Tavern—Wm. Palmateer, Lexington.
Wickliffe's Tavern—Chas. Wickliffe, Lexington.
Mason's Inn—Peter Mason, Mt. Sterling.
Kentucky Hotel—Cuthbert Banks, Lexington.
Spread Eagle Tavern—Dr. Roberts, Maysville.
Mt. Sterling Hotel—Joseph Simpson, Mt. Sterling.
Old Ironsides Tavern—Elijah Noble, Lexington.
Brennan's Tavern—J. Brennan (also Postlethwait), Lexington.
Weisiger's Tavern—Capt. Daniel Weisiger, Frankfort.
Sign of the Buffalo Tavern—John Downing, Lexington.
Traveller's Hall—Andrew Biggs, Mt. Sterling.
Eagle Tavern—Wm. Satterwhite, Lexington.
Sign of the Ship Tavern—Luke Usher, Lexington.
Cross Keys Tavern—Middleton Bros., near Shelbyville.
Bush Tavern—Philip Bush, Frankfort.
Chambers Tavern and Ferry—James Chambers, Limestone
(Maysville).
Moore's Inn—Zedekiah Moore, Paris.
Taylor's Inn—Richard Taylor, Frankfort.
Sign of Square and Compass Tavern—Sam'l January, Limestone.
Indian Queen Tavern—George Webb, Winchester.
Langhore's Tavern—Capt. Maurice Langhore, Paris.

Swan Tavern—John Jones, Cynthiana.
Sign of Sheaf of Wheat Tavern—Thos. T. Tibbaits, Lexington.
Cross-Keys Inn—Hugh Duffine, Millersburg.
Watkins' Inn—Isaac Watkins, Shelbyville.
Wagnon's Inn—John P. Wagnon, Lexington.
Love House—Thomas Love, Frankfort.
Netherland's Inn—Benj. Netherland, Nicholasville.
Goddess of Liberty Tavern—John Current, Ruddell's Mills.
Eagle Tavern—E. Stapp, Georgetown.
Traveller's Inn—Anthony Sheriff, Millersburg.
Landscape Inn—O. S. Timberlake, Greensburg.
Talbott's Hotel—Daniel Talbott, Millersburg.
Sign of Rising Sun Tavern—Wm. C. Connett, May's Lick.
Boone's Tavern—Jacob Boone, Maysville.
Russell's Tavern—Jos. Russell, Paris and Winchester Road.
Clemen's House—Jeremiah Clemens, Danville.
Miller's Tavern—Col. John F. Miller, Richmond.

PRINCIPAL TAVERNS OF CENTRAL KENTUCKY, 1820–1860*

Pratt Tavern—cor. Court and Broadway, Georgetown, 1820–60.
Boswell Tavern—Hart Boswell, Newtown, 1840.
Mayo's Tavern—Wm. Mayo, Versailles, 1835.
Golden Eagle Tavern—John Roberts, Bardstown, 1834.
Foster's Tavern—Thomas Foster, Jett, 1832.
Cole's Tavern—Nugent's Cross Roads, Woodford County, 1830–40.
Eagle House—John C. Orrick, Lexington, 1833.
Stone Tavern—Bardstown, 1820–50.
Burnt Tavern—James Smith, Bryantsville, 1830–50.
Coleman & Humphrey's Tavern—Williamstown, 1837–40.
Kendall Tavern—Wm. H. Kendall, Frankfort, 1843.
Sublett Inn—Shyrock's Ferry, Woodford County, 1840.

---

*This list of inns and taverns was compiled from newspaper advertisements, suits, old letters, and other documents. Whenever known, the name of the proprietor and the date of operation is given.

Buford's Hotel—Nicholasville, 1840–50.

Keene Hotel—Keene, Jessamine County, 1835–55.

Lucas Tavern—Rich'd Lucas, "Slickaway," Fayette County, 1860.

Perkins' Tavern—E. Perkins, Lexington, 1839.

Watkins' Tavern—F. H. Watkins, Versailles, 1826.

Sign of Rising Sun Tavern—John L. Moore, Frankfort, 1829.

Sign of Bell Tavern—A. S. Moore, Paris, 1827.

Calvert's Tavern—S. Calvert, New Liberty, Owen County, 1827.

Union Hall Tavern—John Ward, Winchester, 1820–25.

Porter's Inn—R. W. Porter, Lexington, 1826.

Sanford's Inn—J. P. Sanford, 8 miles east of New Castle and
8 miles west of Frankfort, 1820–30.

Sign of Golden Bell Tavern—John Dudley, Winchester, 1823.

Eagle Tavern—William Hardin, Shelbyville, 1820-23.

Shelby Hotel—J. Hendley, Lexington, 1826.

Cross-Keys Inn—Benj. Ayres, Lexington, 1820.

Eagle Tavern—G. Pickett, Cynthiana, 1822.

Brenham's Tavern—Robt. Brenham, Shelbyville, 1825.

Sign of American Eagle Tavern—John Buzzard, Lexington,
1825.

Sign of Golden Bell Tavern—John Williams, Crab Orchard,
1827.

Ewalt Tavern—Samuel Ewalt, near Cynthiana, 1830–40.

Candy's Tavern—J. Candy, Lexington, 1839–40 (later Mc-
Cracken's).

Indian Queen Hotel—Henry Timberlake, lower Blue Licks, 1823.

Golden Bee Hive Tavern—S. Buckner, Shelbyville, 1822.

Eagle Tavern—Wm. M. Samuel, Millersburg, 1823.

Cross-Keys Inn—Joel Wallingsford, Lexington, 1822.

Henry and McGirk's Tavern—"Slickaway," Fayette County,
1848.

Washington Hotel—R. Nelson, Maysville, 1839.

Lexington Hotel—J. Keiser, Lexington, 1839.

Peel's Tavern—Samuel Peel, Lexington, 1837.

Kelley's Inn—Joseph Kelley, Winchester, 1849.

Farmer's House—H. S. Hastings, Shelbyville, 1847.

Washington Hall—J. S. Murphy, Shelbyville, 1849.

Oldham House—J. T. Burton, Frankfort, 1852.

Mansion House—Ben and John T. Luckett, Frankfort, 1852.

Redding House—M. Redding, Shelbyville, 1852.

Penn House—Mrs. Susan Penn, Frankfort, 1855.

Georgetown Hotel—Nathan Jones and James Barkley, Georgetown, 1849.

Farmers and Traders Hotel—Thos. B. Megowan, Lexington, 1849.

Shelton's Hotel—Col. Medley Shelton, Versailles, 1847.

Martin's Tavern—Edward Martin, Millersburg, 1811–42.

Lee House (Hill House)—Peter Lee, Maysville, 1840–55.

Moreland's Tavern—William Moreland, Bourbon County, 1837–60.

Delph's Tavern—Jeremiah Delph, Delphton (Donerail), Fayette County, 1837.

Chiles' Tavern—Rich'd Chiles, Chilesburg, Fayette County 1835–50.

Hammett's Tavern and Ferry—R. E. Hammett and Captain Samuel Fitch, Camp Nelson, Jessamine County, 1837.

Colbyville Tavern—Colby Taylor, Lexington-Winchester Road, 1840–60.

White Ball Tavern—Jack Willis, Sr., Mt. Sterling-Winchester Road, 1850.

Blue Ball Tavern—Mt. Sterling-Winchester Road, 1840–58.

Bright's Inn—William Bright, near Stanford, 1825–60.

Hallock's Inn—near Hutchinson, Bourbon County, 1840–43.

Traveller's Rest—Charles C. Green, Nicholasville, 1832.

Sherman Tavern—Lexington-Cincinnati Road, Sherman, 1835–50.

McCracken's Tavern—John McCracken, Lexington, 1830–37.

Weisiger's Tavern—Daniel Weisiger, Frankfort, 1820–40.

LaFayette Coffee House—John Candy, Lexington, 1834.

Bruen House—A. S. Morrow, Lexington, 1830–40.

Bell's Tavern—William Bell, Glasgow Junction, "Three Forks," 1830–58.

Kinkead Tavern—A. Kinkead, Versailles, 1825–30.

Sign of Golden Bell Tavern—T. Q. Roberts, Versailles, 1825.

Broadway House—Wm. H. Kendall, Frankfort, 1847.

Shield's House—N. S. Shields, Danville, 1844.

Sign of Bee Hive Inn—John S. Robson, Junction of Shelbyville-Harrodsburg Road, 1824–26.

Washington Hall—Thomas Q. Roberts, Harrodsburg, 1834.

Chiles' Tavern—John G. Chiles, Harrodsburg, 1840–50.

Bassell's Tavern—James Bassell, Millersburg, 1840.

Goddard's House—Mrs. Goddard, Maysville, 1835–58.

Porter's Inn—R. W. Porter, Lexington, 1826.

Owingsville Tavern—Mrs. Lightfoot, H. Owings, Owingsville, 1827.

LaFayette Temperance Hotel—John B. Higbee, Lexington, 1835.

Sign of Black Horse Tavern—James W. Henderson, 4 miles from Lexington on Frankfort Road, 1822–30.

Talbutt's Hotel—Charles Talbutt, Paris, 1838–40.

Jones Tavern Stand—John and Frank Jones, Lexington-Cincinnati Road, Scott County, 1850–55.

Getty's Tavern—John S. Getty, Lexington-Cincinnati Road, 10 miles north of Georgetown, 1854.

Preston's Tavern—Frank Preston, half-way house, Maysville-Mt. Sterling Road, 1840–50.

Forrest Retreat—Governor Metcalfe, Junction Carlisle-Maysville Road, 1825–40.

Brent House—Richard Brent, Lexington, 1844.

Browning's Tavern—Foxtown, Madison County, 1840.

Todd's Hotel—B. W. Todd (formerly J. Keiser), Lexington, 1839.

Phoenix Hotel—known as Postlethwait's, Brennan's, Keen's, Wilson's and Chiles, Lexington, 1820–60.

Blue Licks Springs Hotel—Mrs. C. A. Pryor, Blue Licks, 1839.

Sign of Genius of Liberty Tavern—Jacob Gudgel, Lawrenceburg, 1825.

Bourbon House—Alex. S. Morrow, Paris, 1840–54.
Sign of Golden Eagle Tavern—D. Caldwell, Russellville, 1825.

HOTELS OF LEXINGTON, 1864–65

Brent House—east side Mulberry Street (Limestone).
Broadway Hotel—northwest cor. Short and Broadway.
City Hotel—southwest cor. Vine and Mulberry.
Curd House—south side Vine between Upper and Mill.
Fayette House—northwest cor. Short and Mulberry.
Phoenix Hotel—southeast cor. Mulberry and Main.
Megowan Hotel—Short between Upper and Mulberry.

1875

Ashland House—13 West Short Street (Drake Hotel).
Carson House—62–64 East Short Street.
City Hotel—69 East Short Street.
Phoenix Hotel—Main and Limestone Streets.
Curd House—13 East Vine Street.
Sheppard House—221 West Short Street.
St. Nicholas—67 East Main Street.

APPENDIX B
STAGE-COACH OWNERS AND OPERATORS IN KENTUCKY, 1800–1900

Dickey & West—Milus W. Dickey and Preston West: Lexington-Cincinnati, 1838–45.
Kentucky Stage Company—Thomas H. Irvine, Silas Wolverton, William H. Winn, Augustus Rogers, M. Hayden Jouett: numerous lines in central Kentucky, 1855–65.
Edward P. Johnson & Co.—Edward P. Johnson, Philip Swigert, Jacob Swigert, John H. Hanna: numerous lines, 1835–50.
Irvine & Hawkins—Thos. H. Irvine and Cary A. Hawkins: Lexington-Crab Orchard, and others, 1852–60.
James Johnson: Lexington-Louisville, 1818–25.
John Kennedy: Lexington-Olympian Springs, Lexington-Frankfort, 1803–5.
Abner Gaines: Lexington-Cincinnati, 1818–23.

Augustus W. Gaines: Lexington-Cincinnati, 1838–42.

Charles H. Burton: Monticello-Burnside, 1890–1912.

Irvine & Field—Thos. H. Irvine and David J. Field: Paris-Maysville, and other lines, 1852–56.

Edward P. Jarman: Lexington-Estill Springs, 1850–55.

John G. Chiles: Lexington-Harrodsburg, 1834; Burnt Tavern-Danville, 1838.

Pratt & Gaines—W. Pratt and A. W. Gaines: Lexington-Cincinnati, 1836.

Witherspoon & Saffell—John Witherspoon and Joseph Saffell: Louisville-Frankfort, 1858–60; Lexington-Crab Orchard, 1856.

Griffin & McArchran—Pierce Griffin and William C. McArchran: Lexington-Louisville, and other lines, 1836–42.

McNair & Weaver—Col. Dunning R. McNair and John W. Weaver: Lexington-Louisville; Maysville-Lexington, 1836–42.

William Elder: Lexington-Danville, 1844; Lexington-Owingsville, 1842.

John S. Finley: Lexington-Cincinnati, 1842.

Crozer & Marshall—David Crozer and Alex. K. Marshall: lines out of Stanford and Danville south, 1840–55.

Robinson & Thomas—W. J. Robinson and J. H. Thomas: lines south from Harrodsburg and Somerset, 1840–50.

John C. McHatton: Lexington-Cincinnati, 1840–44.

Johnson, Weisiger & Co.—Edw. P. Johnson and Daniel Weisiger: Lexington-Louisville, 1836–40.

Irvine & Scott—Thos. H. Irvine and Silas P. Scott: Lexington-Cincinnati, and other lines in Kentucky, 1850–60.

Irvine & Berry—Thos. H. Irvine and Samuel Berry: Maysville-Mt. Sterling, 1850–53.

Hough, Carter & Thomas—Joseph H. Hough, Daniel F. Carter, and Samuel B. Thomas: Louisville-Elizabethtown-Nashville, 1845–55, also Louisville-Bowling Green-Nashville, 1846–55 other lines south.

Alex. K. Marshall: Lexington-Harrodsburg, 1849; Danville-Nicholasville, 1846–48.

Samuel B. Thomas: Munfordsville-Bowling Green, 1842.

Thomas C. Shouse: Lexington-Danville, 1850.

Hawkins & Co.—Cary A. Hawkins, Thos. H. Irvine, David J. Field, Joel J. Walker: Lexington-Cincinnati, 1850; Lexington-Richmond, 1852, and other lines in central Kentucky.

Wolverton & Hopkins—Silas Wolverton and Robert S. Hopkins: Maysville-Paris, 1858–60.

Pierce & Douglass: Louisville-Nashville, 1850–55.

Herndon & McHatton—Edward Herndon and James A. McHatton: Lexington-Cincinnati, 1840–42.

McConnell, Smither & Co.: Lexington-Frankfort, via Versailles, 1847.

E. M. Munford & Co.: Louisville-Bardstown-Bloomfield-Shelbyville-Harrodsburg, 1850–59.

McAtee & Eastham: Louisville-Bardstown, 1842–45.

Wolverton & Beck—Silas Wolverton and A. M. Beck: Georgetown-Lexington, 1872–76.

Weedon & Co.—O. M. and F. M. Weedon: Maysville-Mt. Sterling, 1840–46.

Irvine & Pigg—Thos. H. Irvine and Wm. W. Pigg: Lexington-Richmond-Irvine, 1883–87; Lexington-Versailles-Lawrenceburg, 1883–87.

Irvine & Wilkerson—Thos. H. Irvine and Tevis Wilkerson: Lexington-Richmond-Irvine, 1887–89; Lexington-Versailles, 1887–89.

Andy McCoy: Mammoth Cave-Cave City, 1870–83.

Joseph Thomas: Danville-Harrodsburg-Perryville, 1875.

Culbertson & Case: Maysville-Lexington, 1836–39.

Davidson & Co.: Springfield-Lebanon-Campbellsville-Glasgow, 1855.

Charles Moore: Lebanon-Springfield, 1900–10.

John D. Hastings: Louisville-Shelbyville, 1849.

Fred Meyers: Lexington-Richmond, 1854–55.

John W. Turner: Georgetown-Newtown-Paris, 1842.

APPENDIX C

William Adair
James Allen
Len Ballard
Charlie Bean
Henry Benge
Samuel Berry
June Biggerstaff
George Borders
Lloyd Borders
Mack Borders
Robert Borders
Billy Botts
Alvin Brown
George A. Brown
Isaac Brown
James Brown
John Brown
Lewis Brown
Thomas Bruce
Joseph Bryant
Charles H. Burton
Mack Burton
James S. Carson
Miles G. Chelf
Joseph Chipman
Robert Christie
Thomas Cogswell
John Cole
John H. Curd
Samuel Curd
William Dailey

William Darby
James Darling
William Daugherty
Samuel Davis
Pete Depp
Billy Devore
John Dongan
Nelson Dorsey
Alex Douglass
Peyton Douglass
Larkin Edge
Strong Edmiston
David Evans
Bob Fitch
Ben Fowler
William Fowler
John Goodnight
Bob Goodrich
John Griffith
Seth Griffith
Billy Hall
J. Morton Hall
William Hastings
Alex Hawkins
Cary A. Hawkins
Robert Hawkins
John W. Hazelrigg
Newt Hazelrigg
Rolly Hazelwood
Allen Herez
Overton P. Hogan

Jack Hook
Reuben Horton
John Huffman
John Ireland
Thomas H. Irvine
Ham Jones
Broadwell Keith
Alfred Kendall
Dick Kincade
Creed King
John King
Tim King
Harry Kinley
Isaac Laughlin
Hiram Lawrence
George Laws
Ben Lucas
John Martin
Joe Mays
Alonzo McClelland
William McKinley
Isham Merryman
Charlie Moore
James Mudd
Lock Mudd
Daniel Nash
Robert Nelson
Frank Parker
Thos. C. Patterson
James Payne
George Pierce
Wm. W. Pigg

Jack Reid
Turner Reid
Billy Richardson
Bob Richardson
Daniel Roberts
John Roswell
Robert Sayres
Ike Settles
John Showalter
Charles Simpson
Joseph Smith
Mose Smith
Jacob Snyder
George Sowerbray
John Stepp
James Stone
Richard Sullivan
Ben Townsend
Thos. Tyler
Harry Waller
James Waterhourd
Bob White
Billy Wilkerson
Alex Winans
Zach Wines
John Wise
James Withrow, Sr.
Lee Withrow
Silas Wolverton
William Wood
Jeff D. Young

BIBLIOGRAPHY

Allen, James Lane, *The Bluegrass Region of Kentucky*, New York, 1892.

Ambler, Charles H., *A History of Transportation in the Ohio Valley*, Glendale, Calif., 1932.

Ashe, Thomas, *Travels in America*, London, 1808.

Baker, Ira O., *Roads and Pavements*, New York, 1912.

Baird, Rev. Robert, *Emigrants and Travellers Guide to the West*, Philadelphia, 1832.

Banning, Captain William and George H., *Six Horses*, New York, 1930.

Barnes, Demas, *From the Atlantic to the Pacific Overland*, New York, 1866.

Boyd, Lucinda, *Chronicles of Cynthiana, Kentucky*, Cincinnati, 1894.

Brown, Samuel R., *The Western Gazetteer*, New York, 1817.

Buel, J. W., *The Border Outlaws: Frank and Jesse James and their Comrades in Crime*, Cincinnati, 1882.

Cassedy, Ben., *History of Louisville*, Louisville, 1852.

Chatburn, George K., *Highway and Highway Transportation*, New York, 1923.

Chevalier, Michael, *Society, Manners and Politics in the United States*, Boston, 1839.

Clark, Thomas D., *The Beginning of the L. & N.*, Louisville, 1933.

Clemens, Samuel (Mark Twain), *Roughing It*, Chicago, 1872.

Cleveland, Catharine C., *The Great Revival in the West*, Chicago, 1916.

Coffin, Levi, *Reminiscences of Levi Coffin*, Cincinnati, 1876.

Cole, Robert E., *Stage-Coach and Tavern Tales of the Old Northwest*, Cleveland, 1930.

Coleman, J. Winston, Jr., *Masonry in the Bluegrass*, Lexington, 1933.

Collins, Rich. H., *History of Kentucky*, 2 vols., Covington, 1874.

Conclin, George A., *A Book for All Travellers*, Cincinnati, 1855.

Conover, Charlotte R., *Concerning the Forefathers*, Dayton, O., 1902.

Cotterill, Robert S., *Pioneer History of Kentucky*, Cincinnati, 1917.

Coulter, E. Merton, *Civil War and Readjustment in Kentucky*, Chapel Hill, N. C., 1926.

Cramer, Zadoc, *The Navigator*, Pittsburgh, 1817.

Crocker, George C., *From the Stage Coach to the Railroad Train and the Street Car*, Boston, 1900.

Cuming, Fortesque, *Sketches of a Tour to the Western Country*, Pittsburgh, 1810.

Dana, E., *Geographical Sketch of the Western Country for Emigrants and Settlers*, Cincinnati, 1819.

Darby, William, *The Emigrants Guide to the Western and Southeastern States and Territories*, New York, 1818.

Daviess, Maria T., *History of Mercer and Boyle Counties, Kentucky*, Harrodsburg, 1924 (reprint).

Davis, Darrell H., *Geography of the Bluegrass Region of Kentucky*, Frankfort, 1927.

Dearborn, Henry A. S., *Letters on the Internal Improvement and Commerce of the West*, Boston, 1839.

Dillin, John G. W., *The Kentucky Rifle*, Washington, D. C., 1924.

Disturnell, J., *Guide through the Middle, Northern and Eastern States*, New York, 1847.

Drake, Daniel, *Pioneer Life in Kentucky*, Cincinnati, 1870.

Dunbar, Seymour, *A History of Travel in America*, 4 vols., Indianapolis, 1915.

Earle, Alice Morse, *Stage Coach and Tavern Days*, New York, 1900.

Espy, Josiah, *Tour in Kentucky and Ohio*, Cincinnati, 1871.

Fairbank, Calvin, *During Slavery Times*, Chicago, 1890.

Fearon, Henry B., *Sketches of America*, London, 1818.

Felton, William, *A Treatise on Carriages,* London, 1796.

Field, Edward, *The Colonial Tavern,* Providence, R. I., 1897.

Filson, John, *The Discovery, Settlement and Present State of Kentucke,* Wilmington, Del., 1784.

Flint, T., *Letters to America,* London, 1818.

Gaines, B. O., *History of Scott County, Kentucky,* 2 vols., Georgetown, 1905.

Gorin, Franklin, *The Times of Long Ago,* Louisville, 1929.

Gregory, J. W., *The Story of the Road,* New York, 1932.

Hafen, LeRoy R., *The Overland Mail,* Cleveland, 1926.

Hall, Captain Basil, *Travels in North America in the Years 1827 and 1828,* 3 vols., Edinburgh, 1829.

Hall, James, *Legends of the West,* Philadelphia, 1833.
> *Sketches of History, Life and Manner in the West,* Philadelphia, 1835.

Hamilton, Captain T., *Men and Manners in America,* 2 vols., Edinburgh, 1833.

Harris, Stanley, *The Coaching Age,* London, 1885.

Haycraft, Samuel, *History of Elizabethtown, Kentucky,* Elizabethtown, 1921.

Hindley, Charles, *Tavern Anecdotes and Sayings,* London, 1881.

Hulbert, Archer B., *The Old National Road,* Columbus, O., 1901.
> *Historic Highways of America,* Vol. VI, Cleveland, 1903.

Johnson, L. F., *History of Franklin County, Kentucky,* Frankfort, 1912.

Kerr, Charles, *History of Kentucky,* 5 vols., Chicago, 1922.

King, Maude E., *Round About a Brighton Coach Office,* London, 1896.

Lathrop, Elise, *Early American Inns and Taverns,* New York, 1926.

Lethem, J., *A Review of Lexington as She Is,* New York, 1886.

Littell, William, *The Statute Law of Kentucky,* 5 vols., Frankfort, 1809–19.

Lyell, Charles, *Travels in North America in the Years 1841 and 1842,* 2 vols., New York, 1852.

Melish, John, *Travels through the United States,* London, 1818.

Meyer, B. Henry, *History of Transportation in the United States before 1860,* Washington, D. C., 1917.

McCabe, Julius P. B., *Directory of the City of Lexington and County of Fayette for 1838–39,* Lexington, 1838.

McDougle, Ivan E., *Slavery in Kentucky,* Lancaster, Pa., 1918.

McElroy, Robert M., *Kentucky in the Nation's History,* New York, 1909.

Michaux, F. A., *Travels to the West of the Allegheny Mountains,* London, 1805.

Mitchell, S. Augustus, *Travellers Guide through the United States,* Philadelphia, 1836.

Monette, John W., *History of the Discovery and Settlement of the Valley of the Mississippi,* 2 vols., New York, 1846.

Morse, J., *View of All the Present State of the Kingdoms, States and Colonies,* Boston, 1812.

Niles, H., *Niles Weekly Register,* Baltimore, 1812–43.

Perrin, Wm. H., *History of Bourbon, Scott, Harrison, and Nicholas Counties, Kentucky,* Chicago, 1882.

Peter, Robert, *History of Fayette County, Kentucky,* Chicago, 1882.

Pierson, Rev. H. W., *In the Brush, or Life and Adventures in the Southwest,* New York, 1882.

Pusey, William A., *The Wilderness Road to Kentucky,* New York, 1921.

Railey, William E., *History of Woodford County, Kentucky,* Frankfort, 1928.

Ranck, George W., *History of Lexington, Kentucky,* Cincinnati, 1872.

Reid, Richard, *Historical Sketches of Montgomery County, Kentucky,* Lexington, 1926 (reprint).

Ringwalt, J. L., *Development of the Transportation System in the United States,* Philadelphia, 1888.

Rogers, Fairman, *A Manual of Coaching,* Philadelphia, 1900.

Root, Frank A. and Wm. E. Connelley, *The Overland Stage to California,* Topeka, Kan., 1901.

Searight, Thomas B., *The Old Pike: A History of the National Road*, Uniontown, Pa., 1894.

Shaler, Nath. S., *American Highways*, New York, 1896.

Smith, J. Soule, *Art Work of the Bluegrass Region of Kentucky*, Oshkosh, Wis., 1898.

Smith, Z. F., *History of Kentucky*, Louisville, 1886.

Staples, Chas. R., *The Little Town of Lexington*, Unpublished MS.

Strathorn, Carrie A., *Fifteen Thousand Miles by Stage*, New York, 1911.

Stratton, Ezra M., *The World on Wheels*, New York, 1878.

Straus, Ralph, *Carriages and Coaches*, London, 1912.

Stuart, James, *Three Years in North America*, 2 vols., New York, 1833.

Swem, Earl G., *Letters on the Condition of Kentucky in 1825*, New York, 1916.

Taylor, Ben. F., *The World on Wheels and Other Sketches*, Chicago, 1874.

Thrupp, George A., *The History of Coaches*, London, 1877.

Toulmin, H., *Description of Kentucky*, London, 1792.

Townsend, William H., *Lincoln and his Wife's Home Town*, Indianapolis, 1929.

Tristam, W. Outram, *Coaching Days and Coaching Ways*, London, 1914.

Trollope, Frances M., *Domestic Manners of the Americans*, 2 vols., London, 1832.

Verhoeff, Mary, *The Kentucky River Navigation*, Louisville, 1917.

Walker, Thomas L., *History of the Lexington Postoffice, 1794–1901*, Lexington, 1901.

Ware, Francis M., *Driving*, New York, 1903.

Williams, C. S., *Lexington Directory, City Guide and Business Mirror 1859–1860*, Lexington, 1859.

Williams, W., *Southern and Western Travellers Guide*, New York, 1853.

Willis, George L., *History of Shelby County, Kentucky*, Louisville, 1929.

Wilson, Samuel M., *History of Kentucky*, Chicago, 1928.
      The First Land Court of Kentucky, Lexington, 1923.

Wilson, Violet A., *The Coaching Era*, New York [1922].

Wood, Henry Cleveland, *The Night Riders*, Chicago, 1908.

Wortley, E. Stuart, *Travels in the United States during 1849 and 1850*, New York, 1851.

Wright, Richardson, *Hawkers and Walkers in Early America*, Philadelphia, 1927.

Young, Bennet H., *History of Jessamine County, Kentucky*, Louisville, 1898.

Young, V. B., *History of Bath County, Kentucky*, Lexington, 1876.

INDEX

INDEX